Between the Desert and the Deep Blue Sea

A Syrian Journey

Gill Suttle

The Long Riders' Guild Press

www.classictravelbooks.com
www.horsetravelbooks.com

ISBN: 1-59048-246-8

Other books by Gill Suttle:

Jailbreak (A slow journey round Eastern Europe) 1998
Steppe by Steppe (A slow journey through Mongolia) 2000

Both published by Scimitar Press, P.O. Box 41, Monmouth, NP25 3UH, Great Britain, and available on Amazon.co.uk and Amazon.com.

DEDICATION

to
Basil Jadaan
and
Madfaa

*With immense gratitude to you both for making this
journey possible*

PREFACE

Syria isn't at the top of every tourist's hit list, although it may be high on that of George W. Bush. What attractions does a country trodden by some of the most famous warriors in history - from Alexander, via Saladin and the Mongols, to T E Lawrence - have to offer today's traveller beyond the study of life under a totalitarian government, or a fast-track to membership of Hizbollah? What pictures to illustrate the holiday brochure but the obligatory presidential portraits, dangerously illegal snapshots of military hardware, or endless vistas of sand punctuated by the odd camel?

Isolation fosters extravagant myths. Syria's contemporary image abroad couldn't be further from reality. Certainly, this story travels through desert landscapes, and relates the occasional passing collision with secret policemen. But it runs mostly through pine forests where mountain streams bubble among sacred groves; among radically differing communities whose pacifism and peaceful co-existence are a lesson to the West; with individuals whose good humour and tolerance towards their neighbours is exceeded only by the geniality of the welcome which they extend to the eccentric traveller.

A long-held passion for Arab horses and an obsession with Lawrence set me on the road to Damascus in 1978, while the current Ba'athist regime was still in its infancy. Two decades and several visits later, I thought it high time to gain a deeper acquaintance with the multiplicity of peoples, religions, cultures and landscapes which blend to form one of the most fascinating and diverse countries in the world.

Nearly a century ago the young Lawrence, as an undergraduate researching a history thesis, roamed the Levant, staying with villagers and laying the foundations of an empathy with the Arab peoples which, in time, would lead him to become a part of their history himself. These early wanderings of his were an inspiration, a pattern I longed to imitate.

To travel, like him, on foot wasn't possible, as ill-health leaves me unable to walk far. I decided instead to go on horseback. Horses had served me well during earlier journeys in Mongolia and Central Asia, where I had gone seeking the present legacies of three thousand years of mounted nomadism. And so my previous experiences merged with my present dream, to forge a template for the exploration of Syria's backwoods. My road was long and slow, with few advance plans; my accommodation provided by spontaneous, generous hospitality - or the nearest haystack; best of all, my sole travelling companion, thanks to the generosity of a friend, was that of my childhood fantasies: an Arab stallion.

And so I - or, rather, we, for Madfaa and I became an inseparable team - spent nearly three months and covered many miles sifting through the pieces of an intricate and many-dimensioned mosaic. Through river, mountain, coastal and desert places; among Christian and Muslim, Sunni and Shi'ite, heretic and orthodox; from places fought over many millennia ago to those disputed in the last couple of decades.

While occasionally and briefly informed by history, Islam and its offshoots, geography and - where absolutely unavoidable - politics, this is principally an account of the people of Syria, surely the most generous and charming of the Arab peoples; and perhaps the least known. Despite eventually getting plenty of sand in my boots (and chatting up a few soldiers), I failed to encounter a single camel, let alone run into any terrorist organisation. Instead, I found a lifetime's worth of new friends; and lost in the process a few more of my own preconceptions.

August 2006

I

THE RIVER

The man in the cornfield paused and straightened, letting the scythe fall to his side. The neat stacks of barley about him threw hard golden light up from the evening sun, now falling slantwise across the oasis gardens.

"Are you going on a journey?"

He had seen me ride out each afternoon from Fayiz Aridah's yard on the edge of the *Ghouta* - the Damascus Oasis. But this was the first time that Madfaa, the little bay Arab stallion, had carried saddlebags.

The man was gently teasing me. He knew by now that I would ride for just an hour or two, returning as the sun set behind clouds of dust thrown up by the minivans coming home laden with alfalfa for the cows' evening feed, or by the donkey carts laden with watermelons for tomorrow's market. I would hardly need saddlebags for a saunter through the outskirts of the gardens. And they would be a positive hazard when I reached Babileh, the cramped chaotic suburb of narrow streets where concrete block tottered precariously on a foundation of mud brick, and low archways carried two or even three storeys across the street on sagging, sunbleached beams.

For a moment, set in the habit of the last few days, I wriggled in embarrassment, a dude indulging in silly pretensions. Then I remembered, and the blush stopped halfway up my neck. There was a very good reason for trying out my saddlebags tonight.

"Yes," I answered. "I am going on a journey. Tomorrow."

*

Salah-ad-Din lay inside a wooden casket in a modest chapel near his former citadel in the Old Quarter of Damascus. In death, he showed no more love for pomp and circumstance than he had in life. Too little altogether for Kaiser Wilhelm II, who nearly a century ago marked the growing rapprochement between Germany and Ottoman Turkey by presenting an engraved marble sarcophagus. Rather than replacing the original, it now lay alongside.

I mustn't idle away the morning like a tourist, I reminded myself sharply. I had errands to perform. But it seemed proper to pay my respects to Saladin before setting out. He more than most had known intimately the mountains, valleys and deserts I was intending to explore; he had stamped their history with his own personality, and a name that would ring down the centuries.

Emerging from the quiet courtyard, I could faintly hear the distant hubbub of hooting cars from outside the walls, the manic din that is the background to all Damascus life. The heart of the old city tugged at me like a gravitational pull. I had a couple of hours to spare, enough time to lose myself briefly in the Old Quarter and still do my shopping.

A walk through old Damascus is an odyssey through a succession of sensory experiences. Down the carpenters' *souk*, where a mixture of thuds and electric whines echo from the dark interiors of half-shuttered cubicles, and wrinkled old men sit in the street hammering out wooden stools; into the comparative quiet of the street of the goldsmiths, blinking when the sun, sneaking through a rare open roof, bounces off a display of glittering baubles and straight into your eye; right turn into the souk of the spice sellers, its air heavy with the whiff of near and distant lands, where the suggestion of islands and oceans and exotic shores is scooped into a tiny bag and presented to you for a handful of *qirsh*.

Escaping a narrow and crowded street, I plunged into a doorway and found myself in the central courtyard of an old *khan*. Once a caravanserai for pack animals, it still served as a merchants' depot;

under the multiple domes of its roof, stacks of Damascus silk stood hard by crates of plastic bottles in a seamless juxtaposition of old and new. I crept furtively up a stairway to find the former sleeping quarters of the upper rooms now turned into offices and workshops. Their doors open, the occupants greeted me with a smile and a wave. In this country there are no intruders, only welcome guests.

About to go back down, I found my hand given a conspiratorial tweak by a young boy. He led me to another dark stairway, and I climbed up to find myself out on the roof.

Rooftops fascinate me. The Olympian glimpse they give on to the world below embody one of the great delights of travelling: that of seeing the world from an unexpected perspective, of going where most people don't bother. Perhaps, even more satisfying, going where you're not supposed to, seeing what you're not meant to. An open door to a ruined minaret; a single rail barring the stairway to a dungeon; a workman's ladder leading to the closed upper gallery of a temple; all, but especially anything leading up to an aerial view, irresistible temptations. Their indulgence is the visual equivalent of village gossip, their incentive the feeding of that insatiable appetite of the traveller: curiosity. Was it not "for lust of knowing what should not be known" that James Elroy Flecker took the Golden Road to Samarkand?

An almost unbroken surface stretched away westwards from under my feet to where the tin oval lid of the Souk Hamidieh, Old Damascus' cheap and cheerful bazaar, poked its head up. Turning, I could look back across the roofs of the Christian Quarter to Bab Sharqi, the East Gate. South of me, ongoing demolition had unveiled a long-covered street to leave it almost indecently exposed under a few remaining arch frames, sticking up like whalebone from a decayed corset. To the north, framed against the slopes of Mount Kassioun, the Great Mosque filled the horizon. Between, a pimply roofscape sprouted domes like toadstools, and the twin trees of an open courtyard reached upwards for light and air. Satellite dishes outnumbered the minarets on the Mosque. Secular Syria was finding new ways of scanning the heavens.

It was time to rejoin the world below. Stumbling as my eyes readjusted to permanent twilight, I found my way to Bab al-Faraj - the Gate of Deliverance - and out into the saddlers' souk, where my business lay.

Only a few saddlers still trade here. Most of the merchants' booths stock hardware, kitchen equipment and garden tools. But tourists supplement a few local horsemen to maintain a handful of shops, where tasselled breastplates, cotton bridles sewn with cowrie shells, gorgeous saddle hangings and other traditional Bedouin saddlery make up the bulk of the stock. I had to burrow in the back to find the bread-and-butter goods I was looking for.

I came away with a strong headcollar of bright blue cotton, six metres of tether rope and a handful of spare leather straps. On an impulse, remembering the fragility of the straw hat I'd brought with me, I added a wide-brimmed scout hat to the pile. It was blue, nicely complementing the headcollar. I might as well start off with matching accessories. I was going to be scruffy enough after a few days on the road.

*

"Ask about the neighbour before the house," cautions an Arabic proverb, "and about the companion before the journey." My companion was Madfaa, a pure-bred Arab stallion. If you lifted his thick black mane you found the freeze-brand hiding underneath in his coat of gleaming mahogany: a white swirl of Arabic calligraphy that attested his blue blood.

His name meant Cannon. Cannonball might have been more appropriate, for he was small, round and tough. With flaring nostrils and a bright, knowing eye peering out from under the thatch of his forelock, he was more a creature of Thelwell than Haroun al Rashid. Here was the real McCoy. This was no pampered western darling bred with exaggeratedly dished face and long legs to spend a lifetime posturing in the show ring, eyes seductively darkened with vaseline; but, rather, a true son of the desert, hard, enduring and indestructible.

He had been bred eight years before by the Shammar Bedouin in their spring pastures of the Jezira, the land beyond the River Euphrates. His present owner Basil Jadaan, a leading figure in the Arab horse world, had come to know Madfaa's breeder during the registration of Bedouin horses for the Syrian branch of WAHO, the World Arabian Horse Organisation. The man had subsequently fallen foul of bad faith in a client to whom he had sold a mare, and Basil had stepped in to help.

Custom, but not law, decrees that the first foal of a mare after she is sold should be given to her original owner. The purchaser, however, had reneged, demanding a price for the foal. Fearing to lose his blood-line but unable to pay, the Bedouin had asked Basil if he could intervene.

"My business was doing well at the time, *al-hamdu li'llah,*" said Basil quietly, "so I was able to help him." Thus, self-deprecatingly, he dismissed an act of typically Arab generosity: Basil had actually bought the foal himself and presented it to the Bedouin. Gratefully, the man returned his gift with another horse - Madfaa.

I'd known Basil for ten years. WAHO had put me in touch with him when I was researching an article on Arab horses for *Riding* Magazine, just as Syria's affiliation to WAHO was being negotiated. He in turn introduced me to the country's leading breeders, the men who were enabling their country to take its rightful (and long overdue) place in the international world of Arab horse-breeding.

Basil, then, was an Opener of Doors. From the moment that I first began to consider this journey in realistic terms, I knew that he was the man who could make it happen for me. When I approached him for help, I was thinking of contacts and information; perhaps he had a friend who might lease me a horse for a few months, or could tell me where I might buy despite my limited means.

"Don't worry; I can find you a horse," he'd told me. I little dreamed that he would lend me one of his own pure-bred stallions.

Basil kept Madfaa by the Ghouta at Fayiz' farm. The yard was an oasis within the Oasis. You stepped out of the heat of the lane into a cool, twilight zone shaded with tumbling vines and paved with cream tiles. Here under a row of graceful arches lived Fayiz' string of prize Arab bloodstock. Madfaa crunched fresh alfalfa in one of these stables, next to Fayiz' best racehorse, who was being prepared for Hama races the following week. Although I was going to Hama I would miss the race meeting: if all went to plan I would be far up the Orontes valley before the big day.

My pipe-dream of travelling through Syria with an Arab horse was now on the point of realisation, thanks to Basil. Hoping to experience as much as possible of the cultural and geographical diversity of this unusual country, I intended to join the River Orontes at Hama close to where it enters Syria from Lebanon, and follow it north almost to the Turkish border. From there I would find my way through the coastal mountain range to Lattakia, where old friends would give me a rest from the road. Then it would be back into the mountains, working my way ever southward until Lebanon barred my way. Skirting its border, I would then head due south for Damascus, bringing Madfaa home along the very edge of the Badiat ash-Sham, the great desert which stretches to the Euphrates and on into Iraq.

According to the proverb, I had done it the wrong way round; I had planned my route long ago, with no foreknowledge of my companion. But from my first meeting with Madfaa, I knew I had had the luck to get away with it.

*

He travelled up to Hama in Fayiz' open pickup truck. Three hours under a blazing sun; but at the end he skipped over the lowered tailgate as if he had just been for a jaunt up the road. The racecourse stables received him and, content that he had all he needed, I departed with Mofa, my host for the night, to see the sights.

Syria's fourth biggest city, hiding beneath the surrounding uplands in a gash carved by the Orontes, is a strangely schizophrenic place. The modern bars and restaurants along its waterfront sit oddly opposite its hallmark *norias* - the ancient wooden water-wheels which until recently watered the entire town. The tourists on its street brush awkwardly against the black drooping crow figures of women wearing the *aba'a*, a black cloak covering the body from head to foot. There are more of the latter here than anywhere else in Syria - unless you count Iranian tourists visiting Damascus' Great Mosque - for Hama is Syria's most conservative and devout city, and once the gravitational centre of *Sunni* fundamentalism. Until 1982, that is.

I asked Mofa whether he had been here in 1982. He pretended not to hear and changed the subject. I didn't press him. Trauma often runs not far below the surface of Hama's citizens.

It was in 1982 that escalating Sunni fundamentalist terrorism culminated in armed rebellion here by the Muslim Brotherhood, a Sunni party, who held Hama for four days. The revolt was put down ruthlessly, with many innocent people losing their lives along with the rebels, and parts of the city obliterated. Hama still bears the emotional and architectural scars.

How could this cosmopolitan-looking, colourful, pleasant town be the scene of such extremism? It was hard to imagine. Yet when Mofa led me along the river and plunged into the otherworld of the alleyways, it made more sense. Narrow and secretive, passing now and again into vaulted tunnels, their Ottoman architecture and black-and-white stonework recalling a past of Turkish beys and pashas, they might have breathed intrigue and revolt for generations. Had not the men of Hama risen to throw off the occupying Assyrians nearly three thousand years ago? Robin Fedden, observing only fifty years back how riots had closed the souks twenty-one times in three years, described it in his book *Syria: An Historical Appreciation* as "a place of fanatical certainties and uncertain passions".

Across a lane and into another cramped alley, beneath a vine where the grapes were just beginning to hang heavy, and under a structure like half of Hertford Bridge. We emerged into the sunlight by a weir where three norias revolved by pitted brick aqueducts. Swimming boys braved the wheels, grabbing the paddles to ride halfway up and leap from the apex of the curve into the green water beneath. It was a perilous game. Age and algae greased the wheels, which turned with relentless speed. One slip could have been fatal. They shouted with the thrill, but not a word reached us, for the creaking roar of the wheels drowned all other noise. This was the defining sound of Hama, as the flash of sunlight and rainbow through the arcing streams of water was the defining sight.

"You know," said Mofa as we made our way back to his flat, "the people of Hama cannot sleep if they cannot hear the wheels."

*

Madfaa and I left the racecourse stables next morning at six-thirty, while the traffic was still light. We descended the hill to the heart of the city, where I meant to join the river and follow it as closely as possible downstream.

This was harder than I'd thought. A main road took us past some water-wheels and westwards along the bank a little way, but it soon peeled away up the hill leaving only the narrow alleys for access to the

Orontes. I funked taking a horse through these, and found a wider street close by. It led to the base of the citadel, a severed outcrop of the surrounding plateau with a commanding view over a loop of the river.

A left turn to cut off the loop took us uphill into roads increasingly distant from the Orontes. No matter; I should have realised that, in Hama, it would be like this. Time enough to look for a towpath when we had escaped the metropolis.

Syria doesn't have benefit of Ordnance Survey maps. At least, it undoubtedly does, but not for public consumption. I had a couple of the usual tourist maps, showing major roads and the bigger towns; and, for topographical detail, an aeronautical map, produced, according to the legend, "under the direction of the Director of Military Service, Ministry of Defence, United Kingdom, 1981" but certainly originating from information gleaned by American spy satellites. I was keeping that one strictly for backup. It would probably be quite helpful if you wanted to avoid flying your Tornado into a mountain; but I knew from bitter experience that it would be hopelessly unreliable for navigation at anything much under ten thousand feet. There would be no detailed mapwork on this trip; just a lot of guessing, like now.

This particular guess led us straight past the Great Mosque. Site of a pagan temple then a Byzantine church, and once one of the more notable of Syrian antiquities, Hama's holiest place had been a stage for one of the great dramas of 1982. People describe in hushed voices how the authorities had declared an amnesty for all who laid down their arms and collected here; and had then shelled the site into rubble, burying all inside. You would hardly guess, now, what had happened on this spot. Once more the slender minaret probed the heavens. Only the gleaming new marble hinted at the extent of its rebuilding.

I could hardly visit it like a tourist, accompanied by a horse; but perhaps I could glimpse inside a little. I attached my brand-new tether rope to Madfaa's bridle. Then, leaving· him at the head of the steps which led down to the interior, I descended to the extent of the rope's length until I could see to where the green dome of the reconstructed treasure house rose above the scrubbed stones of the courtyard. No further; for a sudden clatter sent me scurrying back up. Although our acquaintance was so recent, Madfaa had already accepted me as his friend and ally. Where I went, he was determined to follow; and he was slithering down the stone steps trying to do just that. With difficulty I turned him around and coaxed him back up to the street. Chastened, I made a mental note to be more careful in future.

When Hama at length released us, it was on to the dual carriageway to Tartous and Lattakia - a far cry from the gentle meander along the banks of the river that I'd envisaged. At the first opportunity I turned off downhill, on a road signposted "Khattab", leading down to a bridge over the Orontes. A track branched off into the rich gardens and orchards enclosing the river. This looked more promising.

It took me straight down to the riverbank, where a motorised pump sucked out life from the Orontes and distributed it liberally through a mixed orchard of figs, apricots and walnuts. Then it stopped dead. I was wondering what I would do next, when a pleasant young man in khaki army fatigues came over to ask the same question.

For thirty years I've struggled to learn Arabic. No linguist, I'd painfully mastered the ten consonants that English doesn't bother with, and had practised my syntax while talking to my horses, my cat or the occasional tree. Inconsiderately, none of these had ever given me an answer; so I could speak the language moderately well, but not understand when spoken to. The Syrian dialect, moreover, was vastly different from the classical written Arabic I'd learned from my books. From now on, though, it was sink or swim. I squeezed every brain cell, and managed a conversation of sorts.

Mahmoud was the owner of the orchards. Yes, of course I could spend a few hours resting here, he said. He showed me where I could tether Madfaa to graze, and spread a mat for me under a walnut tree.

I settled down to laze away the afternoon. After an hour Mahmoud, his day's work finished, invited me to his house to meet his family. I was reluctant to move Madfaa from his grazing patch of fresh lucerne, but couldn't refuse without being rude. So I fetched my tack and saddled up again, flung my saddlebags over, and followed Mahmoud back up the road to his house.

For Madfaa there was a dark stable, which he entered rather nervously; for me a warm welcome as Mahmoud introduced me to his mother, father and five sisters. Although I'd already eaten, a cloth was spread on the floor and a feast brought in. Mahmoud's mother was a strong-featured lady of about fifty, headscarved and cowled. She groaned with pain as she stooped to lay dishes of tomato and cucumber on the floor, holding a hand to her back. I thought then that she must be ill. It was only later that I learnt how rural Syrian women, often mother to ten or more children, almost invariably suffer constant back pain, their lumbar muscles worn out with constant childbearing.

The whole family were curious about their unexpected visitor. The questions flowed in what was to become a predictable order.

"Where are you from?"

"How old are you?"

"Are you married?"

"What are you doing?"

"Why are you following the *Nahr al-'Asi* (River Orontes)?"

England, forty-four, no, travelling round Syria on horseback… yes, really… I was to become fluent very quickly in communicating at least this much.

As for following the Orontes, I was already beginning to wonder why myself, as it was proving so difficult. Mahmoud, to my disappointment, told me that it would remain so; that - as I was beginning to realise - there were no tracks to link the orchards and gardens which so closely hugged the river. There was no towpath, no riverside path of any sort. I would have to settle for tracking it as nearly as the roads would allow.

So when I saddled Madfaa to leave in the cool of late afternoon, I prepared to continue up the road to Khattab rather than returning to the spot where Mahmoud had found me. One of his young sisters picked me a bunch of garden flowers, which I tucked into the top of my saddlebags. The whole family clustered around as I mounted up; but Madfaa, upset by his dark confinement in a strange stable and unnerved by so many strangers, reared suddenly, scattering them. It was no time to hang about, so I gave him his head and set off smartly up the lane, calling my thanks once more over my shoulder.

The way to Khattab took us through a rolling downland of cornfields. The grain had been mostly harvested already, although this was early June. Piles of chaff and unthreshed corn lay about the fields. Stubble fires belched smoke across the landscape, as they would have done in an English September of a couple of decades ago before legislation extinguished them all. I felt disorientated, as if I had been whisked away by magic carpet to the wrong country, the wrong year, the wrong month. The green line of the river, curving its way languorously through the valley below, anchored my thoughts, reminding me what I was doing and where I was going.

At regular intervals, norias raised their heads above the surrounding fruit trees. Some of them were in good repair; occasionally only the brick pyramid of supporting framework or a part-ruined aqueduct showed where they had once stood, scooping up the green, greasy water to spread abundance over the gardens and fields. Nowadays this work was performed by mechanical pumps. The clatter of the water pumps, never more than a couple of hundred yards apart, was the definitive sound of the Orontes valley, as the whirr and creak of the water-wheels remained that of Hama.

There was much here to remind me of travelling in the irrigated lands of Central Asia. But whereas in Turkmenistan I had seen much that was neglected and in disrepair, here all was well-ordered. The water was pumped carefully to where it was needed, in neat tidy channels which wasted nothing. Concrete cisterns gathered any surplus. I guessed that some of these were filled from underground springs, for they contained clear, clean water into which Madfaa gratefully sank his nose. I would have given a lot to rip off my clothes and plunge in myself.

Khattab was quite a sizeable town. The country lane gave way to dusty, crumbling pavement; the stone and brush roadside to a solid blank wall of houses, turning their backs to the street and their faces inward, doors heavily barred. Here and there an open wooden gate gave a glimpse, as through the looking glass, on to a completely different world: a garden shady and cool with vines and perhaps a fountain; and flowers, everywhere flowers.

I turned downhill for the bridge and ran into the local *shebaab* - gang of boys - hurling jeers, insults and the odd stone. Extricating myself and Madfaa with difficulty, I escaped across the river by a bridge crossing below the remains of an old Ottoman khan. Just beyond, a track led off beside the river. A good, firm track showing every intention of going somewhere. At last. I turned on to it with relief.

It wound through a cornfield, where late workers gleaned stray ears or collected sheaves for threshing in the cool of what was now early evening. A car came bumping along the track back towards Khattab, and I swung Madfaa aside to let it pass. I wanted to get by, and on; but its two occupants were in the mood for a chat.

"Where are you going?" asked the driver.

"I'm travelling along the Nahr al-'Asi to Sheizar."

"You can't go on to Sheizar tonight. It's another twenty-five kilometres. There's nothing on the way, nowhere to stay; it's just desert. You'll have to go back to Khattab."

No way, I thought. I was now following my personal Yellow Brick Road, a path hard by the river, and making good time on a glorious evening. Nothing was going to halt this idyll prematurely, to stop me pressing on.

"No problem. I'll sleep out. I've got food, I've got my tether rope. I've got everything I need."

"You can't sleep out. What about the *wahash*?"

I didn't know what *wahash* were, but as I scrabbled for my dictionary, I thought I could guess. This close to the river, they had to be mosquitoes.

"I don't care about the wahash," I answered breezily.

The other man spoke for the first time. "You can't sleep out; the wahash will get you."

"The wahash can't hurt me." I played my trump card. "I've got a mosquito net!" Now I had found wahash in the dictionary. It meant wild animals.

"So, what kind of wahash?" I tried to make my laugh convincing. "Elephants? Monkeys?" Hardly a witty reply, but the only wild animals my meagre Arabic could run to.

"There are *wa-wa*," said the second man, with relish.

Against my will, I was beginning to be impressed. "What are wa-wa? I'm sure they can't be anything that terrible."

"They come and bite you. They tear at your legs. They'll go for the horse," said the first man.

I tried to argue, but the trickling away of my bravado was fast becoming a landslide. I started to worry about what might happen if my bluff were called. I didn't like the sound of the wa-wa at all.

The man sensed that I had cracked. "You'll have to come back to Khattab," he said, with the air of one moving in for checkmate. "You'll have to come and stay with us!"

*

Musa lived behind one of the blank walls just off the main street. His young wife Alhaam received me with gentle courtesy and the sweetest smile under her *hijab*. Below the veil pinned tight under her chin to show only the oval of her face, she wore a severe black dress. She came from Hama, obviously of a very devout and conservative family like so many in the area. Musa himself, once home, changed his tracksuit for a white *dishdasha*, the long shirt which is the usual clothing for an adult male.

The other member of the household was a middle-aged man with hair unusually black for his age, horn-rimmed spectacles and the air of a slightly seedy prep-school Classics master. He was the rather unlikely teacher of the young toughs I had encountered earlier at the bridge. I half expected him to speak to me in mediaeval Latin.

"Welcome. Do you speak the French language?" he asked, peering at me intently over the horn-rimmed spectacles.

"You can put your horse in here," said Musa, stepping down into a dark doorway in the corner of the yard.

"I'm afraid I don't, but I'll do my best to try and understand it," I said over my shoulder to the schoolmaster, juggling with saddlebags and headcollar and falling down the twelve-inch step in the gloom. Madfaa, tumbling down behind me, was received by an elderly man in a white *keffiyah* and iron-grey dishdasha, and tethered to an iron ring in the mud-brick manger. Mice scrabbled and leapt to get out of his way, and six new-born kittens mewled on a sack in the corner.

"Do you have an International Baccalaureate?" demanded the schoolmaster.

"You must come to the *hammaam* and have a bath," said Alhaam with kindly concern as I brushed grime and chaff dust off my arms. Madfaa was now chomping happily away in his corner.

"Where and what did you study? I'm afraid I don't have any of the English language," added the schoolmaster sadly to my departing back as Alhaam led me away.

The hammaam was combined boiler-house, laundry-room and shower-room, with a tap giving directly on to the marble floor, angled to drain into a gap in the corner. I scrubbed myself viciously, then repeated the treatment on my sodden clothes, while fresh sweat mingled with the bathwater still running off my body. I came out considerably cleaner but no less sticky than before, and slightly nervous of the next item on my schedule: the ordeal of coffee with the schoolmaster.

We seated ourselves under a vine at the domestic end of the yard, and Alhaam brought us coffee and black, syrupy tea.

"I have three serious questions to put to you," he began, as if consulting the Delphic Oracle.

"Firstly, how old are you? Secondly, where are you travelling to? Thirdly, have you been to Damascus, and what do you think of it?"

He put them with the severity with which he might have ordered a spelling test; but it was a mock severity, self-deprecating, masking an obvious kindness and a sense of humour which I had completely failed to spot earlier.

Without the ear to pick up the *kelaam 'adi*, the common speech, I answered, stumbling, in classical Arabic, the exact equivalent of the mediaeval Latin that had sprung to mind when I first saw him. He listened with impenetrable courtesy while I mangled my verbs, or searched interminably in my dictionary for the right word; when he corrected my fumbled inflections, it was with a gravity that was wholly tongue-in-cheek. He was a delightful and entertaining companion, the sort of man you might meet over a glass of port after dinner at one of the older universities, or one of a dying breed of rather eccentric public school housemasters. He was entirely satisfied with my answer to his third question.

"I love Damascus," I told him. "It's one of my favourite cities in the whole world."

"I also love Damascus, better than anywhere else," he answered. "It is such a rich city: ancient and modern at once. It has such a wonderful history.

"And I studied there," he added, "which makes it special for me." For a moment the professional façade dropped, and the young man looked out from underneath, full of energy and optimism. It was that rare gleam which sometimes emanates from the ageing intellectual, otherwise dulled by the coarseness and indifference of his students.

Throughout our conversation he was the complete professional, speaking to me slowly and in easy language to help me understand him, displaying under a slightly arch exterior the endless patience of the dedicated teacher enlightening an exceptionally dim pupil. What, I wondered, had drawn this refined and cultivated man from his beloved Damascus into exile here, to cast the pearls of his wisdom among the young barbarians of Khattab bridge?

"What would you say is the one main reason why you travel?" he asked, giving me a fierce intense sideways look, like a crow about to pounce on a squashed hedgehog.

"Curiosity," I answered, the talk of Damascus bringing the reflections of last week to the surface of my mind. "Wherever I go, I always want to know what it is I haven't seen yet, what's hiding round the next corner. So I have to keep moving to find out."

"And what would you say is your biggest fear when you're travelling?"

"I'm afraid it's a very boring answer to that one," I answered, after another endless consultation with the dictionary. "I'm terrified that something will happen to my horse. I'm completely responsible for him, and my worst fear is having to go back to his owner, and say that in some way he's been harmed."

"That is my last question," he said, "because I know you're tired and want to sleep."

*

The discussion surrounding the schoolmaster's last question broached a subject which was to cause some friction later that evening. I had promised Basil not to tether Madfaa at night unless I had to; that if I did, I would stay within sight of him. The little stallion was used to being tied, but not for long periods. There are all sorts of hazards for the tethered horse. He may catch his foot in the rope, or suffer rope-burns trying to get free; he might even trip himself and fall; in the worst-case scenario break a limb... So I asked to sleep in the yard near his stable.

Poor Musa was affronted, insisting that, as his guest, I should sleep in the best room in the house. But I dared not. I still didn't know Madfaa, and he was spending his first night in a strange place. It was imperative that I keep an eye on him. So, begging Musa to excuse me, I held out for the *al fresco* option.

I felt guilty and embarrassed; already I was breaking the unwritten rules binding host and guest, under which I should have accepted with gratitude the best of Musa's hospitality. Two things came to my help. One was the support of the schoolmaster, who understood my anxiety. The other was the imminent start of a World Cup football match, for which Musa reluctantly abandoned the argument. He retired to an upper room to watch the game, and I bedded down comfortably within earshot of the stable, getting up from time to time to peer inside and check that all was well.

At three in the morning the call to prayer sounded from the town mosque. Despite their late night over the football Musa and the schoolteacher rose to pray, flitting round the yard like ghosts in spotless white dishdashas as they washed at the garden tap, then letting themselves out quietly into the street. Footsteps from outside the walls indicated that they were not the only devout people in Khattab. It was further proof of the piety of the men of Hama and its environs.

*

The shebaab still infested the bridge next morning, and when I reached the fields the stubble fires were burning already. I set off along the riverside track in anticipation of Musa's twenty-five kilometres of uninhabited desert; but it was not so. Just round the corner where he had fielded me, a small settlement stood on a rise from which I could look across to several more, following the thread of the river, whose surroundings were as green and fertile as ever.

Too fertile for my purpose. Soon a field of maize barred the way, and Madfaa and I had to exchange grass for tarmac to find our way past. But it was a tiny, pleasant lane, and we had it to ourselves as we climbed up and up, ever higher above the river.

Now I had a comprehensive view of the Orontes valley. It was a landscape of sharp contrast, the dull sepia of the surrounding plateau giving suddenly to green where it hit the extremities of the irrigation. Sometimes the desert reached almost to the river, falling suddenly over a cliff to meet it; sometimes it blended with the stubble-fields in a bleached, empty landscape running seamlessly from the river-bank into the far distance. Elsewhere the dark green of orchards and gardens flaunted their fertility. Back and forth across the gardens ran a network of stone and brick aqueducts in varying stages of decrepitude: here just a brick missing, there an entire section in ruins. The constant noise of the pumps mocked their obsolescence; while intensive dredging work kept the precious water flowing through modern pipework. But it was still manpower which directed their combined output. Wherever I looked I saw people carefully working the irrigation, opening or damming channels, allotting to each growing thing its own particular need. Just so much and no more, with a judgement that no machine would ever match; judgement perfected over a few thousand years of trial and error.

Another track led me off the road below a field of sunflowers, heads the size of dinner plates, down to where a man in a red keffiyah was hoeing a cottonfield. Here, above a mill-race, one last water-wheel was still working, slopping water inefficiently but doggedly into a much-repaired aqueduct. Alone, it was inadequate, and a modern pump supplemented its efforts. The regular thump of the engine was an alien sound alongside the steady groan of the wheel. Caves pitted the hillside opposite. Strange to think how they would have already been old when the norias were at the cutting edge of technology.

The next village showed rural Syria at its best. Mud-brick houses, half-hidden under vines and surrounded by roses, stood among orchards of walnut and orange trees. Nest-holes ate pockets into the wall of a granary, while rollers - big, brash birds with the colour of a kingfisher on the body of a crow - tipped their heads sideways and inspected us from the telegraph wires. Towards the far end was a shop selling choc-ices.

That did it. Time for lunch and siesta. A little way past the village I found a thicket hard by the river where I could draw water and tether Madfaa out of sight of the road. But our passage had been noticed. Within minutes the village children found us, clustering round Madfaa to pat his nose nervously, and overwhelming me with questions which I couldn't understand. I pleaded the need to sleep, and closed my eyes firmly. When I opened them some time later the children had gone, and a circle of apricots and oranges, picked from the village orchards, surrounded me.

For a few more miles, the road followed the Orontes. Decision Time came at a junction by a bridge, where the choice lay between a lane and a main road. The lane clung to the river, while the road swung away hard left over the bridge; but I knew that to get to the village of Sheizar I needed to be on the opposite bank. There might be more bridges, but time was getting on and I couldn't risk being stranded on the wrong side.

Reluctantly I turned my back on the river and set Madfaa at the long uphill haul beyond. Long before the top the wind was rising, and as we came out on to a ridge it hit us squarely in the face: a cool unremitting blast straight off the sea via the distant grey mountain ridge which now rose ahead. This was my first glimpse of the *Jebel al-Alawiyiin*, the Mountain of the Alawis, which runs from the Turkish border south to the Lebanese marches then, after a brief dip, rises greater than before to become Mount Lebanon itself.

Between the near plateau and the mountain there was something missing; the sense of a gap, a hollow hiding behind the near horizon. No more than a sense, for a sizeable town now stood in our way, barring the view.

Mahardah took me by surprise. It barely featured on my map beside Sheizar, which itself was only a village. Here the road split to enter the town in a dual carriageway, its central reservation painted in yellow stripes and planted with oleander. Shops lined the main street. I stopped to buy biscuits; then hurried on again as a rapidly-forming crowd of boys began to surround Madfaa.

The setting sun streamed down the street into my face. I needed to go north; must find a right turn. When it came it led into the Christian Quarter. The streets were quiet, as today was Sunday. At the far end the market place, still twitching with late stallholders packing up, straddled a main road leading down the hill out of town. New building sprouting along its length linked Mahardah almost indivisibly with the first houses of Sheizar village.

As Madfaa and I trod wearily down the hill we emerged from the long shadows of the town. The ridge to our right glowed deeper and darker as we plodded down and down. At its end the long crest they call the Cock's Comb was mercilessly illuminated, the fierce red light of the dying sun picking out every broken stone, every breach in the walls, every tumbled parapet of the great ruined castle perched on its summit.

*

Mohammed Kharouf was a generous and attentive host. Too attentive; you would never have sent your maiden aunt to take tea with him. I'm sure his intentions were entirely honourable - certainly the presence of his wife and daughters, hovering nearby to refill plates or teapots, rendered them perfectly innocent - but he thought that a guest should be petted and stroked like a new puppy. It made hard work of sharing his breakfast.

Determined that I would eat only the best, he would not allow me to choose my own food from the *mezzeh*, the plates of assorted food, that lay before us. Whipping a piece of bread from my hand, he flung it behind him without looking - unerringly finding the open window from which it probably bounced not more than twice before hitting the river hundreds of feet below - and rammed a cucumber between my teeth as I opened my mouth to remonstrate.

Worse, he confiscated my teacup, handing me instead a small sealed glass with a pipe in the top and filled with what looked like dead grass. Sucking obediently on the pipe, I filled my mouth with a liquid tasting like stewed compost. It was my first taste of *mâté*, the traditional drink of South America, which is undeservedly popular in this part of Syria. It certainly hit the spot with Mohammed; for he sat back comfortably sipping with a look of rapture, from time to time emitting on a long sigh, *"Aaiii-WA...!* YeeessSS...!" as if he had just seen the apple fall, or unzipped the double helix.

Finally he seized my comb as I tried to tie up my hair. (I'd got up early to check on Madfaa and, returning, had found my bed gone and breakfast spread in its place before I'd even washed or dressed properly.) Dismissing my protests he raked my head vigorously, knotting the existing tangles. I managed to repossess the comb, whereupon he seized a pot from the sideboard and dolloped a splodge of Brylcreem on to my head. It was time to escape. Making noises about checking on Madfaa, I fled into the garden.

Mohammed was the headman of Sheizar village. A tall man dressed in spotless white keffiyah and dishdasha, he had beautiful liquid, brown eyes. At first I had thought those eyes full of wisdom, the eyes of a sage or a prophet. It was only when you looked deep into them - a liberty which in the circumstances I took sparingly - that they struck me as disappointingly vacuous after all.

Last night I had trudged up the long hill to the castle hounded by the worst swarm of boys yet. Big boys, small boys and all sizes in between, they had buzzed Madfaa on bikes, jeered at me, thrown stones at us both. Madfaa had withstood the assault well, but was shivering with antipathy; I was feeling frankly murderous. Meanwhile their parents, used to tourists here, had looked on with indifference. Feeling like an exhausted, wounded knight in a rather depressing mediaeval romance, I'd ridden up to the castle for sanctuary, only to find its gates barred against me; for the gatehouse was reached by a steep flight of steps, impassable for Madfaa. My hopes of camping inside the castle were dashed. Instead I must find somewhere in the village for us both.

The kindly family living right under the steps had rescued us from the hostile army. Shooing the boys away, they led Madfaa into a gash in the rockface, revealing a cave with a manger hollowed out in the rock wall. They swept out the dust to make a clean space for his feed, then led me off and revived me with tea. Of course I could stay the night, they said. But very soon a holloa sounded from the terrace below. Looking down over the wall I saw Madfaa, kidnapped by Mohammed from the cave, tethered in his own garden and now standing hostage for me. As a foreign guest, I represented a trophy which Mohammed wanted for himself. After a brief futile argument I took the easy option, sleeping on his veranda from where I could watch the little stallion. If I'd realised then that Mohammed was a few cucumbers short of a mezzeh, I might have objected more forcibly.

His house occupied the prime position in Sheizar village. On the very prow of the ridge above a bend in the Orontes, it overlooked the river on two sides. From the garden, one false step would send you tumbling over a precipice some couple of hundred feet to the hillside below. The bottom windows of the house were strongly barred against sleepwalkers or small children, for their outlook was even more vertical than that of the garden. On the third side the land fell away in a steep hill among houses down to the wall which had once encircled the outer ward of the castle. Only on the fourth side did the view fall uphill, to the monumental gateway and ruinous stones of what had once been a massive fortress. Sheizar Castle, sitting like an eagle on its crag to spy over the river valley far below, is surely the most romantic of all the castles in Syria.

The fortress here must have been ancient when warrior Pharaohs first inscribed its name in hieroglyphs upon their temple walls. But the account of the mediaeval soldier-scholar Usamah ibn Munqidh brings its past most vibrantly to life. It was Usamah's grandfather who finally wrested Sheizar from the Byzantine Emperor for good, after many centuries in which it had passed like a shuttlecock from Arab to Byzantine hands and back again. Recording his memoirs in the first century of the Crusades, Usamah draws a colourful picture of life in Sheizar when the only fit occupations of a gentleman were fighting and hunting, or - for a rainy day - making copies of the Qur'an.

Written in the style which inspired the later mediaeval romances of such as Malory, his book is a treasurehouse of knightly tales: of daring exploits against overwhelming odds, of capture and ransom, of chivalry and occasional duplicity. A friend of both Saladin and the Frankish King Fulk of Jerusalem, Usamah presents war as a sporting league, where the Crusaders were just another away team along with the Isma'ilis of Masyaf and the Lord of Afamia and the men of Hama, where a severed limb was as much an accepted occupational hazard as a torn hamstring, where you might go to a man's wedding one day and bludgeon his brains out the next, with no offence meant and none taken. He opens a window on to a world seemingly of fairy tale and make-believe; a world which came to a premature end for his family when an earthquake toppled the castle, burying most of his relations.

It must have been a colossal tremor, for it twisted the foundations of the keep some ten degrees out of true, a fault which not even the later Mameluke overlords sought to remedy. Otherwise they rebuilt mightily, for more than eight hundred years later the tower is intact to its roof - the only part of the castle, other than the gatehouse, which survives. From its top I could see how the plateau ended abruptly above a vast plain, the nothingness that I had felt beyond the ridge of Mahardah. It was a parched landscape of bare stubble-fields and shrivelled grass under a baking sun, striped green by the river and its surrounding irrigation. Far away the blue ridges of the Alawi Mountain shimmered in a heat haze that was intensified by stubble-fires burning vigorously even now, in the early morning.

One turn anti-clockwise, and I could see how Sheizar's promontory was isolated from its parent mountain by an immense man-made ditch; lying across the parapet I could just make out the distortion in the lower stones of the tower. Another turn, another permutation of geography, another world: the Orontes gorge far below, with the green-blue line of the river disappearing in the long tail of an S-bend through a deep cleft in the surrounding plateau. A few goat-tracks scored the scree at the foot of the gorge, giving out altogether at the point of the bend. Belatedly, I thanked my stars that I had slogged through Mahardah rather than trying doggedly to follow the river. I would have had to retrace my steps an awfully long way to escape from that gorge.

*

Checking that Madfaa was still securely tied a safe distance from Mohammed's hollyhocks, I took the easy route down to the river. How many times had Usamah ridden this way, down through the lower town of the citadel to the riverside gate, with a sword at his belt or a hawk on his wrist?

The Roman bridge beneath marks the point where the Orontes spills out at last from the confines of the plateau into the wide, fertile valley called the Ghaab. The river crossing, the crag, the strategic position controlling the valley: it was the combination of all these that made Sheizar so formidable. For extra security, someone - maybe Byzantine but more probably Arab – had built a square tower at the near end of the bridge. A pity the river had other ideas; for today the Citadel of the Bridge is marooned on the far side of the river, commanding a bridge which has itself been left high and dry as the fickle Orontes shifted some fifty yards to the south.

But for the dislocation of river and bridge, I might have been back in the time of the Crusades. I picked my way among sheep and goats grazing the watermeadows to where a group of women were washing fleeces. Skirts kilted up to their knees, they stood well out into the stream, beating their soggy bundles with heavy wooden paddles to drive out the the dirt and compress the wool. They sang as they worked, with a harsh nasal chant whose rhythm kept time with the rise and fall of the paddles.

A cry sounded from above. I looked up to see Mohammed waving to me. He had untied Madfaa, led him to the very edge of the cliff and was now sitting astride him, looking over the precipice and yelling for my attention. Speechless with horror, I could only return his wave; then turn my back and walk quickly away, hoping that he would stop playing dangerous games if there were no-one to notice him. Fifty yards on I glanced quickly over my shoulder, and heaved a sigh of relief to see that he'd disappeared.

From the bend, the lower loop of the S where the river entered the gorge, Sheizar Castle was spectacular. I realised that when I'd climbed the steps to the gatehouse I'd been walking on air, for two great arches spanned a deep cleft between castle and village. Following goat tracks which climbed at a hairy angle sometimes high above the river, sometimes on its very bank, I reached the point opposite the keep; and could go no further without wings.

*

As Madfaa's small, hard feet clattered across the stones of the ancient bridge I tried to imagine myself as a Saracen knight, riding out on my Arab stallion to confront the men of Antioch who had "pitched their tents where they used to pitch them" - that is, in the water-meadows beyond the river, the habitual changing-rooms of the visiting team. It was hardly the most defensible position for an invading army, but to have changed the rules would have been rotten sportsmanship.

Half a mile further on was the original crossing point. Just beyond the wide natural ford one last noria spun lazily, slopping a few drips of water into a ruined aqueduct that stopped short of the nearby olive groves. Nothing remained of its twin on the opposite bank but the stepped pier which had once supported the frame. Beyond, a soft track gave us a brief glorious canter beside the river; but it soon petered out, dumping us back on to asphalt. A major road, what's more, the main thoroughfare of the Ghaab. It was time to abandon the Orontes, which would soon lose its identity among a sophisticated grid of concrete channels directing every drop of water to irrigation. I took the first turning north, heading more or less to my next landmark of Afamia.

As the day wore on I began to look ever more urgently for somewhere to stop and allow Madfaa to rest and graze. But away from the river there were no trees, no shade from the burning sun. On the plus side, every mile or so furnished a block pumping station, where water bubbled up into a cistern and then gushed out into an aqueduct watering the surrounding fields. A constant wind off the Alawi Mountain kept the temperature bearable. It was a warm wind, though - at times almost a hot wind by the time it had passed across the Ghaab valley; it parched face and skin even faster than the sun alone would have done.

As in Central Asia, I was constantly passing old city mounds. There also I had been in natural oasis, the scene of early agriculture and settlement. Were there even more, here? I couldn't tell, as the agriculture broke up the landscape, altering all sense of distance. Certainly they were bigger; did that mean they were older, more layers of mud-brick houses crumbling to give their soil to the foundations of the next generation? It came as no surprise to find such intensive evidence of early occupation in what must be the most fertile area of the Levant.

I stopped at a roadside café for a Coke, and the owner brought a hose and a bucket to give Madfaa a long drink. A crowd quickly gathered around the stallion. A lady with a basket of cucumbers handed them out to the children to feed to him. Soon he was standing in the middle of a spreading green puddle of juice and pulp, while the shopkeeper began to look more and more dismayed at the mess.

I asked whether I could buy barley, having by now used up the stores with which Basil and Fayiz had seen me on my way. The answer was negative. At least I could fill my sack with *tibn*, the straw chaff which is the staple feed for anything with hooves in the Middle East; for piles of it filled the fields about, and the farmers who were busy lifting sugar beet or hoeing the cotton waved me to take all I wanted, refusing payment.

In the village of Jubbayn a girl came running after me, calling out in German. Farida's two uncles worked in Germany and she spoke the language well, disappointed when I answered in English. I gratefully accepted her invitation to stay at her house, stabling Madfaa in a half-finished building like a cross between a garage and a bus shelter. For me there was a bath, a welcome meal and a long sleep in a cool, shaded room.

Farida nodded in approval when I pinned out my underwear discreetly under a shirt on her rooftop washing line.

"Do you know," she said with wide eyes, "in Germany, they hang up their undergarments quite openly." I rolled my eyes in obedient horror; though in fact it was only a few days since Alhaam had taught me this courtesy, smiling in gentle reproof when I'd hung my knickers in full view within the privacy of her garden.

That evening Farida showed me photographs from the family album. I was surprised to see that, instead of the tightly-pinned scarves they now wore, she and her sisters were dressed in jeans and T-shirts.

"Where was this taken? In Germany?"

"Oh, no," she answered. "We wear western clothing whenever we visit our friends in Mahardah. Here in the village, we dress like everyone else."

Mahardah - just a few miles up the road. How effortlessly this girl moved between two cultures! And her answer banished any lingering fears that my own clothing might raise eyebrows in the conservative village climate. Not that I was unduly exposed; my jeans were loose-fitting and my sleeves usually long (although the heat often drove me to roll them up). As for my hair, a tight plait and a wide-brimmed straw hat preserved my modesty. Though the cover provided by the latter was diminishing by the day, as Madfaa reckoned it fair game and took every chance to make a grab at it. Soon I'd be reduced to the scout hat, presently squashed at the bottom of one saddlebag.

I longed to ask Farida if she found the village dress code irksome after the freedom of the town, but didn't want to seem rude about the local custom. Besides, her English was as limited as my Arabic. We talked of superficial things, comparing our lifestyles as best we could. Just before we went to bed, I had a sudden thought.

"By the way, what on earth is a *wa-wa*?"

It was a question which had been haunting me ever since Khattab. Perhaps the lions which Usamah spoke so casually of hunting were long gone, but who knew what creatures still lurked in the caves I'd seen high on the cliffs of that terrifying gorge? Maybe even now there were wolves, or lynx, perhaps vampire bats...?

Farida looked puzzled at my anxious face.

"A wa-wa? It's an ant."

*

On the outskirts of Jubbayn a woman was winnowing grain. Lifting it high above her head in a wicker basket, she tipped it slowly on to the mat at her feet, while the wind gathered the husks and whipped them into a cloud above her head.

I asked her the way to Afamia, and she pointed me right at the next crossroads. It was the wrong way, for it meant that I did a dog-leg and came on it from the east. It wouldn't have mattered, but for the fact that, since my maps had been drawn, someone had had the ill grace to dump a new reservoir in the way. The road curved down and round in a long detour, and unwisely I tried to cut the corner across the fields.

Madfaa and I crossed a field of stubble where the Bedouin-style sacking tents of yesterday's reapers huddled under an old city mound. Soon a field of cotton barred our way and I had to admit defeat, tracing a loop back to the road along a track edged with wild oats where Madfaa, like Christ's disciples, fed himself by gathering the ears as he passed.

From above, the reservoir glittered in the sun, looking good enough to swim in. At its edge, though, I found myself in a hostile landscape of quarried limestone chunks, blinding white in the midday heat. Madfaa picked his way among them in distaste; then, refusing to be daunted by the sharp hill opposite, tackled it with a small buck and great gusto. At the top I at last saw what I was looking for: a long line of Roman columns marching across the distant hillside.

Along a track past one last arm of the reservoir; then up a goat path across a slope strewn with flints. At its top a crack opened in the old city walls to receive us.

*

Afamia was founded by Seleucus Nicator, Macedonian heir to this part of Alexander the Great's empire. But it was his Roman successors who built for posterity, and up whose colonnaded street I now rode. Madfaa must have sensed the ghosts of the past more strongly than I, for two millennia ago horses outnumbered people in the plains and foothills hereabouts: the military stud of the Seleucids, once more than thirty thousand head of cavalry remounts.

As I tethered Madfaa to a chunk of fallen masonry in what had once been the *agora*, my main worry was water. I washed him off with a thimbleful, gave him most of the rest to drink then, settling him with a large feed, tipped the last drops into my billycan to cook the wonderful, stodgy tin of pasta I'd been dreaming about all day. I was just beginning to think about getting up to go in search of more water when the kindly man from the ticket office came back.

He had sought me out earlier, for I hadn't realised that by entering a tourist site by the back door I'd missed paying an entry fee. He had waved away my apologies and handed me a ticket. Now he was back, with two large water cans to show that he had anticipated my problems. By the time he had emptied them, Madfaa's bucket, both billies and my water bottle were brimming.

He stopped smiling, though, when I asked if anyone would mind if I spent the night here.

"You can't sleep here." He had a little English, but not enough to say what was on his mind. "It's... bad."

"What's the matter with it? It looks like a great place to me."

"There are... There are... "

"Wa-wa?" I supplied helpfully.

He frowned. "Snakes," he said gravely.

It was the same later with the *gardiens*, the officers who keep the tourists from damaging the site or, in my case, the site from damaging the tourists. But, besides being thrilled with the thought of sleeping among these ancient stones, I was far too exhausted to saddle up and move on. Anyway, there was nowhere else to stay. I promised to keep an eye open for hungry-looking reptiles, and they reluctantly left me to it.

There was plenty of rubble here to make my hearth, and with a chunk of masonry to block off a chimney I brewed pot after pot of tea while I considered the options for laying out my bed. The fluted alternating spirals on the columns opposite turned yellow as a peach while the sun slid behind the Alawi Mountain; then faded to grey. An owl began to stir from its perch under a pediment, swivelling its head to keep a wary eye on me.

I was very tempted to spend the night right here - nowhere would the ghosts be more sociable than in the ancient meeting-place - but the paving slabs were dangerously worn and slippery for a horse. So I went a bit further down the colonnade and found a perfect place near the old Christian Quarter.

I nearly tied Madfaa to one of the columns; but was afraid that his impatience might accomplish what two thousand years and a good few earthquakes had so far failed to manage. So I tethered him to a piece of fallen masonry with a belay fit to hold a twenty-stone mountaineer; then spread my things on a section of the main pavement which wouldn't have given cover to an earthworm, let alone a snake. I tied my more valuable things together for security, finishing by knotting my stirrups to the bag of tibn which doubled as my pillow. Finally I gave Madfaa another big feed, his third in as many hours, wishing I hadn't lost my torch at Sheizar as it was now completely dark. I was just falling into blissful sleep when the gardiens came back.

They had changed their minds.

"You can't sleep here," said the older of the two. "It's a bad place."

"I know," I said. "There are snakes. Too bad."

They were offended that I hadn't taken them seriously. "There is the *dad*."

"What's the dad?" I had a strong sense of *déjà vu*.

"The dad." He repeated darkly. "It'll eat you. It's fifty metres long."

Oh yeah, I thought, and I bet it wears a tartan beret.

"Just think, madame. Fifty metres long."

Here we go again, I thought. Playing for time, I brought out my dictionary. The dad wasn't among its vocabulary, but it made amends with a splendid centrefold showing the natural history of the Arab world. The younger man took it, scrutinising the bestiary. For a moment his finger hovered lovingly over the picture of the Nile crocodile; then, obviously realising that this might be pushing his luck a bit too far, he closed the book with a shake of his head and handed it back. It seemed the dad had so far eluded the notice of the world's zoologists.

But I wasn't going to win this argument. Mutinously admitting defeat, I undid my careful knots and repacked my saddlebags; then, trailing a bemused Madfaa who had just begun to nod his head in a doze, followed the two young men away from my Perfect Place. They led me past the pillars and pediments of the main avenue, by a goat track running across a small hillock, to a one-roomed blockhouse by a field of sunflowers. Unlocking its padlocked door, they took out their night things then, indicating I should do the same, locked the rest of my gear away safely and prepared to spend the night in the cool of the rooftop.

To tie Madfaa, they offered me a rusty angle-iron sticking eighteen inches above the ground. Tutting at my quick-release knot, one of them undid my careful tether and retied him, too short, the rope held by a Gordian knot. I stood back and said nothing; easier and more tactful to put things straight when they had gone to sleep.

But I was to have no chance of that. They stood and waited for me to climb the roof-ladder first, clearly determined that I shouldn't escape. It took me several embarrassing minutes to retie the rope properly, then take my sleeping bag inner and pad the dangerously sharp iron, winding it round several times and securing it with a braid of baling twine. The two men watched intently, their disapproval deepening with every coil of the twine.

At last Madfaa was as safe as I could make him, and I preceded my now deeply frowning hosts on to the roof. It made a lousy start to the night, and it was no surprise that it became one of the most miserable nights I've ever spent.

Poor Madfaa, upset by the changes, couldn't rest. Back and forth he paced, unsettled and anxious, knocking over his feed bucket; although even in his anxiety he kept his wits about him, remembering that he was tethered, remembering that he might go backwards and forwards but must never go round and round. But for his intelligence I would have been up and down the ladder a score of times to unwind him. Nevertheless I watched him all the time, going down to check him more closely every hour or so. At last, exhausted, he quietened down. But still I couldn't sleep.

By now a wind had got up. The air had been still at dusk, but now a keen breeze sliced through my single sleeping bag. Its direction was the opposite to that of the day. Dimly I remembered school geography lessons: wind flows from the sea to the land by day, from the land to the sea by night. This was cold air off the night-time deserts of Iraq, winging its way home to the distant Mediterranean in time to reverse the performance next morning. I shivered, regretting the extra layer wrapping the rusty post.

At five it got light. One of the gardiens tapped me on the shoulder.

"Wake up, madame. Morning."

I had to get up, wind up my bedroll and descend the ladder to get my things out of the hut before they re-locked it and went on their way. I gave another feed to Madfaa, who was now standing hunched in an exhausted doze, then returned to the roof and slept a little as the temperature slowly climbed off the floor.

At six, the early sun hit the distant Alawi Mountain, creeping down its side until it reached the plain, and firing the sunflowers like molten bronze.

At six-thirty a herd of goats crashed suddenly out of the sunflowers, startling Madfaa so that he shot sideways and cannoned into the iron post. By the time I reached the bottom of the ladder he was standing on three legs, with blood pouring from the fourth.

*

The lady at the tourist restaurant wasn't too happy to be woken at the crack of dawn. But she kindly didn't grumble as she gave me the clean water that I urgently needed to wash the wound.

It was a nasty cut, bleeding copiously, and the leg was already starting to swell. But it wasn't too serious, and should mend quite quickly. That was lucky; but for the padding on the tether post, the damage might have been catastrophic. I bathed it until the bleeding stopped, and bandaged it to keep out the dust; then crashed out for a merciful couple of hours while I worked out the next move.

There was no question of travelling on. I needed somewhere to lie up for a couple of days, somewhere where Madfaa and I could both rest and eat comfortably, while I waited to see how well the leg healed. So I turned my back on Afamia's ancient stones, and took the tourist road to the sizeable village at the foot of the former citadel, Qala'at al-Madiq.

Within minutes Madfaa had attracted attention, and I asked the first people who spoke to me where I might rent a room and a stable. I sat on the stone wall surrounding an olive garden while kindly people went and enquired. Within an hour, Madfaa was comfortably installed in a large, rather dusty but cool stable from which the winter's supply of wood had been hastily evicted, and whacking down a good feed. I had the luxury of a room to myself. I lay peacefully digesting a wonderful lunch of fish straight out of the Orontes, of which ominously wrote the seventeenth century traveller Henry Maundrell: "Its waters are turbid, and very unwholesome, and its fish worse; as we found by experience, there being no person of all our company that had eaten of them overnight, but found himself much indisposed the next morning."

My fish were entirely wholesome, and the next morning I was very well disposed.

*

Officially, my host was the village schoolteacher, Hassan Koko. But my real hostess was his daughter.

Bada'a, at fifteen, was newly designated a woman. She wore the hijab with gravity and pride, as the badge of adulthood which she was proud to have had conferred on her. Self-consciously demure under the nun-like wimple, she was still young enough to be childlike. Her cousin and constant companion, Manal, a year or two younger, was not yet thus encumbered.

Encumbered; so, involuntarily, I saw it. It disturbed me to find in myself this narrow western view, this judgement on another culture. Yet it disturbed me, too, to see Bada'a's childhood curtailed; her hair and neck hidden, like something shameful, inside the closely-pinned scarf; her spontaneity curbed by the need to behave with adult gravity at all times. She seemed like a butterfly buttoned firmly back into a chrysalis. Yet Bada'a was clearly happy with her adult status. She felt more honoured than encumbered. Who was the more encumbered by their culture, she or I?

Bada'a spoke very good English, clear and careful, and was delighted to practise it on me. In turn she coached me a little in my Arabic, with a patient awareness of my difficulties that she might have learned from her schoolteacher father. Obviously studious and academically gifted, she wanted to go to university. I found myself hoping that by doing so she might achieve some freedom, might escape to some extent from the narrow limitations of her village life. Immediately I banished the thought in contempt. Here I was, actively setting out to enter her world myself. Who the hell was I, to be arro-gantly wishing my own on her? Perhaps it was her disconcerting resemblance to my own teenage niece, my constantly recurring vision of Katie rebellious within the veil, that dislocated my judgement.

Bada'a's father and uncle lived side by side, their two houses giving on to a single yard, their two large families mingling so that it was impossible to tell who was whose child. Especially now, with half the village children coming in to see the horse and the foreigner.

They pressed around Madfaa while I sat in the yard holding a gently trickling hosepipe to the injured leg, so that the cold water might cleanse the wound and reduce the bruising. Soon they were taking turns to hold the hose, or bringing Madfaa titbits from the kitchen, or asking me searching voracious questions about my journey, while I struggled to understand and to answer and Bada'a helped with translation. For the first time the gang surrounding me was entirely friendly. I found myself wondering why kids could be such monsters on the streets and so entirely charming at home. Were they aggressive because they felt insecure away from home, threatened by something foreign? Or was it the presence of their sisters that civilised the boys - or the knowledge that adults lurked behind the curtains within call?

In the evening Bada'a and Manal sang for me, their young voices ringing out a folk song with bell-like clarity. Then they rather shyly asked whether I would like to see a dance they had been taught at school.

"We don't dance with the men," they said. "We learn to dance with each other; it's more becoming."

I had expected something a bit dull, a stately minuet in line with the proprieties to be observed by teenage girls. What followed was a revelation. It was a wild, joyful romp with elements of tango and rock'n'roll jive among the more obviously oriental steps. The girls went at it with gusto, whirling and twirling in and out of each other's arms with all the high voltage of western kids at a disco - but much, much more skill. So much for western preconceptions about repressed Arab females, I thought ruefully.

*

There was no easy way up to Qala'at al Madiq. It was a truncated cone, a natural fortress, cut off from the plateau on which Afamia had grown up.

As I trudged up the long zig-zag to the single entrance in its girdle walls, I wondered at the three great arches in the stonework. Was this part of the original entrance, an arched bridge like that at Sheizar? If so, it had long ago fallen out of use; now the road skirted its foot and houses perched dizzily on top.

From the heights, looking west across ten miles of absolutely flat land to the mountains beyond, you could appreciate the citadel's strategic importance. At this point the Orontes valley turns from north-west to north, as the river sets course for Antioch and the sea; sitting on the inner corner of the bend, Qala'at al Madiq, the Castle of the Narrows, commands the whole valley. Together with Qala'at Burzey at the foot of the Jebel al-Alawiyiin, it made a formidable pair of obstacles, a Scylla and Charybdis which any south-bound army must negotiate, driven through the fertile valley by the need for provisions. Perhaps it was the combined threat of these two giants which drove the first wave of Crusaders further east, skirting the dangers, to fight and starve at Ma'arat an-Nu'man on the desiccated and hungry plateau. They must surely have regretted their choice, for there they committed one of the most grisly acts of a grisly campaign: in their desperation, they ate the Saracens they had killed.

Qala'at al Madiq remained a thorn in the Crusader flank, and its capture was a priority for Bohemond, first Prince of Antioch. Maybe he raised the stones which I now clung to as I picked a cautious path round the outer walls. Great honey-coloured stones, probably purloined from Afamia, they made a fierce contrast with the deep green of the occasional fig-tree clinging to the bank. In the valley beneath, orchards and cornfields repeated the green-and-gold pattern into the far distance.

A handful of gravestones, overshadowed by oleander, lay under the walls. What a splendid place to bury your dead, I thought as I carefully edged round them; and what a view to rise to at the last trump! Until then they would lie peacefully, undisturbed; for the only way up this side of the hill was for goats.

Inside the walls was a tangle of higgledy-piggledy streets, most of them no wider than a laden donkey and some a good bit narrower. Twisting and turning, I lost my sense of direction at once and wandered in confusion, not knowing whether the next turning would bring me into a main street, end in someone's back yard, or take me under an archway into a shed of rusty machinery. Long habitation had utterly absorbed the castle. I glimpsed it only where flagstones replaced the usual dust and rubble underfoot, or where the concrete block of modern building sat astride huge foundation stones left over from a distant century. Near the highest point a rose bush poured pink blossom from what might, with a stretch of the imagination, have passed for the base of a keep; and several hundred goldfish swam in an ancient cistern.

At a shop by the entrance gate I bought a Coke, and sat drinking it on the edge of the scarp looking over the mosque to the graceful square of the old Ottoman khan in the town beneath the citadel. A roar sounded behind me, and a gleaming motorbike powered through the ageing gateway. Its riders, two men with white dishdashas drawn up to their knees so that they could sit comfortably astride, looked like sleepwalkers on a mission.

*

An hour out from Qala'at al Madiq, and travelling straight as a die across the dip between the two ranges of mountains: the plateau behind, its skyline broken by the outline of the citadel; and the dramatic escarpment of the Jebel al-Alawiyiin ahead. The land about me utterly, utterly flat, and rich with corn of every description, sunflowers, potatoes, beet...

But absolutely no grass. The fierce sun had long burned off any excess growth, and the irrigation water was so carefully directed that none escaped; no odd puddles, therefore, to be colonised by greenstuff doing its own thing. A pity, as poor Madfaa was becoming browned off himself with dried food. But this land had once been wet, very wet. The roadside was littered with what looked like seashells. Or perhaps the locals ate snails?

The mountains looked as far away as ever; except that, slowly, I began to pick out detail. Dark green growth covered their steep slopes; dry bushes, rather than trees. Tracks snaked up the gentler valleys, with the occasional burst of rubble, falling like scree, to show where the bulldozers had been particularly active.

Looking back, I could see for the first time the full extent of Afamia's city walls, their heavy stonework framing the columns that marched for more than a mile across the hillside. Imagine being a legionary - or a knight-at-arms - sweating up to the citadel in full armour in this heat.

It wasn't too bad today, in fact. By now Madfaa had completely rubbished my straw hat, and I'd had to throw it away and use the narrower one I'd bought in Damascus, but I didn't feel troubled by the heat. Was I getting acclimatised, or was it simply, as Manal had forecast yesterday evening, less hot today? I stopped at a shop and begged water for Madfaa; then, his needs seen to, sank a couple of cans of Coke myself.

"Do you have any oats? Barley?"

"There is *durra*," someone said. It rang a bell. In Egypt I had seen horses fed on durum wheat, small round grains mixed in with the tibn. Could this be the same?

"Yes, please. Could I see?"

It turned out to be crushed maize with a generous helping of wheat. It wasn't what Madfaa was used to, and wheat isn't the best grain for horses. But I knew that he liked it, since a generous host had fed him the odd handful; anyway the proportion was small enough to be safe. I tried it out on him, and he seemed to approve. I bought three kilos, and both of us were satisfied.

It made for heavy saddlebags, as Madfaa already carried a big stuff-sack full of tibn. But as there was no grazing it was imperative to carry provisions. And my own necessities didn't take up much space. They were organised into drawstring or plastic bags, easy to shift from one side to the other so as to balance the weight. Clothing – spare shirt and trousers, and a couple of changes of underwear; sleeping bag; food and cooking things; washbag and small towel; medical kit and essential veterinary supplies – antibiotic spray, Animalintex dressing and a puffer bottle of sulphanilamide powder. Then there was my Useful Bag, named with memories of childhood story books and filled with miscellaneous necessities: matches, comb, superglue, plastic tape, soap powder, needle and carpet thread, compass, and so on. Plus one completely useless object. A tiny wire saw, two rings joined by a length of toothed wire which at a pinch, and with much time and sweat, might cut through a twig if it was half-dead already. I'd never yet found a use for it in three journeys; but it intrigued me, and it weighed nothing. Besides, there might come a time when I'd need to build a shelter of bamboo stalks, or improvise a bow-and-arrow, or weave Madfaa a wicker feed-basket…

It was a short, slow stage today, no more than ten kilometres. The leg was healing well but still swollen, and mustn't be worked for long. But Madfaa was quite sound and stepped out vigorously, fresh from a couple of days' rest. And the mountains were having the decency to creep visibly nearer.

*

Evening. A herd of goats come home driven by a small boy; they champ at the stubble as they go, and raise a cloud of dust in their passing. Half a dozen ladies walk down the road carrying plastic water bottles on their heads. A girl lays another bundle of twigs on the heap beside the oval mound of a mud-brick oven. Little boys swim naked in a bright green pool of second-hand Orontes water, laughing and shouting, diving with a splash under a tangle of slimy duckweed, while the low sun ricochets off their wet, glistening bodies. The incessant noise of the pumps finally dies, as one after another is shut off. Over against the mountains, little pockets of light spring up in the angle between the plain and the scarp.

Another dusty stable for Madfaa, sheep and chickens scattering as he picks his way carefully inside. A long, cool drink, and a manger full of feed.

Problems. A few mouthfuls of *durra*, and he pushes it aside, nosing through the tibn for something more to his liking. Must, absolutely must, find some barley tomorrow.

*

Right turn, and north for a bit. Left turn, and west for a bit. The roads were like a grid. Even I couldn't get lost here.

Except for the Orontes; I'd managed to lose that. Surely we should have crossed it again by now? At last a bridge took us across a bare, featureless canal, like those we had crossed already but many times the size. A dredger worked busily, manicuring the edges into a precise slope of forty-five degrees.

This, then, was what remained of the graceful river of upstream, shoe-horned into featureless banks like a young girl into a hijab. I would not see its like again; for the irrigation work which feeds so much of Syria would control it carefully for many miles to the north. By the time the Orontes regathered its waters into one stream to run *au naturel* beneath the bridge at Jisr ash-Shughuur, I would be several thousand feet above it. *In sha'llahu*, I thought, if God wills it.

The road ran straight into the side of the mountain, until I thought it would bury us. Instead it climbed a few feet and joined a larger one running due north along the edge of the plain. Now, thanks to nature and gravity, there began to be water again. I offsaddled where a wide, shallow lake fed a generous patch of grass, and Madfaa gratefully set to for a couple of hours. By the shore opposite water buffaloes grazed, or stood up to their knees in the water. A little further on a village had grown up by a spring which fed a small pool under a grove of walnut trees. It was a picnic spot, busy today with children swimming in the water while their parents stood over barbecues.

Another lush patch brought tiny froglets, exploding out from under our feet with every step. I can hardly believe this is Syria, I thought, as we strolled through grassy meadows with tamarisk on one side and olive groves on the other. Left and right were utterly different worlds, divided by the road. To one side stretched the baking plain, striped by agriculture, barren and empty now that the corn was cut, with a faint whiff of charred vegetation; to the other the cool mountain, its breath fragrant with resin, bristled with pine and low scrub pressing right up to the tarmac. The birdsong, even the sound of the insect life was different. The air positively fizzed with crickets in my left ear, until I was convinced that my aerosol antibiotic spray was leaking and stopped to check.

There was a difference, too, in the villages. Many of the houses were painted. The majority of these were in pious themes, representations of a mosque or the elegant calligraphy of prayers; but in Qassat ar-Ramla the Muslim proscription against representing living forms hadn't reached the Disney figures jollying up the local shop. The general air of loosening up a bit stretched to the women. Where I stayed last night, most of the women had tied their scarves loosely about their necks, rather than pinning them up tightly. One woman actually went bare-headed. And could that possibly have been a female figure in the pair of jeans I'd seen in the distance?

Arriving at the village of Jawriin, then, I was partly prepared for a new set of rules. Nawfal Amiri's family dressed in whatever felt comfortable. Nawfal himself wore a dishdasha for the cool of the evening, and his mother a long dress and headscarf; but one sister wore a shirt and jeans and the other, gowned but bare-headed, openly embraced her boyfriend. Both girls wore open-toed sandals and painted their toe-nails.

There had to be a fundamental cause behind this obviously different culture. "Are you Christian?" I asked Nawfal. In the last few villages I had looked in vain for a mosque.

"No. We are Alawi."

*

I hadn't really expected to meet the Alawi people already, even before leaving the plain. But some of the characteristics of the Mountain seemed to have spilled down on to the edge of the Ghaab just here, and perhaps they had brought the people with them. Or perhaps it was the other way about; perhaps the people themselves, settling here, had brought their own apartness, the scent of their very different world.

The Alawis number just over a tenth of Syria's sixteen million inhabitants, living mostly in "their" mountain, the Jebel al-Alawiyiin. Mostly passed over by history and occasionally oppressed as a heretic minority, they are now in high favour. From the Alawi village of Qir-daha, just over the mountain ridge from Jawriin, came the family of Hafez al-Assad, who rose from a distinguished career in the Air Force to become President in 1971, filling the ruling Ba'ath party with his fellow Alawis.

The sect, secretive and inward-looking, has long defied outside analysis, even by its close neighbours. Its creed is the subject of rumour and speculation. "They worship the sun and the stars," say some. "They believe in re-incarnation," say others. "Oh, the Alawis; they worship only Ali, not God," was a claim I heard more than once. Fedden is more specific: "interesting hermetic faith... controlled by a hereditary priesthood... secret rites and an initiation. They worship a curious trinity, believe in metempsychosis and preserve a rich symbolism whose significance they have forgotten. They have no churches or mosques, but revere the tombs of saints..."

There is only one conventional Islamic pigeon-hole that might be applied to them, and that very loosely: *Shi'ite*, of the *Shii'at Ali* or the party of Ali. Shortly after the death of the Prophet Mohammed, conflict arose over his successors: two sons-in-law, Uthman and Ali, both of whom were ultimately assassinated. The bloody wars between their respective parties - the *Sunna* (those who follow the consensus of contemporary theological scholars) and the minority *Shii'a* (whose creed acknowledges the legitimacy of election or heredity) - created schism in the Islamic world which has lasted to the present day. As for the Alawis, most mainstream Shi'ites would disown them as heretic.

How did they regard themselves? "Are you Muslim? Are you Sunni? Are you Shi'ite?" I asked Nawfal and his sisters.

No, they said, they were none of these. "We respect Mohammed as a prophet; Jesus, too. But whereas the Muslims worship Mohammed, we worship only God. We, the Alawis, go back eight hundred years, but the beliefs on which our religion is founded go back three thousand years."

In other words, well into the roots of Judaeo-Christian faith, I assumed they meant. It was only later that it occurred to me that this time scale would fit equally well with another possible origin suggested for their beliefs: the paganism of the Phoenicians who occupied these coastal mountains for centuries, reaching the height of their power for a couple of centuries either side of 1000 B.C.

From the veranda of Nawfal's house, the escarpment looked sheer, and awfully forbidding. My turning for the hills was just a hundred yards up the road. It would lead into the heart of Alawi territory. There would be plenty of time to find the answers to all my questions.

II

THE MOUNTAIN

A thousand feet above the plain, and already the Ghaab was falling away below me, its green-and-yellow chequerboard dulled to shades of grey by the haze. Was that mist coming off the fertile valley, or just the collective smoke of a thousand stubble-fires, rolled up against the base of the mountains by the relentless night wind?

I had looked forward to getting into these mountains. So far, though, I was crawling along their edge like an insect. At least I was crawling upwards, if painfully slowly. "Take the right-hand road," the man in the village had warned. "The left-hand one is very difficult." This was supposed to be the easy way.

A few terraces tried to tame the feral mountainside, coaxing olive and fig trees from the stony soil. But for most of the way only boulders and pine grew out of the ochre-coloured earth, and the smell of pine resin intensified with every step.

Another thousand feet, and I could look down through a gap between folds of the mountainside to where Qala'at Burzey, no more than a ruinous heap of stones, once guarded the western side of the Ghaab. No doubt from the valley floor it stood out as impressively as its twin Qala'at al-Madiq. From here it looked like an anthill.

By early afternoon I was looking desperately for the pass through which this road would eventually breach the escarpment. The summit of Jebel Nebi Younis, highest mountain hereabouts, came slowly down to meet Madfaa and me as we climbed laboriously upwards. It was only when we had nearly reached its top that the road consented to level out, striding for some five hundred yards along a saddle which gave stupendous views to either side.

I had never thought, as I'd looked longingly at these glorious mountains from the plain below, that I would have to go straight over the very top of them. Now, as I looked to east and west, I might have been in an aeroplane. Thankfully I said my goodbyes to the Ghaab - splendid view though it was, I had been struggling to lose it all day - and took my first look at the landscape which was to play host to us both for the coming weeks.

I saw a land which might have come straight from a children's story -book. Great wild gorges, covered in forest; gentle little patches of cultivation where farmers eked out a living; round, isolated hilltops projecting above the surrounding upland. I half expected to see the towers and turrets of fairy-tale castles on their tops. What pleased me more was that it was all below me. From now on - *al-hamdu li'llah!* - we would be travelling downhill.

The view lacked one essential feature: there were no rural settlements where I could beg a stable for Madfaa. The road broadened, began to run between yellow-painted kerb-stones and led us into Slenfeh, a resort town where the wealthy from the coastal plain came to escape the heat and humidity of high summer. As usual, Madfaa generated a lot of interest. While I slumped on the pavement waiting for an answer to my enquiry about accommodation, people leaned out from the window of the house above, full of friendly questions. A moment later a girl came out of the door and thrust a plate of casserole and rice into my hands. Manna from heaven, and even more unexpected, it was the best food I had ever tasted; but it reminded me that Madfaa, too, must eat and rest.

The answer came back, and was vague: there might be a stable to rent, but it was six kilometres in the wrong direction. Too far if it turned out to be no good. I shook my head, got up and carried on. As we left the suburbs of Slenfeh I began to eye up patches of waste ground among the many new houses which were under construction on the edge of town. At a pinch I could tether Madfaa where there was grazing, give him the feed I had bought in Jawriin and doss down alongside him. But there could well be snakes in all that long grass.

The sun was nearly down. A shop ahead was the last building before a long stretch of empty country. I would ask there; if the shopkeeper hadn't got any ideas, I'd be sleeping under a hedge.

*

"Ooh-kaaay, *yesss!*" Mohammed spat venomously out of the window of his truck, as if he would rather have spat in my face. Then, realising that I was within an inch of opting for the hedge after all, he became suddenly ingratiating. If he tried to inflate his price any more, or held out for me to pay for the barley before I'd seen it, he might lose my custom altogether. Leaning towards me in his anxiety to please, he breathed clouds of garlic into my face. "Ooh-kaaay, *yesss!*" I shrank back into the passenger seat, deciding that I preferred the venom.

Actually, the barley turned out to be very good. It was heavily milled - much better and more digestible than the whole grain I usually had to settle for - and went down a bundle with Madfaa, who buried his nose and ate greedily. I didn't say so to Mohammed, though. He might have put the price up again.

Having driven up to the shop while I was asking about renting a stable, he had become an instant travel agent. As I followed him down the road I wasn't too enthusiastic about enlisting his services, but Madfaa was exhausted and hungry after his prodigious day's work, and needed food and shelter. Mohammed's idea of a stable was the shell of a room in one of the part-built houses springing up along the road. The first two were quite impossible to put a horse in; in desperation I accepted the third, a basement with a wooden table sitting on a floor littered with rubble, wires draped everywhere and no door. Mohammed picked up the table.

"I'll take this outside, ooh-kaaay!" He blocked the doorway with it after I had led Madfaa inside, both of us carefully picking a way over the rubble. At least now I could take off his saddle, rub him down and give him something to eat. I spread my groundsheet over the floor where I put his bucket, for any food dropped into that dust wouldn't be coming out again. Thank goodness I'd found some bran at Jawriin to cheer up the tibn.

As we set off in his truck to pick up the barley included in the deal, Mohammed wrapped the cloak of false civility around his pressure on me to renegotiate the price he'd offered. Carefully he sought a balance, trying not to antagonise me too far, pressing his face closer to mine the more persuasive he became. "Ooh-kaaay, *yesss!*" Then he would break off, muttering viciously to himself, Gollum-like, before returning to his theme.

Once Madfaa was fed and as comfortable as possible, he took me next door to my own billet. A family lived in two rooms next to the basement, and Mohammed subcontracted my accommodation to them for less than half the sum I had paid him. I slept in a bleak room with a bare stone floor, whose only furniture was a couple of sofas and an old treadle sewing machine in the corner. At least in the filthy kitchen next door I could cook my own food, and brew the gallons of tea that I'd been dreaming of all day.

Neither Madfaa nor I got much sleep that night. Restless in his comfortless surroundings, he would take a few mouthfuls of food then pace endlessly round and round the basement, scrunching over the stones. Watching him through a hole in the wall, I dozed only fitfully, the night-long clatter of iron on stone woven into such dreams as I managed.

By morning, I had only one thought: to find somewhere to stay where both of us could rest up after a ghastly twenty-four hours. As we trudged slowly down the road I was urgently spying out the landscape, trying to get the measure of the very different country we were now in.

The problem was that these mountains were too high and wild for much agriculture. There seemed to be no villages, only a few towns like Slenfeh where the city-dwellers from Lattakia and Aleppo had second homes. People here didn't appear to keep goats and donkeys, only cars. It wasn't horse country. Even the rubbish on the roadside was town rubbish: plastic bags, drink cans, plastic bottles of Dreikish mineral water from the south of the Mountain; once, the shards of what had once been an entire tinted windscreen.

Taking it very leisurely - mileage was the last thing on my mind today - I stopped and offsaddled in a cluster of trees surrounding a small pool. A few tombs were scattered around; could this be one of the sacred groves of the Alawis that I'd read about? It was certainly an impressive spot. Below the pool, the land fell away sharply for a thousand feet to a gorge running deep into the mountainside. The sudden opening up of the view, the sense of disorientation as the whole landscape changed from closed and intimate to vast and limitless, the horizon rolling back from a few yards away one minute to infinity the next: all these features were to become familiar over the coming weeks. While Madfaa gratefully dropped his head and grazed, I sat gazing out into the distance, slowly learning the parameters of this new frame of reference.

Another mile or two, and the country softened a little. Below a small group of houses, the first rural settlement of any sort that I had come to since Slenfeh, a lake stood in the hollow of some shallow hills. Grass grew thickly about its edges; calves and goats were haltered around it, and a heifer stood up to her belly in the water. It drew me irresistibly with the promise of peace and plenty, and I thought seriously of tethering Madfaa and bivvying alongside him. But first I would try my luck at the small village.

*

Picking my way carefully up a narrow, stony track, I reached the little settlement and stopped at the first house I came to. Three generations were drinking tea, grouped about a cloth spread under a walnut tree. I put my enquiry to the eldest man, the proper thing to do. While he deliberated, I tied Madfaa up, fed and watered him, then sat down and gratefully accepted a glass of tea from the young woman who was the mother of the four children.

After a seemingly endless consultation, which occasionally included the other adults but was mostly addressed to himself, he said yes. Shortly after, he stood up and went home to a neighbouring house. I never saw him again.

Ghaada, the young woman, took me into the house and showed me where to put my bags. For Madfaa there was a good stable with a manger in one corner, and plenty of feed to buy, as the family kept cows. He could spend the afternoon in the fresh air, under the walnut tree. Soon he collected a crowd of admirers, who seated themselves about him on the polished limestone slabs under the tree.

The house itself grew straight out of weathered limestone blocks; it was difficult to see where nature had run out of steam and man had continued the upward drive. As you went down the hillside towards the lake the rock became rougher and rougher, its cracks and holes here and there big enough to use for fastening a rope. For now, though, all the animals were elsewhere. The garden had another function.

Ghaada and her family grew tobacco. A hundred and fifty kilos of tobacco a year, to be precise. Tobacco was all around. There was tobacco in the fields, tobacco drying in the garden, tobacco spread out in the kitchen, the living room, the bedrooms. Green, newly-picked tobacco filled the hall, where Ghaada sat for long hours threading strings of tobacco, ready to hang them out in the garden for the sun to turn them golden brown. Outside, racks and racks and racks of tobacco stretched like hammocks, turning their own deeply tanned faces to the sky for lack of sunworshippers to lie in them. Even the flowerbeds grew tobacco - ornamental tobacco, spreading great crimson flowers among the roses.

I began to realise how often I had seen tobacco, without recognising it. It was the staple of the local economy. Ghaada told me how it would bake here for four weeks, before being sold on to businesses in Lattakia for processing. This was the famous Lattakia leaf, which in due course would be shipped out of Syria's main port and smoked all over the world.

She worked as she talked, sitting cross-legged on the floor, dark hair pulled back off her face; methodically picking and threading, picking and threading. Gradually the chaotic heap of green leaves was tamed, transformed into neat strips which could be carried out for their turn on the racks. However many such strings would it take to make a hundred and fifty kilos? I wished afterwards that I'd thought to ask her.

It was hard work, but a good life, I thought, in this idyllic little village held in a crook of the mountains, green and fertile even in the height of the scorching Syrian summer. Certainly contentment seemed to be written in Ghaada's face, and her dark eyes were luminous with humour and empathy. The serenity, I was shortly to learn, came from inside her; for her life wasn't after all the idyll it first seemed.

I was wondering if she would allow Madfaa and me to stay a few days here for the rest we both needed so badly, when the first fly plopped into the ointment. A dark, rather Iranian-looking man arrived, yelling at the children and chasing one of them down the garden with apparently murderous intent; rather extreme behaviour, given that it was his own child. This was my first meeting with Ghaada's husband, Hassan.

Hassan was miffed that arrangements had been made without him. Stuck with a *fait accompli*, he tried to assert himself by doubling the price named by the old man. It was a perfectly fair price and, as I knew by now, the going rate. Although I would gladly have paid double to Ghaada herself, he was so unpleasant that I refused. Belatedly I realised that Ghaada had shown me into their own bedroom, so I quickly picked up my bags and absconded to the living room.

"I'm sorry," I said to her, "but I'm very tired, and just want to avoid any hassle. After all, we had already agreed everything."

"Don't worry," she answered. "It isn't his house, anyway. It's mine."

So that was the problem. Hassan was flexing his muscles, asserting his control over his household. The house attached to Ghaada's, I learned, belonged to his mother, whom I'd met that afternoon under the walnut tree. Ghaada had inherited her own property, then married the boy next door.

All too soon it became apparent that the real cross she had to bear was her mother-in-law. The old lady was a harpy. Shrill and vicious, she chased the children and clouted them vigorously, constantly shouting and cursing at animals and people alike. I soon blotted my copybook when I tried to stable Madfaa for the night.

She snatched the lead rope and tied him to the ring in the manger. But he couldn't stay tethered overnight, behind a closed door, while I slept away from him in the house; we had discussed this earlier. Anyway, the stable door was secure, and there was absolutely no reason to tie him. But the minute I slipped the headcollar over his head and let him loose, she stood in the doorway, hands on hips, and unleashed a torrent of invective. Trembling, I quickly tied him again, then went and asked Ghaada to mediate.

With a patience that must have been born of long experience, Ghaada soothed the old woman until Madfaa could be freed. But, outraged at having to yield, the mother-in-law vented her fury on the door in the corner leading to the granary. Madfaa, she swore, would break this down and plunder the tibn store as soon as her back was turned.

With a constant stream of complaint, she fetched various tools and barricaded the door, a statement rather than a necessity.

Here as elsewhere I needed Ghaada's help as interpreter, since I was still plodding along in *fasaha* - classical Arabic. The language of the Qur'an and essentially little changed since the days of the Prophet, this is the medium of Parliament, books, newspapers and even, mostly, television; so most people understand it. But few, even intellectuals, feel comfortable with its old-fashioned formality. Imagine speaking to your friends in the language of the Prayer Book. People invariably replied to me in Syrian dialect, so far evolved from the original as to have to be learned separately. I knew very little. It usually made for a rather one-sided conversation.

It was rare that I met someone like Ghaada, or the schoolmaster from Khattab, who understood my problems and had the patience to try and converse with me beyond a few basic exchanges. Hassan, although he was himself a schoolmaster, couldn't even seem to understand my fasaha, let alone bother to respond in kind. I could hardly have blamed him for the first; except that Ghaada seemed to manage very nicely. When Hassan came into my room later that evening, he used her as his interpreter as heavily as I'd been doing all afternoon.

He was actually trying to make an effort to be sociable, but he just didn't have the skill. Instead, he went through all my baggage, neatly sorted and arranged, and within moments had turned it all inside out with the skill of a two-year-old going through its mother's handbag. As he did so, he fired questions at me about my equipment.

"Hey.... (What's her name?)" this last to Ghaada.

"Gill," she said.

" ...where did you get your saddlebags?"

"I made them." But he'd lost interest already. He asked questions, it seemed, only to gain attention.

"Hey... (What's her name?)"

" Gill."

" ...this is a good coat. I want one like this."

"Hey... (What's her name?)"

"Gill."

" ...how much did this radio cost?"

I was struggling to do some much-needed repairs to my gear. At each "Hey" I answered "Mmm..?" with my attention fixed on the needle. Offended, Hassan gave me a bollocking for my lack of respect. So at the next "Hey" I obediently looked up and answered "*Aiwa?*" - one of the few dialect words which had penetrated my slow brain.

"Say *na'am*[1] when you speak to me!" he snapped. If he had learned one skill as a teacher, it was to bully.

"Hey... (What's her name?) How much did this camera cost? You can't get one like this in Syria. I need one like this. I'll buy it from you."

It was an SLR with a zoom lens, not a cutting-edge piece of equipment but the minimum for my needs. "I'm sorry; it's not for sale."

"But I want it. I'll give you the money."

"It's a tool of my trade. I can't do without it."

"But I want it. I will give you another one as good."

I managed to bite my tongue before jumping on the contradiction. Be tactful, I told myself, for Ghaada's sake. "I'm sorry; I'm used to this one."

"*But I want it...*"

Poor Ghaada. One of them was bad enough.

When Hassan's mother came in, it seemed that things could only get worse. But, for once, the old woman seemed to be trying to be conciliatory. That, I assumed, was why she invited me to spend the night at her house. Wanting to smooth things over I agreed, hiding my disappointment; for I had looked forward to spending the evening with Ghaada, taking a rare opportunity for some conversation. Only much later did I realise that the harpy wanted to exact her revenge over Madfaa and the stable. Fool that I was to have run before such spurious threats as the *wa-wa* and the *dad*, only to lie down obediently with the most venomous creature in Syria.

The first piece of bad news was that I was to share a bedroom with the harpy herself. Five minutes after going to bed she roused herself, uttering a long stream of curses in which only the word "horse" was recognisable to me. I ignored her, thinking that in her sleeping hours she carried over her waking habits, querulous even in her dreams. It turned out, though, that her grievance was that Madfaa was audible next door, moving around in his stable - a liberty which, in the den of the harpy, was insupportable. All night long she complained. Several times, her spleen drove her from her bed to stand over me, cursing. In

---

[1] The Classical Arabic form for "yes"

the end, desperate, I cursed her back, and she subsided into sleep. About her only saving grace was that she didn't snore. I had never in my life wished more heartily that I did; and loudly.

At six she tipped me out of bed and sent me to take Madfaa out into the garden. Tired and fogged from lack of sleep, I did as I was told. Tying him through one of the limestone rings, I lay down beside him to finish my night's rest, and was infinitely more comfortable there.

As I slid into a doze, I was aware of someone slipping past me in the dawn light. Raising myself on my elbow I looked down the hill to where the small, lonely figure of Ghaada was diligently forking hay in the meadow.

*

I abandoned my plan to ask Ghaada whether I might stay longer. I could have moved back in with her, but by doing so would only sow discord which she would certainly reap later. So I packed my saddlebags and prepared to move on.

"Before you go, come with me," she said. "There's something I want to show you."

She led the way across the hilltop. Like her garden, it was a spare and spiky land, the soil spread thinly across the limestone outcrops like skin over an emaciated ribcage. Brambles and scrub clutched at our legs as we skipped from rock to rock like goats. A couple of hundred yards from her house, Ghaada stopped. Below her the ground fell away sharply, ending in a crag.

We stood at the edge of a ravine. The view was stupendous, clutching at my solar plexus. Down and left, the natural fall towards the sea; up and right, a narrowing seam eating into the heart of the Alawi Mountain ridge. The opposite crag was sheer; so, I guessed, must be the one below us.

"It's beautiful," I said inadequately. Her eye gleamed in acknowledgement of the things I wanted to say, but was too inarticulate. This view was the source of her serenity. Ghaada, I thought, was like the landscape which had given her birth: strong, beautiful and able to weather anything.

*

Madfaa and I made slow progress, hopping from one patch of roadside grass to the next. There was no hurry. Saône was only a few miles. Ghaada had pointed from her hilltop to the castle on the near horizon, and told me how to reach it.

One of her neighbours had offered me a place to stay that night, and I was sorely tempted by the idea. Madfaa and I were still both exhausted from the trek up the mountainside, and Madfaa's leg was a bit swollen and stiff again this morning. But, much as I would have liked the chance to spend some more time with Ghaada, it would have been unthinkable to accept the invitation. Decamping from the harpy to her neighbour might have been a delicious snub, but it would snub Ghaada, too.

She had sent me off with a good breakfast, and my "bit" of a couple of loaves and some fruit, for which I was heartily grateful and would be more so that evening. All I needed was water along the way for Madfaa, and I found it on the edge of a village. A cheerful housewife told me to wait, and went indoors to flick a switch. A blue pipe poking out from underground began to gush water, and she filled my bucket before throwing the pipe's end into her concrete cistern to fill it. Now that I knew what to look for, I saw the same arrangement everywhere. There must be a healthy system of springs and natural reservoirs under these mountains.

"You're going to *Qala'at Salah ad-Din*, Saladin's Castle? Two or three more kilometres." She pointed me away up the hill.

Ten more minutes, and we arrived on a sudden open patch of ground. The road plunged over the edge into a ravine. A loose jumble of stones, barely recognisable as a fortress, crowned the opposite hilltop. Trees filled every inch of space in between.

A series of hairpin bends took us down into the forest. A small meadow of good grass hugged the penultimate bend; I called a lunch break, untacking Madfaa and attaching him to a concrete bollard considerately placed to save over-enthusiastic drivers from obliteration. We were now within an arrow-shot of the castle, and I wondered about it as I nibbled a piece of Ghaada's bread.

Why build a castle here, in such an inaccessible place? What was it supposed to guard, away from the main routes through the mountains?

Saladin must have understood its importance, or he wouldn't have bothered to include it in that frenzy of conquest which notched up Lattakia, Saône and Burzey in just four weeks. And why was it renamed in honour of Saladin just fifty years ago? Perhaps, as Syria had then just gained independence after a quarter-century of French rule, this was to spare it the embarrassment of bearing a Frankish name any longer.

A couple of hundred yards brought us to the foot of the ravine, where a bridge spanned a stream bed littered with huge boulders. Slowly, in the heat of the day, we climbed the far side, Madfaa stopping every few minutes to snack by the roadside. The walls of the ravine came down to meet us.

As dressed stone began to appear at their top, they opened suddenly to admit the road, which here turned sharp right into a gap. I followed it round; and stopped. Saône wasn't entirely ruinous after all. But that was the least of its surprises.

*

Picture the shell of an old abbey; the roof long fallen in and rotted away, only the walls of the nave remaining. The transepts have one wall only, and in place of the choir is a steep mountainside. Now take out the mortar and blend the stones seamlessly, so that a single block reaches a hundred feet from floor to top. Where there might have been windows, paint in splashes of creeper or dark green bushes, growing from heaven knows what foothold in those sandpapered walls, so that the only light comes from above, barely reaching the floor. Where the nave altar would have stood, place a single column, a square-sectioned obelisk cut from the same living stone and to the same height as the enclosing walls. Replace the flagstones and chiselled memorial tablets with grass, but keep some of the echoes and all of the awe.

And this is only the castle moat.

People have forgotten who cut this breathtaking ditch, using only mallet and chisel and muscle and sweat. The Byzantines may have had the idea first during their brief tenure here at the end of the tenth century; but the moat as it stands today was conceived by the Frank, Robert of Saône, who held the castle in fief from the Prince of Antioch. He began the reconstruction of the fortress, which was to be completed by his son William. Before he could finish it, he was captured during an unsuccessful assault on Damascus, and opted for death rather than conversion to Islam. The Turkish commander, in the time-honoured custom of his Central Asian forebears, set Robert's skull with jewels as a drinking-cup.

At the further end of the moat, the transition to tourist country was jarring. Visitors' cars were parked in the shade of the trees, and a one-man stall did good business selling tea and cold drinks. A steep flight of steps, longer than those at Sheizar, led to the castle entrance. It was no place to take Madfaa. I tethered him, washed him off and gave him food and water; then found a young lad who would keep an eye on him - and my bags - while I took a look inside the castle.

Here for the first time my path intersected that of T E Lawrence. By the time he reached Saône he had visited, measured and sketched most of the major castles of the Levant, and might reasonably be expected to have become a little jaded. About Robert's fortress, however, he was ecstatic. "It was I think the most sensational thing I have seen: the hugely solid keep upstanding on the edge of the gigantic fosse. I wish I was a real artist." He was less enthusiastic when he began work inside, where he struggled to measure the keep against the twin perils of total darkness and "a lusty colony of snakes".

I was luckier, for the friendly warden was at the entrance. Mahir took charge of me, taking me into corners and showing me what I might otherwise have missed: the cannonballs from Saladin's siege engines lying among the scrub at the bottom of one tower, the cistern of green and slimy water lurking at the foot of the next. Better still, he allowed me to collect the grass that had been recently cut inside the upper ward, and pile it in a corner of the entrance tower ready to take out to Madfaa later.

Far more remained of Saône than I had guessed. Perhaps if I had approached from the south-east rather than north-west, I should have thought differently, for along the ditch and up to the gatehouse the towers looked much as they would have done to Saladin. It was hard to imagine a fortress of such seemingly impregnable strength surrendering after just three days; though I suppose that if I had faced surviving indefinitely on the evil-looking water in the castle cisterns, I would have run up the white flag at once. From the postern beside the keep I looked down into the dizzy depths of the moat and perhaps a couple of dozen yards across the needle to the adjacent uplands; and tried to imagine a battle line of mangonels preparing to hurl tons of death and destruction at me. What price the tremendous moat, against such formidable technology?

Although they found no need for defensive reconstruction of Saône, the Muslims left their mark on it in other ways. They left the church untouched to build their mosque elsewhere, and even after eight hundred years its graceful minaret looks strangely out of place among the heavy, utilitarian stones of the Crusaders. But it was the little bath-house which best showed me the gulf between Arab and Frankish cultures. I sat under the shade of its arches conjuring up the play of water from the fountain, and understanding that there were more civilised accompaniments to life in a mediaeval castle than sweaty armour and sword drill.

*

Arms full of hay, I walked down the steps of the castle and straight into an industrial dispute.

I'd left my baggage within sight of Ali, the one-man drinks stall. Although he wasn't included in the left luggage arrangements, he reckoned that he had prior employment rights, and had bullied the boy into handing over half his wages the minute my back was turned. Now he was very aggrieved at being persuaded to return the lad's money.

He wandered over later, as I was setting up camp, to try and arrange a bonus. I'd found a small spring dribbling from the bottom of the moat wall, and had coaxed enough water from it to fill Madfaa's bucket and brew tea. Madfaa was by now anchored to a boulder; as I told myself that it was the broken remnant of a cannonball I was only half kidding. I hoped he thought the pile of fresh hay was an improvement on the usual diet of tibn. It certainly looked it to me; but then, I didn't have to eat it.

I offered Ali tea and sympathy in lieu of hard cash.

"You're not planning to sleep out here, are you?" he asked. "What about the *barda*?"[2]

---

[2] It was later suggested that he had actually said the *bardaan*, the cold.

Ohmygod, I thought, not again. Knackered, I wouldn't have been kept from my bed that night by a nest of rattlesnakes. I gave him a short answer, and the subject was dropped. He tried another tack, suggesting that I might like to sleep with him instead; but it was said without heart, a formality which must be observed. Once the ritual offer was made and declined, the proper courtesies performed, we could both heave a sigh of relief and get on with our lives.

He rambled off to his stall, wrapped himself in a blanket and subsided. I took a final check on Madfaa, then did the same.

If I had been disappointed in my Perfect Place at Afamia, Saône made up for it in full measure. Lying under those awesome walls, I watched the narrow line of sky darken and the first stars come out. Sparrows rustled in the bushes and crevices, and an owl hooted. A red squirrel on its way to bed scampered about the blank wall as if on suction pads. Now and again a late car came through the moat, and I raised myself on one elbow and used the beam of its headlights to check on Madfaa. So far he had ignored the hay and was eating what grass he could find.

I had to look, because I couldn't hear him moving. For this was the hour of the Free-Wheeling Bicycle Cricket.

The song of the Saône crickets is a perfect replica of the tic-tic-tic made by a free-wheeling bicycle. Starting very slowly and accelerating up to full speed, it then performs with the regularity of a metronome until something disturbs it, or its bowing arm gets tired. Then there is no deceleration, no tailing off: just an immediate hush. Hundreds of them all whirring at once made so much noise that I couldn't hear Madfaa at all. If he stamped, or if a bird flew up, they all stopped in perfect unison, as if ordered by the baton of an unseen conductor. The sudden silence was deafening.

Just before complete darkness fell, there was a new noise. Something howled in the hills behind the castle. At once, from all directions, other somethings joined in. Could it be dogs, I wondered, or was it some other wild animal? Had Ali, and others who had tried to stop me camping out, known something I didn't after all? Or was it just the local shebaab having a laugh at my expense? I yelled something rude, and the noise stopped instantly.

The crickets fell quiet, and Madfaa dozed. Silence rolled down out of the surrounding hills like fog. I tried to make myself comfortable on the hard ground, and longed for sleep. But things walked in the night at Saône.

*

I was drifting off at last, when a hand shook me awake.

"Come," said a voice in English. "Drink tea!"

It was Ali. With difficulty I persuaded him that socialising was the last thing on my agenda, and he went away. I wondered if waking me up was his revenge over not getting paid for not guarding my bags. It was only after he had roused me several more times that I realised the problem: Ali was afraid of the dark, and had elected me his comfort blanket.

Every hour or so he would come back to try his luck again. Sometimes I begged him to go away and let me rest; sometimes I feigned sleep when I heard his footsteps approaching, lying as still as a mouse while he stood over me, hoping he would give up and go away, breathing only when the footsteps receded again.

At last my patience cracked, and I threw off my bag and jumped aggressively to my feet. I wanted to be six feet tall and built like a tank, so that I could seize him by the throat and batter his head against the stone walls; as it was I half-pleaded, half swore.

"For God's sake! I don't want any bloody tea! *Please* can't you let me sleep? - it's the middle of the night!"

"No, it isn't," he answered with gloomy triumph. "It's morning!"

He was right, damn him. Within half an hour the sky was beginning to lighten. I still had not slept for a single moment. As dawn broke Ali was back one last time. This time he passed by me and walked the length of the moat, circling the pillar reverently and singing some hoarse incantation. Perhaps it was a hymn of thanksgiving that I hadn't killed him.

I lay there for another hour then gave up, wearily packing my things, feeding Madfaa and having a bite myself. As I came round the south-east corner for a final photograph I saw Ali on a rock ledge behind his stall, snugly rolled in his blanket and deeply, magnificently asleep. For a moment I fought a violent urge to go and jump up and down on him; then shrugged wearily and went to saddle Madfaa for the road.

*

From here my route lay through one of the quietest parts of the Alawi Mountain. I had to find my way down to the main Lattakia - Aleppo road, which snakes through the Mountain by the line of least resistance, and then up again into the hills around Kassab on the Turkish border. From there I would head south, on a path converging with the coast, to Lattakia, a distance of about forty miles. Old friends there had arranged stabling for Madfaa at the Riding Club, where he could have a few days' rest while I caught up on events with Nabil and Sana.

Haffeh, a few miles north of Saône, was a down-to-earth, workaday sort of town, a relief after the artificial resort villages higher up the Mountain. I asked directions, but still nearly missed my road, for it was a narrow street between high houses which at first glance looked little more than an alley. I crossed my fingers and went for it, and was grateful when, half a mile further on, I came to the reservoir that the friendly man had told me I would pass. A delivery man was making his rounds here on the edge of the village; as he stopped and started, we passed each other repeatedly, exchanging increasingly familiar hallos each time. Meeting me for the last time when he turned round to go home, he presented me with a flower from the garden of one of his clients.

Not all the locals were so friendly. It was here I had my first traffic incident. I was passing a parked minibus when it unexpectedly moved off, forcing Madfaa into the middle of the road. A motorist coming the other way drove straight at us. "*Jahash!*   Jackass! Road Hog!" I screamed at him as he missed Madfaa by a whisker. The little stallion was unperturbed. He was obviously used to such driving. But it was a warning I heeded. Quite soon we would be meeting heavier traffic than up until now. I must remember to be extra careful.

A few miles brought us to the edge of a tremendous escarpment. Below lay the valley of the *Nahr al-Kabir*, the Great River, along which the road and railway cut through the hills.

It was an extraordinary landscape. Dark, dark green with thousands of trees and bushes; not a patch of open ground between them. But clipped, cultivated trees; almost exaggeratedly so. It was as if I were looking down on a vast, densely packed formal garden; or a computer-generated image of how such a garden should look, but one in which the designer had been carried away by the ease of planting trees, trees and more trees at the click of a button - then forgotten to program in the people. From where I stood I couldn't see a single house to break the sense of unreality, the feeling that we were about to enter an alien world. The only sign of human life was the railway, striding across the valley on stilts above the trees, like a statement that the land belonged to real people after all.

That particular viewpoint must have given a distorted picture. When, after a good two miles continuously downhill, we came to the valley floor, the countryside after all seemed normal, familiar. There were people, houses, animals, vigorous life.

Too vigorous; for when we reached the busy Aleppo road, the pace of life was too fast for comfort. The Syrians are a wonderful people, but their driving is often deplorable; especially when overtaking. More than once I was faced with the horrific sight of two cars approaching us abreast on a road only wide enough for one car and one horse. Madfaa became adept at folding himself into the hedge and breathing in tightly. We cracked on up the road at a sharp trot, and I exhaled deeply with relief when we turned off on to the quiet Kassab road, still in one piece.

With every step away from the main road, my blood pressure dropped a few notches. Soon we came to the Nahr al-Kabir, lapping a gentle path between sandy reedbeds edged with oleander. I stopped to offsaddle and water Madfaa, then took a few steps into the river to bathe my feet and splash water over my face, washing off gallons of terror-induced sweat. The water trickled over stones scoured clean by the winter flood, whispering of quiet and solitude. Its message was irresistible, and I made up my mind. I would camp here, tucked away from sight among the oleander. I had enough feed for Madfaa, and there was even some grazing here. As for me, I still had some of Ghaada's bread, and had stocked up on biscuits and chocolate in Haffeh. It was the ideal place for rest and refreshment, and no-one would ever know we were here.

It was a well-inhabited spot nonetheless. Frogs sang throatily as the evening wore on. Freshwater crabs and tadpoles of all sizes scuttled from under Madfaa's feet as he stepped into the water to drink. Later, as

I sat on a rock sluicing my feet for the umpteenth time, minnows came to nibble at my toes, scattering like children when I wiggled them.

Just before nightfall, some local girls found us and fetched their mother. Fayiza was concerned that I was bedding down here in the open. But she made no attempt to dissuade me; the wa-wa, the dad and the barda were not invoked. Instead, she sent the children back with a plate of *laban*, fresh sweet yogurt. The next morning she came with a bowl of warm milk for my breakfast, and the whole family stopped by to wish us on our way.

*

The day began with a long, gentle climb through pine forest. A knot of trees marked the top, sheltering whitewashed tombs and a small mosque. The pattern was becoming familiar; this was another of the sacred groves.

It had been a clammy, cold night beside the stream, and I was grateful when the sun got up. High in these mountains, it was a cheerful friend rather than a hostile fire. A fresh breeze kept the temperature down, and shade was never more than a few steps away.

From now on, we travelled through surely the loveliest country in Syria. Thick pine forest still covered the steeper slopes, but large areas had been cleared for agriculture. Fields in the hollows and flats had already been stripped and ploughed, and immaculate terraces stepped the hillsides. The houses were tidy, businesslike cubes: farmhouses, not the straggling half-built settlements of the tourist zone. This was a Mediterranean rather than a Middle Eastern landscape; though occasionally, crossing lively streams tumbling down between polished rocks where dense brush grew under the pines, I might have thought myself ambling through the lovely Scottish forest of Rothiemurchus on an unusually hot day.

This corner of Syria is a forgotten land. Few of the local holiday crowd come here, let alone foreign travellers. Even the border crossing at Kassab is quiet, its traffic restricted to a few local traders, or the gathering of Turkish-Syrian families separated by a bureaucratic line on the map.

The Hatay, the part of Turkey immediately to the north, is a hybrid land. A narrow strip hugging the coastline of the north-east corner of the Mediterranean, it is historically part of Syria, and its ancient towns of Antakya (Antioch) and Iskenderun (Alexandretta) were major Arab cities. But it was heavily settled by Turks under Ottoman rule, so that a referendum held in 1939 under the French mandate over Syria came out against the Arabs: the population elected to secede from Syria and become a part of Turkey. It remains a bone of contention, however, and Syrian maps still show the Hatay as part of Syria, the *de facto* border marked only by a dotted line. "I think that when the problem of the Golan Heights is settled," Basil had said to me, "the Hatay will be the next disputed area."

*

Hassan and Fatima lived in a single storey house among terraces of olive trees. A trellis of vines shaded the front of the house, and an olive press almost filled the tiny garden.

Yes, they said, we could stop here. Madfaa could spend the night in the barn attached to the house, along with the cow and the couple of black-and-white sheep in whose company he was now grazing happily. The barn had no door, so he would have to be tethered; when I asked to bed down by the stable doorway they raised their eyebrows a little, but made no objection. Fatima brought bread, humous, olives, tomatoes and cucumbers for supper, and we sat in the open air eating companionably as the sun went down, making such conversation as I could manage - no fasaha, here. When it was quite dark fireflies came out, making tiny pinpricks of light flickering like wildfire among the vines.

It wasn't an entirely restful night. At about one in the morning Madfaa lay down. It was the first time he had done so, and the bare concrete floor hardly invited such intimacy. I was worried, and got up to watch him. A few moments later he laid his head on the floor and stretched out fully, pulling the tether rope uncomfortably tight.

I went and stood by him. He didn't move. I was now seriously alarmed; this was unusual behaviour for a sensitive horse in a strange place. He must be ill, I decided. Could he have picked up some poisonous plant by the roadside? Or had the whole grains of barley, always crushed when fed to European horses though never here, given him colic? I searched for the stable light, but couldn't find one.

Poor Fatima was very philosophical at being woken in the dead of night to give me a light. She pressed a switch in the house, and the light came on in the stable. Madfaa still didn't move.

Could I get him to his feet? I twitched the halter rope and spoke some encouraging words. He gave me a pained look, scrambled disgustedly to his feet, then immediately buried his head in his manger and began to eat heartily. False alarm.

In the weeks to come he was to lie down quite often on bare concrete, and I got used to it and stopped worrying. For now, though, I could only grovel apologetically to Hassan and Fatima for disturbing their sleep. They were quite unmoved to find that I'd been making a fuss about nothing. They must have already decided that anyone who would refuse a comfortable bed in the house and sleep on a concrete floor with a horse must be quite beyond sanity.

*

They had a short night, for Hassan rose at ten to five for the morning milking. There was fresh, boiled milk and laban for breakfast.

From here northwards the road was a switchback. We crossed a watershed and came down to where a stream, fighting the sun for its existence, clung to a shrinking path between gravel banks pink with oleander and booming with frogs. Then another watershed, another valley, another stream; each slightly lower than the last. We were gradually losing height.

A flat stretch brought us to a crossroads where a blindingly white mosque stood against a stand of dark pines under a powder-blue sky. It was the first road junction for two days. A left turn led us quickly to the Lattakia - Kassab road. Left again; nothing the other way but the Turkish border.

Suddenly we were back in tourist country. Stalls lined the roadside, selling children's toys and holiday junk. Small grocery stores competed half-heartedly with them to sell biscuits, chocolate and canned drinks. The latter were to be a feature of all the more populous areas to come. I was drawn to them as a moth to a flame. From now on, my progress through the Mountain would be one long junk food trip.

A group of young teenagers gathered about one of the stalls, drinking beer. Old cans littered the verges beside them. They shouted across the road at me, half-friendly, half-jeering.

"What's that," asked one lad as he pointed underneath Madfaa, who was having one of his embarrassingly frequent priapic moments.

"Don't you know?" I returned unkindly, and the boy subsided; which was more, at that moment, than could be said for the stallion.

Now traffic began to threaten again. Luckily the road was wide, despite the very quiet border crossing. Perhaps its width was a measure of optimism that one day the Hatay would be returned to Syria, one day a major road would be needed between Lattakia and its sister port of Iskenderun.

Or perhaps it was just to cater for local tourists, day trippers from Lattakia or even from across the border. This area is Syria's Lake District, where a number of dams collect the surface water off thousands of acres of mountain and store it in a string of reservoirs running halfway down to Lattakia.

It was just a couple of miles to the first and biggest, *Buhayrat al-Balura*, the Crystal Lake. I remembered this from earlier journeys up and down this road, when I had gazed from afar at its shining waters through the window of a minibus or shared taxi. Now I looked forward to closer acquaintance, a picnic on its shore, a swim, perhaps.

It was disappointing. Before, I'd seen it in April, engorged with the spring rains streaming off the hills. Now, in July, it was tired and wilting under the summer sun. The lake had retreated to leave a shoreline littered with all kinds of rubbish. Green and scummy, its water repelled Madfaa, who preferred a plastic-smelling drink from my bottle. Even if I'd wanted to, I dared not paddle, for broken glass glinted dangerously in the shallows. My lunch was brief and symbolic, while Madfaa grazed with care and little pride among rusty tins and old bottles.

All too soon we were back on the road again. This time there were no hills to climb; it was just down and more down, the only variation lying in the degree of slope. As we lost height the pines retreated to the hilltops, which were themselves drawing gradually further away. Agriculture began to encroach on their slopes, nibbling away relentlessly at the forestry. At first, there were just a few terraces lying about the river bed; soon, whole fields and then a succession of fields spread away up the hillsides. One or two of the older men working in the fields wore Turkish trousers, baggy to the knee and close-fitting down the shin. The younger men invariably wore western clothing.

A road leading up to the right was signed for Ra'as al-Bassit. Here, entrepreneurs are cashing in on a spectacular stretch of coastline to build a holiday resort. Disappointed at Buhayrat al-Balura, I thirsted now for my first glimpse of the Mediterranean. Could I justify a there-and-back-again detour? But it was only a few miles, and not much past mid-day. This might be my last chance to see a place which would probably be swamped with tourists in a few years' time.

Of course, I was a tourist myself, and by my own reckoning should stay away. But rules never apply to yourself. I turned Madfaa up the hill.

It was a sharp climb, with pines gradually giving way to smooth slopes of chalky scree. I came over the top to a sudden view of the sea, its rippling wavetops painted silver by the sun. The coastline was all it had been cracked up to be: rolling hills of scrub and the odd pine, ending in dramatic white cliffs dropping vertically to the Mediterranean. Northwards Jebel al-Akra, the southern Hatay's highest peak, hovered in the sea-haze.

Below me, a track led through the brush to a hollow where a friendly knot of pines beckoned. It would have made a spectacular camp. But who knew what nasties might be lurking in all that dry scrub? With regret I turned my back, and we retraced our steps to the road.

*

The track led to a cluster of houses near the top of a hill above the main road. I was only halfway up when a young man came to meet me.

Ja'afar Na'nou and his family were Alawis. This was immediately obvious when his sister Fardoss came down to join us, for she wore a shirt over tight leggings. She led me to a huge stable with a comfortable earth floor, which Madfaa could have all to himself. When I had untacked him and filled his manger with tibn and *alaf* – the floury, heavily milled grain that I'd first seen at Slenfeh - I spent a few minutes talking to him before leaving him alone. As usual he nibbled my hand, licking the salt from my sweaty palms; then, working his way up my arm, he took my forearm between his teeth and held it gently for a moment or two before returning to his feed. This was becoming his habit, his way of deriving reassurance in a strange place by holding on to a familiar figure.

He enjoyed the amenities next morning, for he was allowed to graze under a shade shelter in the yard, which normally belonged to the house cow. I had gone with Fardoss when she did the evening's milking, wondering why she changed her usual clothes for a tracksuit and tightly wound keffiyah, as if she was preparing for some especially dirty and unpleasant job; but my linguistic deficiencies prevented me from asking.

They were a friendly and outgoing family, more hospitable and welcoming even than usual in Syria, and very interested in the carryings-on of their eccentric guest. Although I was only one march away from my base in Lattakia, I asked if we might stay a couple of nights.

The whole village, I learned, belonged to the Na'nous. "There are seven families of us here - and two more across the road," said Fardoss.

It was an insight into how, over time, large areas might fall under the influence of a particular family. Common enough with nomads - the Bedouin, for example, where a whole tribe is an extended family - but obviously possible also for settled people. Particularly where, as here, geography tended to isolate and concentrate small groups of people; where the next valley was a separate world.

I wondered how long the process took; how many generations had been needed to fill this whole valley with Na'nous. "How long have you been here?"

"We've been in Zaghriin about a hundred years," she answered. "At least, Granny was born here in 1917." She turned to Ja'afar for confirmation, and there was a quick discussion, too fast for me to follow. "No, about two hundred and fifty. There are records in the centre nearby."

They had been here, then, when the Ottoman Empire was at its peak. The early Na'nous of Zaghriin could have sold their produce from the Persian Gulf almost to the Atlantic without trade barriers. The old grandmother was alive when Lawrence and the Emir Feisal led their victorious Arab army into Damascus. What upheavals had gone on while she continued to live peaceably in this spot: Turkish rule, the

Arab Revolt, the French Mandate, the early Republic, the Ba'ath revolution...

The method of agriculture they used, dictated by the landscape and the climate, can have changed little over the two-and-a-half centuries of their tenure. It was based on intensive cultivation of small plots, heavily dependent on irrigation and producing a wide variety of crops. You name it, the Na'nous grew it. Fruit - grapes, figs, pomegranates, oranges, lemons; vegetables - aubergines, tomatoes, cucumbers, peppers; olives, sunflowers, tobacco. Most of the fruit and vegetables found their way into the Lattakia markets, via a middle man. Many of the oranges, lemons and olives, though, would end up in Saudi Arabia or the Gulf States.

"How much land have you got?"

"Fifteen *dunums*."

"How much is a dunum?"

"One *fid'an* is four dunums." My dictionary couldn't handle either fid'ans or dunums. I gave up.

Fardoss took me down the hill and across the main road to where Ja'afar was working the irrigation in the orange orchard. Each tree, planted in its own hollow, would be flooded once a fortnight. Barefooted, trousers rolled up to the knee, Ja'afar worked his way down the main irrigation ditch, blocking or opening a side channel with a flick of his spade. As each dam was breached the water rushed in to inundate the tree, sending bubbles fizzing up from the dry earth.

All this bursting growth was the gift of Buhayrat al-Balura and its lesser siblings. I thought of its receding shoreline, of the stagnant, greasy waters of midsummer. "The stream must have slowed a lot. Do you have any difficulties over water at this time of year?"

"No. We can take as much as we need."

She showed me a spring in a bank, which fed the stream. Its generous gush of clear water must have risen from underground, as there was no nearby hill for it to drain from. You can sink a well here, Fardoss told me, at a depth of just four metres.

In the evening, Ja'afar and Fardoss took me further up the hill past the settlement. Here was the family cemetery, a necropolis of Na'nous blending their bones with the limestone of this small lookout ringed by mountains. At the top, a path led away among cool pines. As we walked along it, the hooting of cars on the Lattakia road below faded to a distant "poop-poop".

At the far end, Ja'afar had built himself a bamboo hut, with a small bedroom and a veranda looking out over a hillside of vines to the distant mountains.

"Isn't it a wonderful view?"

I was speechless. He could look out to nearly 360°, minus only the little knob of hilltop behind, of pine-covered mountains scored by the white streaks of scree-slopes. To the south, the black ribbon of the Lattakia road snaked away over a pass.

My route for tomorrow. Next stop, Lattakia.

*

At the top of the hill I paused a minute to look back at Zaghriin, a small corner of the globe belonging utterly to the Na'nous. Goodbye rural Syria, for now. I took a deep breath and plunged back into the traffic.

It got worse as we neared Lattakia. So did the rubbish. Municipal collections obviously didn't reach this far, and the increasing population density made for a problem. In the bigger villages a pall hung over the air, a charnel-house reek of rotting meat that made Madfaa jumpy, so that the traffic threatened us more than ever. It seemed to be the custom here to throw meat bones and chicken carcasses into the hedges and verges for the jackals to come and get them. The trouble was, no-one seemed to have told the jackals.

At least here there were still hedges and verges. A little further, and they disappeared beneath houses and workshops. Now the lorries were zipping past Madfaa with a couple of feet of clearance, and a car driver brushed my saddlebags. I had to find a safer way to get out of Lattakia when the time came. As from today, I thought grimly, Madfaa and I didn't do traffic.

It was a relief to reach the suburbs and have a choice of smaller roads. We didn't have far to go. Our destination was at the northern end of the city. For the last mile I could navigate by sight; the floodlights and grandstand of the stadium stood above the surrounding buildings, a beacon to guide me. The Riding Club, I knew, was immediately next to

the Sports City complex built for the Mediterranean Games in the
Eighties.

A British riding club is a group of people, its nearest thing to a
physical presence being perhaps the Committee. Lattakia Riding Club,
like others in Syria, is a thing of substance: bricks and mortar - or,
rather, concrete – and tanbark. Owned and run by the government but
used also by private individuals for payment, it consisted of three
"American barns" – big corridors of indoor stabling - two outdoor
arenas with showjumps and various other facilities.

Through a word from Basil and a visit from my local friends I had
stabling arranged here for a few days. We were both ready for a break
from the road. Although Madfaa was still rattling along tirelessly his
bad leg, though nearly healed, wasn't helped by daily work on tarmac.
The wound was still swollen from bruising and the tissue surrounding
the tendons "filled" a little. As for me, despite the break at Zaghriin I
was almost incoherent from exhaustion. It was nice to have an excuse
for the incoherence. At least, staying with Nabil and Sana, I could have
the relief of speaking English for a bit.

Within an hour or so I had Madfaa comfortably bedded down on
thick shavings, his tack stowed, his leg newly dressed and a good feed
in front of him. Satisfied that he had all he needed, I shouldered my
saddlebags and went to find first a phone, then a taxi.

III

THE COAST

Nabil pushed his empty plate away, stretched his legs under the table and reached out to switch on the radio.

"What on earth would we do without the BBC?"

It was strange to hear news from home. I had tried occasionally to get the World Service on the tiny radio which was my sole luxury, but had rarely managed a viable signal. Nabil, though, had probably listened every day since his return from Bristol University in the Seventies. Three years there doing his PhD had turned him into a lifelong Anglophile. Ten years later, by then a lecturer at Lattakia University, he had returned on a term's sabbatical with his wife Sana and young family. It had given me an opportunity to return some of the hospitality I have had from the Bizrahs over twenty years.

Sana had laid in a supply of milk especially for my tea, and I sat on the veranda under the fig tree draining pot after pot while catching up with family news. It was wise to sit still while drinking tea at this time of year in Lattakia, for at the slightest movement it would bypass your stomach and leak straight out of the pores.

For most of the year, Lattakia has the best climate of Syria. "Alas for you, ye Læodiceans," despaired St. Paul, "for ye are neither hot nor cold." While actually chiding them for spiritual apathy, he might have been celebrating their weather. At the height of summer, though, the moist sea air hitting the hot landmass turned the place into a sauna. I was actually cooler now than I had been in the Ghaab, but it didn't feel that way. At least a breeze cooled the house up here in the Tabiyaat district. Nabil and Sana lived at the top end, on a spur above the bay. New building had blocked their view over the sea since my last visit, but if I walked to the end of the road I could still look out over Syria's biggest port, its gateway to the Mediterranean world.

Lattakia may be a lot older than the name Seleucus Nicator bestowed on it in honour of his mother, but its history is well hidden under an entirely modern city. There is no trace of La Liche, the fortress subdued by Saladin on his way to Saône; the Classical age fares little better, represented mainly by a Roman arch which I passed daily on my way from the Tabiyaat into the city centre, travelling up to the Riding Club to keep an eye on Madfaa.

The first morning I went with Omar, Nabil and Sana's son. The children's English was vastly better than my Arabic, and they were usually sent with me to act as interpreters - or to make sure I didn't get lost. After weeks of wandering round the countryside I was befuddled in the city, and all Lattakia looked alike to me. It was a bustling, noisy, cheerful place. Its heart lay in the central Jumhuriyya Square, where hooting taxis elbowed a minority of private cars out of the road, and a handful of real Roman columns wreathed in acanthus tottered on false concrete plinths. Behind a bank of fountains a benevolent President Assad presided in marble from his literal and metaphorical pedestal, staring back at himself from a hundred banners draped about every building.

Dodging the frenetic traffic, we ducked into the quiet of a cafe to enjoy a banana smoothie. Syria's most ambrosial drink is a soup of fresh bananas, ice cubes, milk and ice cream, whizzed in a blender and laced with strawberry cordial. Could I be drinking some of the Na'nous produce? Probably not; I remembered Nabil telling me some years ago how one of Syria's ruling military élite had cornered the market in banana imports, earning himself the nickname of "the Banana General".

A bus took us on to the Sports City, and we found Madfaa in good form, his leg quite cool with all swelling gone. To be sure I took him outside to hose it, adding cold water to the benefit of rest. Omar was delighted with him. There was an instant rapport between the boy and the stallion, and I was able to leave Omar on hose duty while I went and cooled my toes in the Mediterranean. The sea was just a dozen yards from the back of the barns. It was a pity that a bank of boulders prevented horse access, for salt water would have been the best thing on earth for that leg.

There was a different sort of rapport on view the next day, when Darine was looking after me. Still only fourteen but already well endowed with her mother's beauty, she immediately grabbed the attention of the young grooms. The lads, teenagers doing their military service rather than horsemen by choice, left brushes and barrows to gather about her like moths round a lantern. She handled them with poise and complete control, like a coachman effortlessly calming a restive team.

The Riding Club was busy that day, well on with its preparations to stage one of Syria's major horse shows. Show-jumping is popular in Syria, and besides Arab horses the club housed a number of western European warmbloods, big horses with the power to jump. Basel al-Assad, the President's son, had been an enthusiatic show-jumper, giving the sport a welcome boost. This Club had been his home territory, for the President's family came from a village in the mountains nearby. It was even named after him, the Basel al-Assad Riding Club .

Basel was more than just a sporting and social personality; he was a major political figure. There was a general understanding that President Assad was grooming him to inherit the position of head of the ruling Ba'ath party and President of Syria. It was seen as a national tragedy, then, when Basel was killed in a car crash in 1994.

*

"Ba'ath" means "Renaissance". The Ba'ath movement, originally built on the doctrine of Arab unity, quickly embraced the ideals of revolutionary Arab nationalism, ideals which led Syria to a short-lived federation with Nasser's Egypt in 1958. Called the United Arab Republic, the federation lasted only three years. The political upheavals in Syria that followed its dissolution saw the Ba'ath party come to power in 1963, with the brilliant Air Force officer Hafez al-Assad named as Defence Minister. After a turbulent few years in which Syria changed its ruler as often as its calendar, Assad took power in 1971. His guiding hand might not be a gentle one, but even his fiercest critics cannot deny the stability and increasing prosperity of his reign. And reign it is, for it is his clear intention that the succession will pass to his second son, Bashar, "the best guarantee of continuing the policies of the President and maintaining stability in Syria".

"The Leader, the Martyr, the Hope." That is the title of the triptych of posters over the road to Qirdaha, the Presidential birthplace. Hafez al-Assad, centre stage; the dead Basel, left; the heir-apparent, Bashar, right. The two younger men wear sinister black sunglasses and their father's moustache. There is to be no defacing of these pictures by mischievous boys, even if they dared, for the traditional clichés are already there.

Nabil was taking me sightseeing, navigating the twisted mountain roads with easy familiarity and many times more horsepower than I was accustomed to. He had driven me high into the Jebel al-Alawiyiin until from a viewpoint we had looked down over the Ghaab, shimmering under the haze of distance and stubble-fire. On the way back he had taken a dog-leg to show me Qirdaha, the village that had put the Alawis firmly on the political map.

Oleander and palm trees surrounded the lavish new mosque under construction in the centre of the town. This was Basel's mausoleum; under the cool, dark interior of the completed dome lay the sarcophagus of the fallen heir. Quite why the victim of a road accident should be considered a martyr, say some privately, is hard to fathom. Though as an Englishwoman I had to admit it was not unknown for a national icon, killed in their prime by a car crash, to be canonised.

*

"Is it true," asked the farrier, "that in England one man shoes a horse unaided?" He was unsurprised, if a little disappointed, when I answered that it was.

"Of course," he added, "you have professional staff. That makes a big difference."

He was right, of course. The grooms at the club were soldiers, voted into horse care by the accident of their place on a list. Good enough lads and hard workers, they mostly lacked personal interest and the desire to get to know their horses and treat them as individuals. One or two were actually scared of horses. It showed in the way they treated them as adversaries, trying to dominate them, losing their temper when they felt threatened by any lack of submission. All bullying is rooted in fear.

The lad holding Madfaa's foot up for the blacksmith was a case in point. Tense, he held the foot as if in a vice, making no allowance for a horse wobbling on one foreleg. His fear passed like a virus into the little stallion. When Madfaa's nerve broke for the third or fourth time and he pulled sharply backwards, jerking the boy off balance, fear spilled over into fury. Swearing, the lad jumped out of the way then spun on one foot to deliver a vicious kick in the horse's stomach. It was too much.

Until then I'd remained in my place as a woman, which was well away from horses while Work was in progress. Now I yanked the lad off, yelled at him like a virago and picked up the foot myself. There was a general hush at my unladylike behaviour; but the blacksmith - himself a gentle and patient man - didn't try to argue. Certainly a familiar face soothed Madfaa a bit; and although he continued to pull back periodically, at least he no longer got punished for it.

The farrier asked Nabil something, and he translated for me. "He wants to know if you would like chairs?"

I was nonplussed. After a quick discussion, Nabil turned to me again. "He says, they will help when the road is slippery." Now the penny dropped. He meant calkins.

In the days when horses pulled carts and cabs on hard surfaces, it was usual to make the shoe with an extra long heel, which was then bent under to make a wedge for better grip. The practice had been superseded in England with fixed or removable studs; but I'd seen the old-fashioned calkins used on gharry horses in Egypt. "Chairs", I had to admit, was a much more logical name.

"Yes, please!" I answered with enthusiasm. Madfaa had begun to slide around on the tarmac as the miles polished his shoes to smoothness. In the weeks to come I would bless the blacksmith's foresight many times over.

I soon had another cause to be grateful to him. It was through the farrier that Nabil managed to find the man of my dreams: someone who owned a pickup truck like Fayiz', and was prepared to transport Madfaa safely out of Lattakia. For now, there would be no more close encounters on arterial roads.

*

Before I left, Nabil took me sightseeing again. This time it was to Ra'as Shamra, a headland overlooking the sea some ten miles north of the city. To its early inhabitants, and in ancient Egyptian archives, it was known as Ugarit.

The Phoenicians, "Canaanites of the Sea" (as opposed to their cousins the Canaanites of the Land, who were displaced by the Children of Israel) were an early Semitic people. Arriving in the Levant from the Arabian Peninsula via the Fertile Crescent, they made their home on the Mediterranean shore about three millennia ago. The businessmen of the ancient world, they learned the arts of seafaring from the Minoans of Crete, whom they employed to carry their cargo. By the time the Minoan civilisation met its volcanic nemesis, Phoenician vessels were trading from far down the African coast to Cornwall. Such was their reputation that it was Phoenician mariners who were commissioned by Pharaoh Necho in the late seventh century BC to circumnavigate Africa. These took more than two years to complete the journey, stopping on the way to sow and reap food crops. Their assertion on their return that they had seen the sun shine in the north met with disbelief from most, including Herodotus, to whom we owe the account of the journey.

The Phoenicians were not a military people, and their skill at business negotiations didn't extend to politics. Instead of uniting, their city states quarrelled with each other, so that the Egyptians, Assyrians and other great powers in turn rolled over them and submerged them. Surviving mostly by meek submission - and, certainly, the value to the taxman of their business empire - they prospered most when foreign empires were in decline. The disappearance of the Minoans and the temporary eclipse of Egypt gave them a golden age around the end of the second millennium BC. It lasted until Tiglath-Pileser fell upon Phoenician Arwad; after which the remaining cities tripped over themselves to offer tribute to Assyria.

This was a period which saw Ugarit's claim to history as birthplace of the alphabet. The idea of letters, vastly more adaptable than Egypt's pictorial hieroglyphics or the syllabic cuneiform of Mesopotamia, is thought to have originated in Sinai; but it was the practical Phoenicians, with their account ledgers and stock lists, who picked it up, ran with it – and passed it on. They even named their letters: A, *Aleph* (ox); B, *Beth* (house) - much as our children might learn A, apple and B, book - which, when envious Greeks took over the idea, became alpha, beta...

You can't any longer see at Ugarit the famous sarcophagus bearing the evidence of this monumental advance. Beyond price, it is safely housed in the Beirut Museum. But the ruins are evidence of a substantial city, greater by far than, for example, its comtemporary, Troy. Like Troy, it has a thick, sloping wall to seaward. A trapezium-shaped postern gate bores a hole through its massive stones; but we entered, as tourists, over its top.

Inside was a maze of streets and houses, bathed in blinding sunlight. Lizards skittered out of our path, or watched us from a safe distance, lifting their feet one diagonal pair at a time to minimise contact with the scorching stone. In vain we tried to distinguish palace from storeroom from warehouse; but only foundations and low walls remained, skeletons giving little idea of the body's substance. Sometimes there was a clue; here a millstone, there a cistern of green water, where frogs paddled and croaked.

We left the place to the frogs and the lizards and walked up to the harbour. Above a small bay of dazzling blue water we sat on the low cliff, trying to picture the Phoenician galleys sailing out to pass the Pillars of Hercules and carry their trade to the limits of the known world.

*

Tartous was even more of a sauna than Lattakia. The air positively sagged with moisture, and although it wasn't unduly hot my shirt was soon covered in damp patches, sticking uncomfortably to my skin.

The town had grown considerably since I was last here. New blocks of flats crowded its centre and extended its outskirts by at least a mile. Over the last twenty years its port had begun to rival that of its northern neighbour Lattakia, while the town itself had retained – indeed enlarged – its status as a Mediterranean resort.

After the fun and games of the Lattakia Highway, I had no intention of riding Madfaa to Tartous. Leaving him comfortably resting in the five-star accommodation of the Riding Club, I'd hopped on a bus and covered the ninety kilometres in just over an hour. My old friend the Ambassador Hotel had just one room left, though sadly not one of the seaward-facing ones I'd had before. My thrill at seeing a fan rotating on the ceiling was premature. Weighed down by decades of dust, it could do no more than creep around churlishly, barely stirring the soggy air.

I soon realised I was lucky to get a room at all. The Tartous Festival was in full swing, and the place was throbbing. As the lights came on in the town, holidaymakers emerged into the cool of the evening to stroll down the Corniche. Long after dark, boats puttered back and forth to the island of Arwad, visible only as single lights bobbing like corks in the waves.

I bought a bottle of wine and washed down my supper of bread and cheese, sitting on the roof of the hotel and watching the lights of Arwad flirting with the rippling waters of the sound.

*

Tartous – Tortosa to the Franks – was the principal stronghold of the Knights Templar, the most famous of the Orders of knight-monks born of the Crusades.

Their birth gave no hint of the glory to come. Founded in 1119 with their headquarters on the Temple Mount in Jerusalem, the "Poor Fellow-Soldiers of Jesus Christ and the Temple of Solomon" initially gathered with the aim of protecting pilgrims to the Holy Land. Within twenty-five years the Order came of age, evolving into a formidable fighting force with Papal support for its autonomy, extensive property in Europe and its own castles in the Crusader Kingdom of *Outremer* – the Land-Over-the-Sea. Tortosa passed into Templar hands around 1152, whereupon they built massively on to the existing Byzantine fortress. The result was impregnable; even Saladin failed to subdue it, and only the disintegration of the Crusader fiefdoms finally persuaded the Templars to yield it to the Mamelukes in 1291.

Two pyramidal towers built into the sea frontage mark the boundaries of the castle today. Otherwise, it is hard to discern its limits, so thoroughly has it been absorbed into the current town. Behind the palms on the Corniche concrete-block flats sprout from the remains of the Templars' walls, the joining seam hidden behind swathes of washing hung out to dry. I climbed through a jagged hole beneath to find myself in echoing cobwebbed storerooms, picking my way carefully over piles of rubble slippery with age and sea-moisture, and stepping round heaped litter. No Templar ghosts walking here.

If I was looking to find them next door, I was out of luck. The great banqueting hall of the Knights had been opened and spruced up. Today a craft fair was in progress; if "craft" was the word. Among delicate inlaid woodwork such as you might buy from deep in the Damascus souks were tables laden with hideous plastic kitsch: fake flowers, garish face masks, religious knick-knacks to hang on your walls… The last catered to Tartous' Christian as well as Muslim populations, for there is a sizeable Greek Orthodox community here.

A back door led me deep into the heart of the old castle. Here, treading a narrow alley or climbing a flight of steps to another level, I at last felt a faint tremor of times past. But only if I kept my eyes down and didn't pry too deeply. For behind the arched gateways lurked scruffy back yards or dingy workshops, breeze block perched above ancient stone and everywhere staircases, their treads hollow with centuries of wear, led up from dark corners to somebody's back door. In a rare open space children played football. Come on, Tortosa United, I thought as someone scored a goal and the boys whooped.

There was no sense of form, no identifiable feature. Fifty years ago Fedden remarked that "little remains of the great keep," which Lawrence found "impossible to get at today, thanks to the existence of the harem of the governor above it." I failed even to find it, among the crammed and confusing passages. It was something of a surprise to step through the walls and find open space that not even the modern town had encroached on.

A moat of some twenty yards width ran along the landward side of the castle, empty of all but rubbish. Above it rose the quadruple line of the citadel in all its ancient and modern glory: a base of solid rock, grown straight from the earth's crust and squared off in perfect right-angles; a layer built in massive blocks of golden-coloured stone, lovingly worked and laid; a third storey of stone again, smaller blocks this time, surely borrowed and relaid from elsewhere in the castle; and a summit carelessly shaped in concrete, that ugliest of all symbols of the twentieth century. Where once flagpoles had flaunted the standard of the Templars, television aerials poked ugly fingers towards the sky and washing stirred to a faint breeze.

It was a short walk uphill to the Crusader Cathedral of Our Lady of Tortosa. Here, on the site of a much earlier church - legend claims that St. Peter once celebrated mass here – the Franks displayed some of the best of mediaeval religious architecture in miniature. That it has survived at all while the castle was so utterly destroyed is only the latest of many miracles attributed to the shrine.

There was nothing remarkable about the exterior; no breath of what lay behind the façade. Pleasant, semi-formal gardens grew about the walls, their clipped hedges and tidy lines of rose bushes (how strange to see a tidy garden in Syria!) tempered by a glorious tangle of hibiscus at their edge. The west front might have been the wall of a warehouse; not so inappropriate, as the cathedral has been just that among its many incarnations. Only the heavy buttresses, the arched windows and the minaret-like tower above the west door reminded you that this wasn't just a municipal building.

On this spot, right before the main entrance, the western world suffered an early collision with Middle Eastern terrorism: the murder in 1213 of Raymond, son of Prince Bohemond of Antioch, by two Assassins, fanatical adherents of an heretical Islamic sect. The murder sealed more than half a century of bitter strife between Templars and Assassins.

Stepping inside the main door, I found a world of illusion. The interior seemed far too tall to fit into its outer shell. Soaring Corinthian columns led to a barrel-vaulted roof, with alternating dark and light stonework pre-empting the typical black and white Ottoman pattern. The side-aisles, rather more elaborately vaulted, housed glass cases of local archaeological finds, randomly exhibited and mostly unlabelled. Otherwise, the cathedral is uncluttered. This, as Fedden notes, is part of the secret of its dramatic impact. "Here is a church naked, largely as the inspired masons left it, and the beauty of fine construction in stone, essentially an architectural beauty, comes home to one with great effect."

*

The harbour, too, can have changed little over the centuries. An L-shaped mole of piled boulders enclosed the bay immediately under the castle walls; it was only at its near end that concrete glued the stones together, making a base strong enough for small vehicles to drive right up to the unloading fishing boats. The serious traffic used the new port a mile or two up the coast.

Fish sellers lined the quay, displaying everything from tiny sardines through all conceivable varieties of striped and multi-coloured fish right up to a whole shark, with a saw laid by to cut off your steak to order. Their stocks were replenished even as buyers depleted them, and on the other side of the harbour you could watch how it was done.

A launch went offshore - a *ghizz,* the traditional Arwad boat - paying out a fishing net in a wide arc round the bay. Four hefty young men stood waist-deep in the sea, bracing themselves on a rope attached to the end of the net and trying, not always successfully, to keep their footing against the waves and avoid entangling themselves in the rope. The launch, meanwhile, completed its semi-circle and returned to the shore fifty yards up the bay, to sit treading water and waiting for the net to fill.

On the stones of the beach, an earlier catch was being turned over. In the net was another shark, three or four feet long. No man-eater, but big enough to take your hand off. I shelved any plans I might have had to swim in Tartous bay.

*

The track led endlessly down between irrigated orchards. Alongside ran an old stone aqueduct, long disused, dropping chunks of masonry carelessly into the undergrowth. The ground became increasingly sandy underfoot, orchards gave way to reed beds and oleander, and ahead the sound of shouting and raucous laughter mingled with the roar of breaking waves. Pop music blared out suddenly from a transistor radio.

No good at all; this was just leading me to the beach. I retraced my steps some way, cast my net wider, and began to trawl the orchards to either side of the road.

Just beyond a farmhouse surrounded by white-painted orange trees I found it at last, appearing suddenly out of a bed of reeds. The Tower of Snails: a strange, alien tower of enormous blocks, each ten feet long, reaching to some fifteen feet high - about the height of an orange tree. No wonder it had managed to hide so effectively.

The orange farmer had left a wide, reverent swathe around it, so that you approached over open ground. I went carefully, looking out for snakes in the long, dry grass. The other translation of *Burj al-Bezzaq* was the Tower of Cobras. If this was the right version, it may have arisen from decorations carved on the cornice, of which only three stones now remained. Below them trailed a wreath of unidentifiable greenstuff, sprouting from a tiny crack.

Inside the lower of two chambers, the ceiling was blackened by what looked like smoke, although it might have been lichen. Carved funerary slots lined the wall, and at the back corner a single valiant reed groped desperately upwards into the darkness.

History has left no record of who was buried here; and few details at all of the Phoenician inhabitants who lived and died among these scattered ruins south of Tartous. Known today as Amrit, the city which the Greeks called Marathus and the Egyptians, Mrt, was known in antiquity as Antaradus: the place lying before Aradus, or Arwad. It shared the name with Tartous, and also quite possibly with other Phoenician colonies lying along the coast in the vicinity of the island kingdom. For it was Arwad itself which was the city-state; local, shore-based settlements were merely its satellites, space for its markets and shipyards and merchants to overflow when they outgrew the tiny island. And space, of course, for its graveyards.

It would be a mistake, though, to presume that the citizens of Antaradus were concerned solely with the mundane and municipal certainties of buying and dying. True, exactly half of its surviving monuments - two, to be precise - are mausolea. The other two, designed for the propagation of one old and one thoroughly modern religion, deserve to rank somewhere near that greatest of all cultural advances, the alphabet. Maybe even alongside; in that both were Phoenician innovations, not a borrowed - if highly developed - idea from abroad.

I scarcely paused to look at the strange, phallic-like tombstones of the Spindles, for I was running out of light. In a desperate race against the setting sun I fought my way over hostile ground knitted with spiky undergrowth and treacherous with old quarry workings, and reached Amrit's temple sanctuary with just enough time left for photographs.

The limestone blocks, discoloured by age, glowed amber in the evening light. As I climbed down the rock walls and walked round the quadrangle of the temple precinct, the frogs were just beginning to croak. Even at this parching time of year the spring continued to flow, completely flooding the base of the *cella*, or shrine, at the southern end. The scent of crushed watermint rose from under my feet, and hundreds of tiny snails trembled on thistle-like flowers, dropping into the water as I brushed past them.

It must have been the presence of the sacred spring which decided the location of this sanctuary to the Phoenician god Melkart, the local Baal. Maybe even of Amrit itself, as the presence of the god usually influenced the place of settlement, rather than the other way round. Archaeology dates the cella at around 700 BC, but the original shrine is believed to have been much earlier, for Antaradus was settled by the early second millennium BC.

Stone pillars marched around three sides of the surrounding ledge, rather as the bluestone circles surround Stonehenge. A few had fallen into the pool, and by stepping from one to the next I was able to pick my way dryshod across to the cella.

Above a solid limestone plinth stood a small chamber. Perhaps it had once housed the image of Baal-Melkart which archaeologists found nearby. The stepped pyramids engraved on the cornice reminded me of the Nabataean tombs at Petra in Jordan; and also of the great Temple of Bel at Palmyra in the Syrian desert. This last is no coincidence.

As with the decoration, so with the underlying form. The little sanctuary at Amrit was to become the pattern for later Phoenician temples, such as the temple of Baal-Zeus at Husn es-Suleiman a few miles away in the Alawi Mountain; and was to be faithfully reproduced by the Palmyrenes on a grand scale. It was a style which would eventually be exported to Rome. But the other idea to which Amrit gave birth was to go much further.

Deliberate planning placed the open side of the sanctuary facing the stadium, Amrit's fourth and last monument; for in ancient times sport was a matter of religious rite as much as entertainment. Sports historian Dr. Labib Boutros of the University of Beirut argues convincingly for a date of around the sixteenth century BC to be applied to the origin of this stadium. This would mean that the Phoenicians were contesting ritual games at Amrit five centuries before history's first sports report.

When Odysseus won the foot-race before the walls of Troy in honour of Achilles' dead friend Patroclus, he may have been taking part in a funeral rite first conceived by the Phoenicians. If so, the prize he won was highly appropriate: "a mixing-bowl of chased silver... a masterpiece of Sidonian craftsmanship, which had been shipped across the misty sea by Phoenician traders..."[3]

But this particular Phoenician legacy far exceeded the idea, and the prize, recorded by Homer in the Iliad. For the dimensions of Amrit's stadium were to be almost exactly reproduced at Olympia, where emigrant Phoenicians had kept a sanctuary to Melkart as early as the sixteenth century BC. At Olympia, Melkart was identified with Herakles, founder of the Olympic Games. "Melkart arrived in Olympia," says Dr. Boutros, "bringing the traditions and culture of Baal, from places where Phoenician worship was deep-rooted, and established the Games of Olympia... These games, originally, were therefore introduced in Olympia by the Phoenicians."

It was nearly dark when I reached what might have been the proto-type for a succession of Olympic stadia. But I could still make out the shape: a long, narrow oval, its near end now merged into the surrounding heath, rough stone seating still visible through the undergrowth. Where once the runners had striven, now goats were grazing, shouldering their way through brambles to climb the frayed edges of the terraces. Instead of massed shouts and cheers, only the odd bleat stirred the air.

I looked furtively around for a shepherd; then, finding myself alone, took up position on imaginary starting blocks, and raised my head to look up the track. Two hundred metres, dead straight. I decided I preferred it with a bend; it didn't look so far.

As I left, I nearly fell in the darkness into a box-like hole in the ground. I thought it was another tomb; then, on a closer look, found it was the opening of a tunnel for the athletes to enter the stadium.

Was there anything the Phoenicians hadn't thought of before the rest of us?

*

------

[3] Reproduced by permission of Penguin Books Ltd.

Tartous jetty was labouring under many times the load it had been designed for. Men were busy unloading a stock of vegetables for Arwad from a large truck, its wheels close to dangling over the side. A small van, its own cargo already in the ghizz, was just leaving. I wobbled nervously on the edge for it to squeeze past, then followed the vegetables on to the boat.

Next to me on the cabin roof sat a woman who, despite the intense heat and humidity, wore a heavy black coat with a black linen bag over her head. The latter was a fairly common fashion accessory among conservative ladies, and I had seen the black bags hanging on the coat stands of some of my hostesses. My companion's husband, I was glad to see, was trendy and pleasantly cool in T-shirt, jeans and a baseball cap.

In a few moments we were off, skimming above an almost flat sea or bouncing like a pebble over the occasional wave, while the speed of our passing raised a stiff breeze that stripped the sweat from my body. It wasn't a straight crossing to the island. A decade or two ago this sound had been clear. Now we had to thread a path through tens of cargo ships, waiting to enter the ports of Tartous or Banias. Outside the murk of the harbour the water turned a brilliant Mediterranean blue-green. The white lazy mushrooms of hideous jellyfish bobbed a few feet below the surface.

Ten minutes and a couple of miles later we cruised carefully into Arwad's little harbour. The island wore a holiday air, its water crammed with small boats and its quayside buzzing with cafés and shops. A troop of ladies with black coats and head-bags making their way down the jetty tried vainly to impart some gravity to the atmosphere. They were helped by a factory of sorts on a disused central mole, pumping out a thin column of black smoke that wrapped itself around a solitary, miniature Corinthian column, half buried under twentieth-century débris.

The third, northern, jetty was the place where ships were born and came to die. Next to the boat-building yards, it was the last resting place for a number of rusty hulks. Among these, lying on the sea-bed with its masts askew and only its bow above water, a twin-masted schooner waited for time and decay to finish it off. The writer Eric Newby, sailing round the world in the 1930s on one of the last four-masted barques to sail commercially, was told by a fellow-sailor that

Arwad was the last place in the world where tall ships were built.[4] Judging by an old aerial photograph taken between world wars, these must have been schooners like the one now rotting in the harbour. Just beyond, though, lay far older evidence of Arwad's seafaring past.

Around the perimeter of a natural ledge forming the northern tip of the island, Cyclopean blocks bounded a man-made harbour hollowed out from the soft rock. In places these still stand to a height of four blocks – perhaps thirty feet – and my imagination strove to picture the harbour as it once stood with this tremendous wall intact. Here was the strength of ancient Arwad. No wonder the island once reigned supreme along this coast; no wonder that when even the impregnable Arwad fell to the Assyrians, local civilisation trembled to its roots, and, rightly despairing of its own future, submitted without further resistance.

A succession of breakers hurled themselves against the ledge, spending themselves in a wash of foam before curling over its lip to lick at the rock towers that the masons had piled above it. Fishermen cast their lines into these waves, taking advantage of the deep water immediately below the ledge. So must the men of Arwad have fished in this surf for tens of thousands of years, long before the harbour was hollowed out and the Phoenician galleys sailed away to bring amber from the Baltic or tin from Cornwall. And so they must have dumped their rubbish here, I thought, grimly watching a tractor bring the island's waste and tip it into the sea. A hundred years ago - even twenty, before the universal adoption of plastic wrapping - it probably dispersed very effectively. Now, Arwad must be filling half the Mediterranean with non-biodegradable waste.

These days, the harbour is mostly above water. As I picked my way among the puddles, the hammering of the nearby boatyards merged with the grumble of the breakers and the shouts of boys swimming off the walls. Climbing the lowest course of blocks, I sat counting the ships in the straits, and fingering the pockmarks in the walls. They were like sponges, pitted with holes which alternate waves and hot sun had filled with a thick crust of salt.

So onwards, in an anti-clockwise circuit of the island. The western seaboard must have been the merchants' suburb, for here nature had

---

[4] The sailor spoke of an island off Banias, further up the coast, but can only have meant Arwad.

been manipulated in a style that was smaller in scale, more intimate, than the main harbour. A double line of walls had been sculpted from the seabed, leaving a channel the width of a small boat. A rowing boat? No, for the corridor left no room for oars. It must have been poled through the narrows like a punt or a gondola. Gaps in the inner and outer walls, far enough apart to baffle a violent wave, allowed these craft to pass from the sea into the channel and then to anchorage. Perhaps the sea-level had dropped in the last few thousand years for, like the harbour, the channel was high and dry. In the low cliff of the shoreline was evidence of long use: the hollowed-out cave of an old warehouse, its interior shaped in a perfect beehive dome; square holes which had once supported beams; ramps and jetties. I pictured fleets of little boats ferrying goods from ships at the main harbour. They had rounded the immense wall at the northern tip of the island, slipped into the shelter of the narrow channel and nosed their way quietly to the merchant's own quay, where a single heave would suffice both to unload and to store their cargo. How many reunions had these slipways seen, of families separated for months, maybe years? And how much better to celebrate them quietly, privately, rather than in the public forum of the crowded quay across the island, heaving with all the excitement of a great trading vessel newly docked.

A group of boys swimming from the walls yelled at me to join them. Why not? I was already soaked with the humid air, which rose off the sea and permeated every stitch of my clothing. Temporarily forgetting the shark and the jellyfish, I took my jeans off and swam in my shirt, stepping carefully off the rock shelf and straight into eight feet of water. There were no ladies in head-bags around to deplore my state of undress, and when I climbed back on to the shelf and replaced my jeans over my soggy underclothes, I felt very little wetter than before.

Nevertheless I was squelching a bit as I left the shore and plunged into the alleyways of Arwad's interior. The tiny, twisting passages were worse than any maze; a good thing I was trying to reach the highest point of the island, for "uphill" was the only sense to my direction. Even so, when I reached the citadel I went round three and a half sides before I found the entrance. For a few lira I was inside, and strolled on the walls of perhaps the Levant's tiniest Crusader castle, looking back to the mainland and Tartous Castle as the Templars had done seven hundred years ago.

Finding my way back down to the harbour was easier; just as well, for "downhill" had too many options. The alleys grew wider and presently gave way to a market stall, where for the second time I came across the crates of apples and watermelons I'd fallen over on the quay in Tartous. Just before the harbour was another fort, even tinier than the citadel. You come on it from a back street, where two stone blocks flank the entrance. They bear the arms of Guy de Lusignan, last King of Jerusalem… with a twist.

It was in 1302 that the Franks finally surrendered this last outpost of Outremer to the Egyptian Mamelukes, eleven years after the loss of Tartous had removed their last foothold on the mainland. It's said that the Arabs, with a quirk of humour, altered rather than altogether removing the Crusader arms. To the Lion and the Palm of Lusignan, they added a chain: the lion chained to the palm, the Christian entirely subjugated to the Muslim. It doesn't quite add up, for the chain is in relief and can't therefore have been added later; but it's a good story.

A couple of dozen more steps brought me once more to the open space of the sea front. Here were shops selling the things you find at the seaside around the world: shell ornaments, driftwood sculptures, carved wooden boats. Although much was factory-made tourist fodder, there were also pieces of exquisite craftsmanship. Arwad's souvenirs were a cut above most. But I wasn't here to go shopping. With an hour or two yet before the last boat back to Tartous, I returned to the northern quay and went to watch the boatbuilders at work.

After a few minutes Mohammed Bahlawan laid down his chisel, beckoned me over and called for tea.

Boatbuilding in Arwad was a family business - and a monopoly. Mohammed's grandfather had graduated from humble carpenter to owner of his own yard, and his sons and grandsons had followed him. Now the family ran Arwad's boatbuilding - and Arwad's boatbuilding ran the family.

"That is my cousin…" he nodded to the young man sitting with us at the table, picking over a tangled fishing net. "That is my cousin…" - over towards the sound of hammering coming from behind a half-built boat - "..that is my cousin…"

He confirmed that Arwad had built tall ships until comparatively recently. "Yes, my grandfather told me all about them."

Mohammed spoke excellent English and willingly supplied answers to my torrent of questions. I quizzed him voraciously.

"How many people live on Arwad?"

"About ten thousand." It was scarcely believable. How could so many cram themselves on to this tiny rock? Mohammed elaborated. "About four thousand are at sea. Another five thousand people from Arwad live around the coast."

"And what do they all live on?"

"Fishing." He hesitated and consulted a cousin. "No, fishing and boatbuilding, fifty-fifty… and then, there's the Merchant Navy."

This, it appeared, was another family business.

"My father was in the Merchant Navy. He went all over the world. He was in England for the coronation of your Queen. He was also in prison for threatening his Captain…" Mohammed left the older generation to its misdemeanours and returned to his own. "I was an engineer. And my brother was a Captain, my other brother was a First Engineer, my other brother was a Second Engineer…"

He led me among the half-built boats, right under the walls of the ancient harbour. "The Phoenicians had a deal with the Egyptians," said Mohammed. "The Phoenicians built ships for the Egyptians, the Egyptians built the walls for the Phoenicians. Yes, it's easy rock to work. Did you know there's supposed to be an underwater passage from Arwad to Hbess?" He gestured vaguely to the south, where a few uninhabited rocks poke their heads above the Mediterranean.

Wood in all stages of working, from fresh-cut logs still seasoning to well-planed board, lay about the yard like litter, filling the air with the scent of pine resin. Shavings and sawdust thickly padded the ground underfoot. We picked a way to where Abdullah and Mustafa Hamoud were caulking the hull of a boat. With wooden mallets they packed soft cotton rope between cracks that were scarcely visible to the naked eye, so perfectly were the planks laid. Afterwards would come a resinous paste to seal the hull, then painting could begin.

"What's your annual turnover?"

"A hundred boats a year. Most go to customers in Syria, but a lot go to Argentina."

"What about Turkey?" Syria's neighbour has a booming tourist trade, especially along its Mediterranean coast. But it was the wrong thing to say. Mohammed didn't like the Turks.

"All Syria suffered under the Turks. Before 1560, we lived in the light. After the Turks came, we lived in the dark." They had set a garrison on Arwad, he continued, sending their bravest men here and paying them extra. The men of Arwad, ran the implication, weren't easy subjects.

"Four thousand years ago, Arwad was king. It ruled from Ra'as Shamra to Hama." He paused for thought, and into the space left by his voice crowded the sounds of Arwad: the thud of the mallets, the hum of the surf, the distant whine of a power tool coming from behind the young skeleton of another boat. Four thousand years since the island was supreme, but the memory of that supremacy endured. Long after its moment of greatness had vanished the island retained an independence, a sense of apartness from the rest of Syria, that it would never surrender. And the nucleus of that greatness, that subsequent independence, was its ship-building yards.

Stepping forward, Mohammed ran his hand appreciatively over the pale new wood of the nearly-finished hull.

"You know," he said simply, "we live from the sea. Without the sea, we are nothing." It might have been any one of his ancestors speaking.

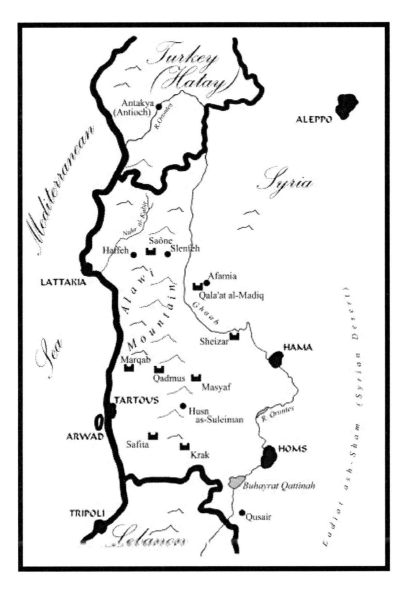

Map of northern Syria

Map of southern Syria

Above: First step on a long journey.
Below: A ninety-year-old craftsman in the Street of the Carpenters

Above: The women of Sheizar beating their fleeces clean.
Below: Ghaada's daily work: threading tobacco leaves for drying.

Madfaa gives a scale to Saone's man-made ditch
and drawbridge pillar.

Above: Krak des Chevaliers, "the best preserved and most wholly admirable castle in the world."
Below: An unwilling passenger at Homs Bus Station.

Above: Hassan Ahmad Salim with his family.
Below: Hungry and hopeful, Madfaa explores the deserted village of Khayza.

Madfaa waits patiently below the convent of Sednaya.

Above: A tourist snapshot: by the Roman arch in the Street Called Straight, Old Damascus.
Below: End of the road: Madfaa returns to Fayiz' yard.

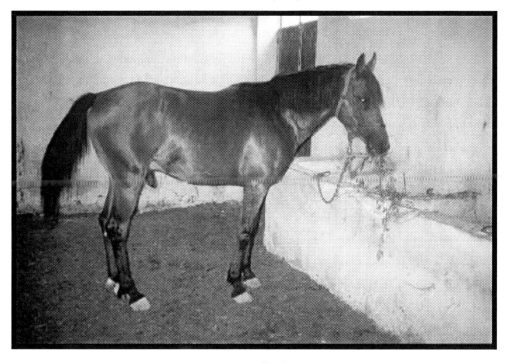

IV

THE MOUNTAIN

South of Lattakia the mountains recede from the coast to leave a wide, fertile plain. This is fruit-growing country, and orchards of oranges, lemons, figs and olives fill the miles leading up to the distant hills. Old farmhouses seem to grow organically from the soil along with the trees, living in comfortable symbiosis with the thick vines that trail all over them. Greenhouses and polytunnels, dotting the spaces between them, bring the picture up to date; otherwise things can have changed very little, except that concrete block has replaced mud brick.

Twice we passed a coffee factory, the aromatic fumes drifting through the open window and clinging to the cab for the next half-mile. Just before Jebleh a military airfield sprouted a thin crop of missile launchers, their long snouts pointing threateningly out to sea.

For the first few miles Madfaa had clashed and rattled alarmingly in the back of the pickup truck, its bare tin floor reacting without sympathy to his newly shod feet. By the time we left the city suburbs, though, he was standing so quietly that I kept nervously looking back to see if we still had him. I felt uncomfortable that I was cheating on the journey by doing a short stretch on four wheels instead of four legs. But the road south was even busier than the road north, and it would have been completely feckless to have tried to ride him through the traffic.

I unloaded him and waved our driver goodbye south of Jebleh. Here the mountains draw close to the sea again, squeezing the road and its accompanying settlement on to a thin strip of coast. This hasn't stopped the town of Banias, perched on its narrow ledge, from developing into a sizeable port. Its rapid growth makes for an unattractive, severely functional place. Nevertheless I thought kindly of it, as its little boys for once were friendly.

An airy bridge took us across the motorway; then at once we were climbing, climbing back up into the Mountain, with frequent rests because of the gradient. Not that Madfaa needed to rest much today. He was raring to go after his holiday. The swollen leg was completely better, and the wound almost healed, with only a small bump to show where it had been. I still kept it bandaged as a precaution against his knocking it, but otherwise could forget it. Already the calkins were proving worth their weight in gold, for the road was newly surfaced and very slippery.

Soon we were among terraces, chalky horizontal gashes in a deep green background of fruit trees. Now, instead of grass, the bloated fingers of prickly pear edged the roadside; and when we stopped for a breather Madfaa had to browse on the dry, dead stalks of wild corn. We came to a village where people called a welcome to me from dark interiors, and boxes of fruit and vegetables tumbled out of a shop doorway. Among crates of oranges and aubergines were huge flat cabbages. I bought one for Madfaa, cutting it awkwardly in half with my rather blunt penknife. He ate one piece with relish, while I stowed the other in the saddlebags for his lunch.

Black bands striping the minaret of the village mosque suggested its Ottoman origins. A random scattering of black stones in many of the houses suggested an earlier history; so did the chequerboard mixture of basalt among the limestone blocks in the olive terraces beyond. This had almost certainly been purloined from the castle which lay up there ahead of us: the great Hospitaller castle of Margat, known to the Arabs as *Qala'at Marqab*, the Castle of the Watchtower.

What would they have thought, those humble monks and laymen who served the Hospital of St. John in Jerusalem at the time of the First Crusade, if they could have seen the heights to which their order would rise? Founded even earlier than the Templars, the Knights Hospitaller had followed the latter by evolving into a military order, while still retaining their original vocation of ministering to pilgrims and the sick. Enriched by donations and bequests from throughout Christendom, the Hospitallers bought Marqab in 1186 from the Principality of Antioch.

As the road wound up and round, the solid black, brooding mass of Marqab began to unfold. It lay on a spur detached from the surrounding mountains, jutting out towards the sea. The road climbed to the isthmus behind, then turned in a right-angle for the final ascent to the main entrance. As I turned the corner to pass under the third side, I found a scattering of stalls selling souvenirs, postcards, food and drink. I shouldn't have been surprised; but the approaches to the castle had been quite deserted, and this sudden little knot of humanity was unexpected.

Unexpected but welcome. I was ready for a drink after the long, hot plod uphill. So was Madfaa, and gratefully emptied the bucket of water I found him. While we both drank and rested, I took a long, hard look at the way ahead. Marqab's access was not like the flight of steps at Sheizar and Saône; more a steep ramp with a series of shallow risers to break the slope. We could manage this one together.

Cautious but trusting, Madfaa climbed steadily until we stood inside the gatehouse. At last I was able to satisfy my ambition to go right inside a Crusader castle with my horse. The warden came to meet us.

No, we couldn't stay the night, he said. *Mamnuu'* - forbidden. But he told me where I could tether Madfaa safely for the afternoon, and I left the little horse tied appropriately to a cannon in the outer ward while I went ahead to check.

I could have got lost for a week in Marqab. Following the contours of the rock from which it grew seamlessly, it was a maze of twisting, angular passages, their width a function of the underlying rock structure, with flights of steps leading off where I least expected them. The entrance itself was designed to disorientate invaders, a Hospitaller speciality. Leading through a massive gateway into the outer ward, the ramp turned back on itself to climb the steps through the inner wall in a series of elbow turns, until it reached another huge arch giving on to the inner ward.

It took half an hour to find the garden that was Madfaa's destination. It was decorated with fine detail, quite disarming by comparison with the grim aspect Marqab had presented so far. Flower patterns were etched into the stones of the windows in the block room along one side, and scallop shells covered the doorway, whose lintel bore a ten-petalled flower. The little square was well-stocked with grass; almost too well, for I'd been warned once again to look out for snakes. When I returned with Madfaa I pulled a dead branch from a bush and used it to beat ahead of him, until I was satisfied that any resident serpents would let him enjoy his Eden without interference. Now I could leave him safely while I went to explore the keep.

More louring black basalt, relieved only where where restoration had seamed the stones with light-coloured mortar. The keep, a square block with a circular tower attached, was built directly over the water source. The bottom floor housed two wells, and clear water trickled from a rock-cut niche in one corner. Much more satisfactory than the evil-smelling cisterns at Saône; they say that this castle could withstand a five-year siege.

An outside staircase led to the first floor, passing under an elegant arched gateway with decorated columns. Inside was a wonderfully light, airy hall; the last thing I had expected to find within that sullen exterior. I looked for a spiral staircase but found a straight flight of steps, leading up under a roof of solid basalt rafters into darkness broken by a tiny gleam of light from above. I groped my way through a couple of right-angled turns on the second floor, and found a final flight bearing me up to welcome light and air on the roof.

I looked over the parapet with a suddenly lurching heart to find myself way above even the highest terraces. My gaze fell over the bastion of the outer wall, to follow the narrow thread of road leading away along the crest of the mountain. There, a couple of miles away, was a village where I might find lodging. In the other direction, I looked over the fig and olive orchards enclosed within the outer ward, and on down to Banias, where white smoke belched from four factory chimneys. Beyond, a blue sea melted into the heat-haze. Even to the east towards the mountains, little but mist limited the field of view. No wonder they called this the Watchtower.

Up here, I could see the layout as if it were drawn on paper. From either side of the colossal fortifications opposite the hill - the castle's weakest point topographically - ran two massive pairs of parallel walls. Hugging the contours of the hill, they spread out to enclose a narrow triangle, blunt end to the sea. In Marqab, and its sister fortress Krak des

Chevaliers, the Hospitallers brought military architecture to new heights, building on to original Byzantine ideas the latest concepts from France. The concentric castle exemplified here is a fort within a fort: if the outer walls were breached, it should still have been possible to hold the inner ward. Impregnable in theory, Marqab was never put to the ultimate test. Even Saladin, to whom fortresses such as Saône fell like dominoes after his decisive victory at the Battle of Hattin in 1187, took one look and marched away. It wasn't until 1285, when the writing was on the wall for the Kingdom of Outremer, that the Knights were finally persuaded to abandon Marqab, marching out with their heads held high under safe-conduct from the Mameluke Sultan Qalawun.

The warden was waiting for me at the foot of the tower.

"Mamnuu', mamnuu'," he said, reading my thoughts as I eyed up the pile of tibn in a side room: someone had evidently kept a donkey here. From then on he and his deputy kept an eye on me, popping up continually beside me in my ramblings around the castle, as if they thought I might disappear with Madfaa and hide in a dungeon overnight.

*

The road ran eastwards along the crest of the hill, with magnificent views down to the valleys either side. To the left, a succession of villages and terraces and more villages and more terraces; to the right a land more sparsely furnished, with seams of rock bursting through the thin soil like ribs of the underlying skeleton. More than one hilltop was crowned with a white mausoleum; the shrine of some local saint, now tinged pink with the setting sun. Even the black stones of Marqab, growing smaller on its ridge behind, seemed softer at this hour.

In the village of az-Zawba I asked at the shop for possible lodging. Abd al-Aziz Sukariya, who was running some late errands, overheard me and volunteered himself.

Abd al-Aziz - Abid to his friends, among whom he instantly included me - installed Madfaa in a huge stable with a window giving on to panoramic views. He filled the manger generously with tibn and barley, then led me off to my own supper. He and his wife Maryam were a close couple. Unusually, here, Maryam dressed like a European in blouse and knee-length skirt. Most of the Alawi girls wore jeans or tracksuits, and - with the exception of Ghaada - changed to long, loose robes when they became wives and mothers.

Word got round of a foreign visitor, and after supper half a dozen callers arrived. Madyan, a strikingly good-looking young man with a clipped black beard, spoke good English. I seized the chance to ask him more about the Alawis.

"Firstly, we believe in the legitimacy of the twelve *Imams*," he answered. Starting with Ali, cousin and son-in-law of the Prophet, he listed their names. "These were the heirs to Muhammad, upon him be peace." Only through the line of Ali and, through his wife Fatima, of the Prophet himself, he explained, could a leader legitimately rule over the world of Islam and infallibly interpret the Qur'an.

So far, Madyan had told me nothing to define the Alawi people. The creed he had defined so far was that of the Twelvers, mainstream Shi'ites, who awaited the return of the twelfth Imam, or his heir, in the person of a *Mahdi* or divinely guided one, a Messiah who would usher in a reign of justice and the destruction of all wickedness.

But I'd already been told that the Alawis didn't consider themselves Shi'ites. "So what makes you different from the Shi'ites? You have different beliefs, don't you? Special rites?"

"We are quite ordinary Muslims, just like the Sunnis and the Shi'ites," he answered defensively. "People don't understand us, they don't know about us, so they tell silly stories about us." He continued with rising passion. "The only difference with us is that we love Ali more than the Shi'ites do, and we love the Prophet, upon him be peace, more than any of them. We have a few differences in doctrine, like you Christians, but that's all."

There was to be no insight into secret rituals. Disappointed but not surprised, I tried another tack. "Do you consider men and women equal among the Alawis?"

"Yes, of course. But although men and women receive the same instruction in school and college, men tend to feel their faith more deeply than women. Men are more inclined towards philosophy than women."

"That's interesting," I ventured, "because in Britain, more women tend to maintain their Christian faith than men. Perhaps," I ventured cautiously, "we're not talking so much about the difference between men and women as the difference in the faiths themselves?"

I was dangerously close to the western stereotype: the mis-apprehension that Islam is male-dominated; that the Muslim woman is regarded as an inferior being. I desperately wanted answers to some of the many questions which had been buzzing around like flies in my head throughout the journey. This articulate, devout man was someone who might provide them. But I was pressing the wrong buttons.

Madyan became heated, his struggle to express himself in English adding frustration to his urgency. "Muhammad, upon him be peace, gave women importance. For instance, women had no right to property before his time. He said that a woman should inherit property - one share for a man's two. Before Islam, women were nothing!"

His friends saw him becoming more excited, and tactfully steered the conversation into calmer waters. Artlessly they asked innocent questions: where was I going next, how old was I...

I regretted that I had forgotten to ask him about the sacred groves. It was an opportunity that I mustn't lose again.

*

I tried to make up for it the next morning.

"Is that a special place of the Alawis?" I asked a woman by the roadside, pointing to the small knot of trees on a distant hilltop which had marked the skyline for the last few miles.

"Yes, that's ours," she replied.

"How long have those trees been there?"

"For a very long time." She didn't know how long. Conversation faltered, and I longed for Madyan and his excellent English.

I had got away early that morning, well fed and waved on my way by the ever-hospitable Abid. On the outskirts of az-Zawba the road ran alongside a stone wall whose base, centuries old, was of heavy black and white stones underlying a layer of concrete and three courses of breeze block. What a labour, to have hauled all that stone along three miles of mountain roads from Marqab; perhaps even before the days of motor traffic.

They still build in stone, here. Concrete has not entirely taken over as elsewhere. In the houses and garden walls were great square blocks, lovingly crafted with perfect right-angles; elsewhere thinner, rougher slabs, set at an angle in alternating rows, made a herring-bone pattern.

Much of the terracing which laced the gentler hillsides was newly restored; beautifully built, with interlacing large boulders and small stones. From any one vantage point my eye could travel over what must have equated to a lifetime's work in man-hours. The less precipitous areas, where terraces extended themselves into fully-grown fields, were boulder country: large, round boulders lying randomly beside the road, or pushed aside to mark a boundary to the field and make room for the plough; smaller boulders piled in the middle of the cornfield.

The Marqab ridge contracted to a narrow crest, along which Madfaa and I stepped as if through thin air. Spectacular valleys, their sides wrinkled by terracing, fell away to either side. At last the final spur spluttered and died, dropping between a few last, defiant outcrops down to a saddle at the head of a valley. From here we began the ascent to another ridge. Behind it, Abid had promised me, I should see the citadel of Qadmus.

For now, I was more aware of the contemporary military presence. Soldiers congregated at bus-stops on their way to work, and a great radar scanner guarded the hilltop nearby. It was a lesson in the importance of topography in strategic planning. For all the arts of modern warfare, these mountains are as important on today's military scene as they were in the days of the Crusaders.

We crawled along the side of a long gorge with a sheer cliff rising to the right, and olive and walnut groves falling away to the left. Near the top, a group of children clustered around a hollow in the hillside under a small settlement.

One by one, like bees clustered around the entrance to a hive, they disappeared into a tiny cave, to re-emerge carrying full water bottles. When Madfaa approached, they left their work and came to meet us both.

Madfaa wanted a drink, and I wanted a closer look. One of the children led me into the cave. Its entrance was just big enough to let me in. My shoulders blocking the light, I slid down a short slope and found a pool of clear water at its foot. It was only small, but magically replenished itself, like the widow's cruse, as I filled my bucket.

We followed a herd of goats up the road past the houses and into a dark knot of trees with a scattering of whitewashed tombstones. When had the little spring first attracted settlement and sanctity, I wondered? Certainly long before the Alawis came to the mountains. Probably long before even the Phoenicians. The people of this village were heirs to traditions older than human memory. Surely the Alawi people had, as has so often happened, absorbed into their creed elements of much older local practices. They must have sucked them in with the very air they breathed.

The road emerged from the trees and swung south to follow a tremendous gorge, with cliffs above and terracing below. Another of the sacred groves occupied the far hilltop, and I used it to keep my bearings as the road lurched in crazy swerves, following the contours. Where the opposite hillside finally converged and joined forces with our own, we found ourselves suddenly among the high stone walls of another village. Another chance to scrounge water, another large crowd gathering; Madfaa was getting more used to being mobbed these days, but still wasn't too sure whether he liked being the centre of attention. As soon as his thirst was quenched I remounted and rode quickly on.

A few hundred yards further, and we brazenly helped ourselves to someone's terrace for a few hours' halt, tying up under a fig tree for tibn and bananas. It was a prime position. Lazing with my back to the tree while Madfaa browsed among the wheat stubble, I looked down an endless vista to where the sea must be hiding under the shimmering haze. A half-turn, and I could trace our path along the morning's ridge to the dim shape of Marqab, levitating in the throbbing mid-day air.

A turn in the other direction, and I could see another castle, just as Abid had promised I would. Qadmus, first of the castles of the Nizaris. I was entering the territory historically associated with a sect so secretive and enigmatic that it made the Alawis appear positively evangelical.

*

Marco Polo, whiling away the hours in his Genoese prison by dictating his memoirs to Rustichello, told a strange story of a sect of northern Persia. He spoke of a society of heretics led by a "Sheikh of the Mountain", who made an art of assassination. Since the young zealots sent on their murderous missions often didn't return, they were first brainwashed in a bizarre way.

"The Sheikh... had made in a valley between two mountains the biggest and most beautiful garden that was ever seen, planted with all the finest fruits in the world and containing the most splendid mansions and palaces that were ever seen, ornamented with gold... There were fair ladies there and damsels, the loveliest in the world, unrivalled at playing every sort of instrument and at singing and dancing. And he gave his men to understand that this garden was Paradise."[5]

The Sheikh's acolytes, Marco continued, were drugged and carried to the garden, where they enjoyed its pleasures for a time; then again drugged, and brought away. Back at the court of the Sheikh, they discussed their experiences, declaring that "this was in truth the Paradise of which Mahomet had told their ancestors... They longed for death so that they might go there." Thus, when the Sheikh desired the death of an enemy, he would have many young men at his disposal, all ready and willing to undertake suicide missions.

Marco - or, maybe, Rustichello, who is thought to have sometimes exceeded his brief as ghost writer - was repeating tales which had been current for a century. Certainly, the sect he described had long been known for political murders, and Arab as well as western writers sought desperately to explain the religious fanaticism which led some of its adherents to sacrifice themselves for their leader. To an age unfamiliar with the concept of the Kamikaze pilot or suicide bomber, there could be only one explanation: drugs. Opiates or hashish; either used as Marco described, to play an elaborate trick; or to induce a religious ecstasy in which the killer became a missile to be pointed at his target. Contemporary Muslim writers, to whom such men were an heretical anathema, labelled them *hashishiyiin*, hashish users. Among the Franks, the word became Assassin.

The Assassins were a branch of the Isma'ilis, themselves schismatic Shi'ites. Dispute over the legitimacy of the Seventh Imam led to the supporters of the candidacy of Ismai'il distancing themselves from mainstream Shi'ites. Known as "Seveners" and denounced as heretics, they became a mainly underground movement, only acting openly when they were strong enough to show themselves. Such a situation arose in eleventh century Egypt, where the rise of the Isma'ili Fatimid dynasty to the Caliphate gave them their finest hour. More typical was their small enclave in northern Persia, based on a number of almost impregnable fortresses.

---

[5] Reproduced by permission of Penguin Books Ltd.

It was from here that Rashid ad-Din Sinan was sent as *da'i* (missionary) to unite and galvanise the fractured Isma'ili communities of Syria. Mostly small groups existing under a local warlord, these communities were under increasing threat from the encroachment of Sunni Turkish rulers. An astute and ruthless politician, Sinan played off the local powers against each other so skilfully that by the end of his tenure the Frankish chronicler William of Tyre numbered the Syrian Isma'ilis at sixty thousand, based around ten castles. One of these was Qadmus.

It dominated the road from now on, jutting out on its crag above the surrounding village. It didn't look big enough to be one of the more important Assassin castles; but perhaps anything would seem small after Marqab.

The outskirts were those of a modern resort town. As I rode deeper in, though, the streets contracted and the houses, older and shabbier, drew more closely together. Many were built from suspiciously well-cut blocks. Tiny alleys and staircases led off the main street towards a crumbling, jungly acropolis. This was no place for a horse.

I left Madfaa tethered with food and water under the eye of a helpful shopkeeper, and set out for the citadel on foot. It was like negotiating a maze. More than once I found myself in a blind alley leading to someone's back yard. At last a flagstoned passage took me up a zig-zag and under a small archway, barely large enough for a horse ever to have passed underneath.

Lawrence's dismissal of Qadmus (and its sister fortress of Masyaf) as "absurdly weak" seemed unnecessarily scathing. The top of the crag was quite small, but magnificently fortified by nature: the near side inaccessible enough, the far one a sheer rockface of perhaps thirty feet. Ordinary houses had long since obscured any trace of the castle. The only street, its broad steps comfortably overgrown with grass and weeds, must once have been the main passageway through the fortress. Fig trees and hollyhocks grew about it. With their elevated position and wonderful views, the people who lived in Qadmus Castle today were perhaps some of the luckiest in the Alawi Mountain. But I couldn't help wondering how the hell they got all their shopping up here.

*

Hot and thirsty, I couldn't refuse the invitation to tea. And, looking out of the shuttered first-floor window of the old house, I could just see down the street to where Madfaa dozed lazily in the shade.

My hostess was an Isma'ili descending (like most of the population of Qadmus) from the Assassins. Describing her forefathers as *Nizari*, she related how the murder of Nizar, an eleventh century successor to the Egyptian Caliphate, had created schism parting Egyptian Isma'ilis from those of Persia and Syria. The many religions of north-west Syria are greatly complicated by a multiplicity of names for each. The Alawis are referred to as *Nusayris*, after their founder Muhammad ibn Nusayr; while *Nasara* is the plural of *Nasrani*, or Nazarene - that is, Christian. Since it's often the case that Arabic vowels are a courtesy of dialect, which itself is a function of the local community, there was enough ambiguity here to confound the keenest Arabic scholar. It made my crash course in local religions rather hard going.

Besides, people were always more anxious to gossip about their neighbours' faith than discuss their own.

"Their women know nothing about religion," said my hostess contemptuously of her Alawi neighbours, "only of child-bearing." I wondered what Ghaada or Fardoss would have made of that; and gave up the subject altogether.

"Have your people been here since the time of Rashid ad-Din Sinan?" I asked her.

"Of course. Rashid ad-Din lived in our castle at Qadmus."

I knew that his headquarters had been further across the Mountain at Masyaf; but of course he would have visited all the strongholds. My skin prickled to think of the half-legendary figure climbing the path under the gateway that I had passed that afternoon, and looking across the same landscape that I had surveyed.

The lady was pleased that she had so obviously impressed me. She tried a bit harder.

"Richard the Lionheart lived here, too," she added brightly.

It was time to move on.

*

I spent the night behind a haystack, at what must have been the highest point of the Jebel al-Alawiyiin hereabouts. There was a biting wind - the same wind which I'd felt for the first time on the Mahardah ridge, here compressed to demonic strength as it passed over the mountain-top - but I was buried snugly under a mountain of duvets kindly lent me by the owners of the stack. Madfaa dined on the armfuls of unthreshed straw they brought him, crunching the grain fiercely from the heads and then chewing more leisurely on what was left.

He set off like a cannonball the next morning. Although he had had eight or nine pounds of barley over the last twenty-four hours, he had gone short of bulk food and felt hungry. Lots of calories but a tight stomach; the formula for preparing a racehorse. He was ready to run, and it was to the disappointment of both of us that before the haystack was out of sight the road took a downward turn. It stayed that way for two hours; and on gleaming new tarmac that was as slippery as glass. So progress was slow and careful, and for now all that energy went to waste.

Down and down we went, through a long, desolate valley where only scrub grew among huge limestone boulders. The wind funnelled viciously down the decline, laughing at our slowness. At last I caught a glimpse of the Orontes plain ahead of us, as if we were coming out of the mountains and down to the sea.

Now the valley widened out and signs of habitation started to appear. An old, stone-built village clung to the top of the scarp, while modern, resort-type houses spread around its foot. I asked for water, and was directed off the road along a track running sharply downhill to a little valley. Houses surrounded a small meadow planted with walnut trees. Springs gushed from every available crevice, spilling water so generously over the grass that it was difficult to walk dry-shod, and making a series of rivulets running in parallel to join the stream at the bottom. Several families of ducklings paddled communally, and beyond a low stone wall on the far side of the valley a man was ploughing with a donkey.

Children clustered rapidly as Madfaa began to tear hungrily at rich clover. They brought him armfuls of greenstuff, placing it reverently under his nose like a burnt offering. One gave him a big bundle of deadly nightshade, which had me moving rather quickly.

He did equally well further down the main road, at a shop where I stopped to buy my own breakfast. The kindly shopkeeper gathered all the cucumbers which EU regs would have rejected - the bent ones, the knobbly ones, the mouldy ones – and Madfaa demolished them with gusto, dribbling green sludge all down my shirt front.

At last Masyaf began to unroll itself in front of us. It was almost at the foot of the mountain, barely higher than the Ghaab. So much for the Old Man of the Mountain, I thought, dreading the long pull back uphill that lay in front of us on the next leg of the journey.

That was how Crusaders referred to Rashid ad-Din, pre-empting Marco Polo - for *Sheikh* means "Elder". And the castle at Masyaf was his headquarters. From here he ruled over his Nizari populace, surrounded by enemies - for the local Powers were Sunni almost to the last man - skilfully playing off Turk against Frank, Sunni against Christian, dispatching his lethal envoys to deliver death to those who offended his perception of the world order, and gathering rumour and fantasy about him until the very word "Assassin" became a synonym for a political killer.

*

I came through a mediaeval gateway into what remained of the old walled town. Inside was a warren of streets; it wouldn't take hashish to confuse someone, here. The citadel stood well above the level of the housetops, beckoning me through the cobbled lanes until I finally stood underneath it.

I led Madfaa round a circuit of the walls. They formed a series of angles, zig-zagging along the contour of the underlying rock. From here it appeared that they made a double line of defence. Could the Assassins have learned from the Hospitallers, producing at least the semblance of a concentric castle?

As ever, Madfaa was gathering a crowd of small boys. If I were to leave him while I explored the castle, I had to make allies of them. Backtracking to the nearest shop, I suborned them with sweets, promising more if they took care of him for me. As a diplomatic man-oeuvre it was pretty basic, well below the standards previously set inside those grim walls; but it paid dividends, for the lads took Madfaa into the warden's garden, where there was grass to eat and a tree for shade, and promised to look after him well.

A steep flight of steps led to a massive wooden door. Bleached by centuries of sunlight, it might have dated back to the time of the Old

Man himself. It led to a blank wall with an immediate right-angled turn, then a choice of two exits: one leading to store chambers, the other to the outer ward and the entrance to the Great Hall. Above this entrance an Arabic inscription stood out in relief on white marble, between slabs of basalt. The floor was hewn straight from the underlying rock, filled and levelled by great blocks of limestone, with a basalt threshold.

Everywhere basalt and limestone; though limestone predominated. It gave a pleasant lightness to an otherwise austere building, as a rather grim hospital might gleam under a cheerful layer of emulsion. Decorative carving twisted its way up the short columns inside the doorway. The Old Man had an eye for more kindly arts than killing.

I climbed as high as I could reach, and sat looking out at the mountain behind and the plain ahead. Barely in the foothills of the Jebel, this fortress rather knocked my preconceptions of a remote eyrie perched on top of a crag. But there were obvious strategic advantages in controlling an area so close to the fertile Ghaab. And strategy, rather than military strength, was ever the forte of the Assassins. It wasn't the force of Nizari arms that compelled Saladin to withdraw from the siege of Masyaf after just one week. It was probably diplomacy; but the myth that was by now attaching itself to the secretive sect was more colourful. Saladin, the story went, had awoken in his tent to find a poisoned dagger lying on his pillow and a Nizari token by his bed. Unnerved by this eloquent message, he had instantly sought forgiveness and reconciliation with Rashid ad-Din, and lifted the siege.

There was some fire behind this smoke. Saladin had already survived two assassination attempts, attributed to the Nizaris. The Franks weren't so lucky.

They first felt the Assassins' knife in 1152 when Raymond II, Count of Tripoli, was struck down by a Nizari band inside the gates of his own city. Some twenty years after this, with the Sunni threat ever growing, the Nizaris began to consider the benefits of reconciliation and alliance with the Crusaders. The balance of power was fragile, and the Franks were open to offers. It is fascinating to speculate what might have followed if the Nizari embassy to Jerusalem, well received by King Amalric, had not been ambushed and wiped out on its way home by the vengeful Templars, still mindful of Raymond's murder.

It was a further twenty years before the Nizaris struck back. By the murder in 1192 of Conrad of Montferrat, one of two claimants for the disputed (and by now purely theoretical) kingship of Jerusalem, they deeply rocked the Kingdom of Outremer - and threw mud which stuck to one of the most romantic figures of the Crusades. For the survivor of the two assailants, before the mob lynched him, swore that it was Richard, King of England, who had instigated the assassination.

Richard, said the whispers, had intrigued covertly with Rashid ad-Din. The story was widely believed; for the Franks and Nizaris had by now reached a degree of compromise, and Richard was known to support Conrad's rival as candidate for the throne of Jerusalem. Perhaps it wasn't, after all, quite beyond imagining that Richard the Lionheart had at least been invited to dinner at Qadmus.

*

Immediately east of the castle the ground was quite open, in stark contrast to the teeming streets that pressed up against its walls on the other three sides. Here the city walls were quite untouched, running from the vestiges of a gateway across what is still the main road east, across an open meadow and far beyond my sight.

Above them the castle reared in stark silhouette against the enveloping mountain. How on earth had the Nizaris ever managed to capture such a stronghold? Had they unusually excelled themselves in the arts of open warfare? Or, more likely, had they dispatched *fida'is*, agents who would live like "sleepers" among the people of town and fortress, biding their time perhaps for years until some brief window of opportunity opened? Under the white splash of a mausoleum high on the hillside lay buried the answer to that and many other questions. Rashid ad-Din must have carried more secrets to his grave than most mortals.

Back through the old gateway and left turn: from the first step the road was uphill. Poor Madfaa tackled it bravely, raising a war-dance when we passed another stallion tethered by the roadside. Out of town the surroundings alternated between woods and cornfields. I took the opportunity to rest him wherever the wheat had been cut, taking the bit from his mouth, loosening the girth and letting him browse on the stubble. He got stuck in with enthusiasm; and I soon realised from the scrunching that came from his small, hard teeth that he was picking up not just fallen corn grains, but entire heads that the reapers had let drop.

I joined in, picking up as many heads as I could find and stuffing them in the saddlebags for later. It had never occurred to me before this journey, I thought as I gleaned busily, that this was what "gleaning" really meant; that Ruth, when she stood in tears amid the alien corn, had not after all been searching for individual grains. That had always struck me as a peculiarly hard way to make a living, enough to make anyone weep.

A long uphill pull brought us to Resafa, where I begged water and bought barley and tibn at the first house. Just beyond the village I called a halt to feed Madfaa. We were joined almost at once by four inquisitive girls, who asked all the usual questions. Then,

"Where are you going to stay the night?"

I very much wanted to know the answer to that myself. It was now late afternoon, I had had no offers in Resafa, and our slow uphill speed wasn't going to get us to the next settlement on the map. I answered gloomily that I would make camp in the open.

"Aren't you afraid of the *wahash*?"

Up here, it seemed an entirely reasonable question. I had been trying not to ask it myself for some hours.

"What sort of wahash?"

They conferred, then answered something that sounded like "tiger". This time, though, no-one was winding me up. I gave them the dictionary and asked them to find the word they meant.

After much discussion they pointed to *dibaa'*: hyenas. It was a bit of a jolt, as by now I'd decided that Syria's biggest predator was the jackal, far less frightening than little boys - or big ones in fast cars. I stared apprehensively up the desolate road ahead. We had better push on - fast.

In fact we were slower than ever, for the kindly girls rustled up a couple of kilos more barley. Poor Madfaa sighed as I plonked it in the saddlebags, and sweated as he plodded wearily upwards.

When at last the road levelled out, it was through a hostile landscape: an empty upland where blocks and pillars and needles of limestone pierced a dense, low scrub. Urgently I searched for a spot to spend the night. But for the road itself, there was no open space whatsoever. If I did find one, should I stop or keep moving? Would the presence of a human keep hyenas from attacking a horse? Should I build a fire? Though, judging by the many hummocky bits of fresh-dug earth I could see through all that spiky undergrowth, if we got attacked by anything up here it was most likely to be moles. I had a sudden farcical vision of myself waving a firebrand like a caveman, defending us both from a pack of ravening moles.

The sun dropped the last few degrees to fall behind the mountains with alarming speed. One or two lights began to prick out in a tiny gathering of houses on a hilltop ahead. When I reached it I found the first road junction for many miles and, in this most unlikely of places, a shop.

Five minutes more, and I would have been too late. The shopkeeper, a lady of about my own age, was just locking up. She turned round in amazement to find herself confronted by a dishevelled traveller with a tired, sweaty horse.

"Come and stay with me!" she cried, before I could even open my mouth. That's my house just over there. I've got a stable where you can put your horse."

The hyenas - and the moles - were going to have to do without supper.

*

The keeper of this lonely shop was Najaaf, known to her friends as Umm Wa'il, "mother of Wa'il". It's a common rule that adults are nicknamed as the parents of their eldest son; Fayiz, for instance, always referred to Basil as "Abu Faris".

Umm Wa'il led us, both drooping with exhaustion, to her house across the road. Outside was the sort of stone-walled yard you might find in Cumberland or the Yorkshire Dales. I hitched Madfaa alongside a contentedly chewing cow and fed him: tibn with just a little barley for now, as he was tired. There would be plenty of time later for a bigger grain feed.

Then it was my turn. In the bath-house I stripped off every stitch of my rancid clothing and sluiced myself down with bucket after bucket of water. Supper, instead of the usual mezzeh, was a miracle of cuisine: an enormous tray of chips with tomato ketchup. Although I'd been eating most of the day - Masyaf's shops had been full of biscuits, chocolate, Coke and generally un-ethnic food, which I'd greedily shovelled into my saddlebags - I had no trouble keeping the flag flying in the very British sport of chip-guzzling.

Now it was time to broach, hesitantly, the subject of letting Madfaa loose. If necessary I would leave him tethered and sleep in the yard with him, but it was cold on this mountain-top.

I needn't have worried. "Of course," answered Umm Wa'il readily. Her good humour didn't even wobble when Madfaa, who was becoming very lonely and evidently considered the cow as a sort of proxy horse, lunged at it with lustful intent the minute he was free. I clapped the headcollar over his aspirations and bundled him back to his tether ring; then resignedly looked round the yard eyeing up the best bivvy spot, defined by shelter versus cowpats.

Najaaf, though, wasn't defeated. She and her eldest daughter Sawsen began rearranging the animals in the byre, and I realised that they were making a space for the cow so that Madfaa could have the entire yard to himself. Soon the cow was inside, and Madfaa was loose again and exploring every corner of his new billet.

I followed Umm Wa'il into the barn to thank her. She took one look in my direction, then squeaked with fear and jumped into the manger. It wasn't personal. I heard a step behind me and looked round to see that Madfaa, associating indoors with food, warmth and more food, had come in to case the joint. I grabbed him and bundled him straight out, and he used my big toe as a starting block to launch himself down the twelve-inch step. I wouldn't be going anywhere on that foot in a hurry, so when Sawsen and Umm Wa'il pressed me to stay the next day, I gratefully accepted.

Umm Wa'il was mother to fourteen children. It was the biggest family I ever came across, in a country of big families. In the country areas, that is; among Nabil's city friends it was rare to find more than two or three children, as in western Europe.

Living in two houses on their isolated little hilltop, the family were almost self-sufficient. They grew their own fruit and vegetables and produced half the wheat they needed. Water was abundant, despite the elevation, lying less than fifteen feet below the surface. It never ceased to amaze me how and where water gushed out of brimming reservoirs below these harsh but fertile mountains.

Umm Wa'il spent the day sorting over a huge pile of wheat, sieving every grain to get rid of the dust, checking through for stones, and diligently removing stray oats and barley that might spoil her bread-making. Finally satisfied, she bagged it. "Ten sacks full," she said. "We need twenty to get the family through the winter."

She broke off only to get the lunch: another great tray of chips. I helped as much as she would allow; otherwise I spent the day washing my filthy clothing, then playing first with a very tolerant cat, and afterwards with the latest baby. It was a good-humoured cherub with an elastic mouth and a repertoire of expressions which would have made Les Dawson envious.

*

Now, in the south of the Jebel, the topography was more frag-mented. Further north great, sweeping ridges rose in waves, above a framework that was essentially predictable, although the local views might change rapidly. In these parts, though, every valley differed from the last in some essential attribute, and the dividing hills contrasted fiercely with their neighbours: here, a smooth grassy hilltop, there a pointed cone transplanted from an alien landscape, somewhere else an unnaturally round dome with a fringe of cypress trees and a bare crown, like a tonsured monk.

The road led us south along the summit of the Mountain. To the right, ridge after ridge fell away into a blue haze, somewhere under which lurked the Mediterranean. To the left, the land dropped sharply, with nothing much below us but, I guessed, the upper reaches of the Orontes valley. The wind was vicious; mother and father of that in the Ghaab, but squeezed tight into an icy blast as it streamed across the rocky knife-edge.

A descent among tumbling limestone outcrops brought us down to a small village clinging to the side of the valley. Narrow alleys led off the road; cobbled lanes or flights of steps on a precipitous hillside. A whitewashed mausoleum looked down from a hilltop. A sign by the road told me that I was in *'Ain adh-Dhahab*. The overflowing waters of the mountain inspired even the place-names. Earlier I had passed *'Ain al-Bayda*, the White Spring. Now I was at the Golden Spring - I think. For the notice was damaged at the vital spot above one consonant, so that the dot which would have turned "d" into "dh" was missing.

The next villages were *'Ain al-Baarida*, the cold spring, and *'Ain al-Hayaat*, the spring of life. You can't argue with that one, I thought.

For water meant growth, and growth meant life. And everywhere I went that day growth, measured in wheat and barley, was being converted into life, measured in grain and tibn, by threshers and choppers. This was way above subsistence farming. It was no coincidence that every mile of road I'd passed since leaving Banias was newly asphalted, making poor Madfaa slip and slither even on his cal-kins; that a whole fleet of brand new minibuses served the remotest hamlets, even Najaaf's little settlement of two houses and their unlikely shop. Rural Syria was more affluent than I had seen it in the past. I hoped fervently that the new affluence would remain equal to the strain of family sizes in double figures.

Somewhere very near here Lawrence, too, had observed an exceptionally good harvest.

"…bed for the night in a threshing floor, on a pile of tibn, chopped straw, listening to the Arabs beating out their Dhurra in the moonlight: they kept it up all night in relays, till about 2 a.m. when they woke me up, & said they were all exhausted, would I keep watch because there were thieves, & I was an Inglezi and had a pistol… they told me in Tartous next day that there really were not thieves, but *landlords* about! Isn't that charming? These dear people wanted to hide the extent of their harvest."

I'd set off late, for Husn as-Suleiman was only a short hop away. As evening came on, it brought an unprecedented quality of light. It searched out every terrace, every hilltop, every white-painted mausoleum. I came over the last hill, and there was my goal, spread out before me: the great temple of Baal, every stone glowing pink in the afterlight. Only the sacred grove on the hilltop behind, the less sophisticated temple to another religion, still held on to a few rays of the sun.

*

Reverently I led Madfaa under the temenos gateway, and into the middle of a football match. Football, in the form of the World Cup, seemed to have pursued me all round Syria. That, and little boys. It was just my luck to catch a dose of both at once.

Bad light stopped play as I tied Madfaa up under a walnut tree on the far side of the temple compound. The *shebaab* abandoned the game and gathered round.

"I need barley, or alaf..." I waved a note "...and tibn. I'll pay the first person to bring them."

They scattered at a run. Perhaps it wasn't such a good idea to make a race of it; but it gave me breathing space to unsaddle Madfaa and wash him down while he picked at the grass under the tree. It would surely take them a quarter of an hour to find their parents and persuade them to sell me the feed.

I soon realised how naïve I'd been. The winner was back in five minutes with the tibn, though no-one came up with any barley. The lad had just raided the store without asking, and would keep the money for himself. As for the precious grain, that was evidently under lock and key, and the little bandits couldn't get at it. At least, I thought as I uncomfortably fed the plunder to Madfaa, I had plenty of witnesses that I'd paid for it.

The returning boys brought their friends with them, and the crowd was thickening fast. I was wondering what to do next, when a friendly couple came and rescued me.

Hiyaam and Nafiif were the hereditary guardians of the temple. They took me to the house in one corner of the temenos where their family had lived for generations. They pointed up to where white cubes lay under the sacred grove. Even in death, their forefathers continued to watch over the sanctuary.

The stones of the temple compound formed the back wall of their house. "Some are twelve metres long," said Hiyaam with pride. How did the ancient people who built this place move such blocks, bigger than those at Stonehenge? Trailing vines softened their edges, and flowers grew at their feet, filling the little courtyard with their scent.

They took me up to the roof of the house and gave me *zufa'*, green tea made from hyssop. (Good for the red blood corpuscles, said Nafiif.) From here I could look across to where Madfaa now, at their suggestion, stood tethered to the thick trunk of a vine that rambled all over the south wall of the courtyard. We lazed on the roof talking, while the last of the day faded, the huge bulk of the temple sanctuary slowly dissolved into a shapeless hummock, and lights began to burn in the village.

As the stars came out we discussed their relative names in Arabic and English. "That is *tabbaan*," said Nafiif, pointing to the Plough. Of course; t-b-n: the same root as in tibn. All words constructed around that three-letter base would have related meanings. No matter that my dictionary told me that *tabbaan* was a straw-seller. That was a rotten name for a constellation. Darb at-Tabbaana, I learned, was the Milky Way.

When it was quite dark a chorus of howls arose from all directions. It was the same as I had heard at Saône. "What's that sound?"

"Jackals." So it hadn't been the local shebaab having me on.

"They told me near Masyaf that there were hyenas in these mountains."

"Not here," was the answer. "Only over on the other side, where there are a lot of trees. They live in the pine forests."

Someone brought out a huge tray of food, with slices of fresh watermelon for dessert, and we ate and chatted alternately while various members of the family came and went. When it was nearly time for the football to start - another World Cup match - Nafiif took me to a little reed-thatched hut in the corner of the rooftop. It was a perfect vantage point; from here I could check up on Madfaa without doing more than roll over in my sleeping bag.

Glow-worms bumbled in and out of my field of view, and birds began to sing in the surrounding hills. "Hoot" might be a better word, except for the bell-like clarity of the sound: a single note, at a pitch unvarying from one bird but differing from all the others, and at random timing. Each bird was doing exactly its own thing, without reference to any of its kind. I might have been listening to a quirky piece of avant-garde music, in an unusual theatre.

Just before I slept a late moon slipped above the top of the hill, so that the temple's hulk stepped out of the darkness and reassembled itself, and Madfaa ceased to be a dark crunching blob and took on equine form again. It was all very satisfactory, I thought as I slid into peaceful sleep.

*

It is some two thousand years since the massive blocks of stone were assembled at Husn as-Suleiman, to be felled at leisure by centuries of earthquake, and by such few pilferers brave enough to dare the sanctity of the place and Herculean enough to enact the thought. The style is Graeco-Roman, but the concept and layout belong to an earlier age: that of the Phoenicians, who dedicated the site to Baal.

To the spring below the sacred grove they attached their own blueprint: a sanctuary approached from the spring by way of an altar at the foot of a flight of steps, and surrounded by the large temenos, or courtyard. This was Amrit, reproduced on monumental scale. By the time the Hellene masons had added their work, setting their signature by engraving the morning and evening stars Phosphoros and Hesperos over the pylon gates and writing a Greek inscription over the east wall, the Phoenicians had been absorbed by successive waves of settlers, while Baal had been assimilated to Zeus. It is tempting to suppose that the latter was just the last in a long line of usurpers. These hills and valleys, with their groves, abundance of springs and rich soil, must have been a fertile ground for the gods to go forth and multiply. If the world's great monotheistic religions were conceived in desert places, local deities tend to prefer spots where the living is good.

So it seemed only right that today agriculture encroached hard on Husn as-Suleiman. Terracing pressed hard up against the east wall, rising to half its height; the lighter colouring at the base of the stones showed how recently they had been dug out of the cornfield. Some hundred yards to the north, the colossal blocks of what had probably once been an outer compound supported a terrace twenty feet high. Circling on round, I came to a little subsidiary temple to one side, its main courtyard now an orchard. One of its carved columns had fallen; in its place stood a walnut tree. It lent an air of shambolic irreverence, as if Pan had turned up uninvited and elbowed Zeus out of the way.

Here the shebaab found me, and I reckoned it was time to get back to Madfaa. He was scrumping grapes from his vine, chewing them thoughtfully then spitting them out with disgust. A family of red squirrels raced up and down the branches above his head cursing vigorously at him, each other and anyone else who came into sight. The sun was now full on him, so I moved him back to the shade of last night's walnut tree, tying him to one of the ruinous fallen stones of the sanctuary. While he ate grass I brushed him off leisurely, removing the marks of last night's sponge until his bay coat gleamed once more like a new conker.

The flies were biting that day, and he kicked and twitched constantly to rid himself of their irritation. I knew very well that whenever he did so he would habitually flick a hind leg out sideways; but the lads, with their constant questions, distracted my attention for a crucial moment. I reached carelessly under his tummy to complete the all-over job, just as he aimed at a horsefly.

When I staggered to my feet my sunglasses were broken, so from then on I had to wear them perched lop-sidedly and fixed with a hairgrip; and I had the makings of a splendid black eye. For the next week it shone brilliantly in fluorescent purple, the perfect accessory to my luminous toenail. It said much for the innate courtesy of the Syrian people that not one ever asked me who I had offended.

*

For the next couple of days I struck roughly southward, occasionally asking the way but mostly hoping for the best.

Not far down the road at Dreikish was another spring sacred to a benevolent local deity. Here was a thoroughly modern temple, in the form of a water bottling plant, and the god it served was Profit. To judge from the plastic bottles I'd seen scattered by the roadside throughout the Mountain, he took good care of his acolytes.

There must be a steady flow of pilgrims, for suddenly all roads seemed to lead to Dreikish. I knew only that I didn't want to go there. So at every junction I perversely took the other option. It was the only clue I had. Route-finding among these valleys was a nightmare, the twisting roads defying accurate mapping, so that I had to plod on blindly and ask "Safita?" on the rare occasions I passed someone.

Burj Safita, Safita Tower, is the intact keep of a Templar stronghold to which a sizeable town has attached itself. At the top of a high hill, it is visible for miles around. Early on the second day it materialised on the skyline, and helpfully remained there. Very soon there was no more need to ask for directions.

The way ran a little below the main ridge of the Jebel al-Alawiyiin, the north-south spine from which all the lesser ribs and valleys ran westwards down to the sea. It meant that we must ride a switchback, where poor Madfaa panted and puffed up sharp gradients then minced anxiously on the slippery surface of the downhill, until I dismounted and walked.

Over another ridge; and surely the valley to the south was marginally lower and less dramatic? Away to the south-west, there was a definite sense of the Mountain losing its grip and beginning to fall away. Easier territory ahead, I hoped. Straight ahead, far to the south, something insubstantial seemed to hover above the low cloud. Could it possibly be my first sight of the Lebanon ranges, or was it just mist?

This was the real beginning of Crusader territory. Marqab had been a foretaste, that of an outpost guarding the narrow coast road which linked the Kingdom of Jerusalem with the northern Principality of Antioch and the Christian lands of Byzantium beyond. Now I was coming closer to the heart of Outremer. Tripoli, centre of a Crusader Dukedom, was just down the coast, and a high density of castles in the southern slopes of the Mountain protected its hinterland - as well as the Homs Gap. And the Homs Gap, the fissure between the Jebel al-Alawiyiin and the mighty Mount Lebanon, was the only practicable route through to the interior of Syria.

I stopped to buy barley from an obliging shopkeeper. As I tipped it into the saddlebag Madfaa repaid me by treading on my foot, for the second time in three days. That put an end to any walking, and it was from the saddle that I saw Safita slowly rising up before me.

*

The town was wealthy, to judge from the order and cleanliness of its houses and the multiplicity of jewellers among its shops. The castle soon became hidden behind the dense buildings, but reaching it was a simple matter of heading uphill.

As Madfaa and I left the modern suburbs and penetrated into the the Old Quarter, tarmac gave way to paving and cobbles, modern buildings to graceful, rather decayed old houses in French Colonial style. Near the top the blocks of the castle itself appeared in the foundations of today's houses; here, as at Qala'at al-Madiq and Qadmus, the new had continuously absorbed the old. A narrow alley led us off the main street and into a surprisingly large courtyard. The tower beyond it was intact to the very last stone of its roof.

It was busy today, with scurrying people criss-crossing the yard, panting up the flight of steps and disappearing into the small side door at the foot of the tower. Not tourists, but people with a purpose. People carrying, among other things, sheaves of flowers.

"There's going to be a wedding," someone told me. I looked after him through the door, and understood. This was Safita's secret, the pearl in its oyster. The grim old Templar castle was now a church.

As I tied Madfaa to some railings and untacked him, he was already collecting his usual crowd. Children clustered round him, nervously reaching out to touch him at the full extent of their fingertips, as if he could confer a blessing. A man from a nearby restaurant brought him some left-over bread, and I tore it up and added a good measure of barley to make a proper feed for him. One of the children tweaked a flower from the bundle of gladioli on the florist's truck, and offered it hopefully for him to eat.

The cool darkness of the tower was restful to my eyes after the pitiless mid-day sun on the stones of the square. The three crystal chandeliers above the nave were dim, and little light penetrated the deep slits in the external walls, but the glow from a few naked bulbs allowed me to see plain wooden pews and a row of icons on the east wall. Only the heavily barred and bolted door in the near corner suggested that there was more to this building than was apparent from the ground floor of its interior. I was lucky that the place was busy today, or I wouldn't have got any further.

Someone produced a key and removed the heavy padlock. Behind the door, a flight of stone steps led up into darkness. At their top was a low hall, vaulted in stone and lit only by arrow slits. I groped my way to a further flight of steps, and presently emerged, gasping, on to the roof. Looking over the battlements I could see Madfaa, a tiny figure far below surrounded by children and still eating peaceably. There was no hurry. I could take my time, and enjoy the best views to be had in all Syria.

To north and west the ridges and valleys of the southern Jebel al-Alawiyiin lay spread out below me as if I were flying over them, their valleys creased with terracing or dotted with villages, their summits crowned by sacred groves. In the distance I could just make out the shape of Krak des Chevaliers, the most famous castle of them all, crouched on a mountain-top. Turning, I could see the blue haze of the

Mediterranean. And yes, that had been Mount Lebanon to the south. From here I could see that the haze possessed not only substance but, definitely, snow.

"Do you know the Hill of the Blessed Virgin Mary?" The man had come up the stairs behind me, and I'd assumed he was a tourist. "That's somewhere you should visit."

I'd noticed it from a distant hilltop yesterday; a truncated cone so regular that it looked unnatural. I would have thought it an old city mound, except that it was too big.

"Every year there is a great festival there on August 14th, after a two-week fast. All the Christians from these parts come to it."

David Boulos was a Christian from Safita, now living and working in Kuwait and back on a family visit. This valley, the area within the range of view of the tower - he swept his arm expansively over the four points of the compass - he called the Valley of the Nasara; that is, the Christians.

"This valley was the first place to be settled by Christians driven from Jerusalem by the persecution of the Jews. So it was from here that many of the early Christians spread out. For instance, the Maronites originated from here, although they have now all gone to Lebanon." History ascribes the origin of the Maronites, a seventh-century sect loosely allied with Rome, to the monastery of St. Maron on the Orontes between Homs and Hama; but perhaps that wasn't so very far away.

" ...but we still have here Syrian Orthodox, Greek Orthodox and Roman Catholic Christians."

"And do you get along OK with the Alawis?" For there was also a sizeable Alawi population in Safita.

"Oh, the Alawis live mostly along the coastal side of the Mountain."

This didn't fit what I'd seen over the last few weeks. Inevitably, I returned to the subject which still hovered near the top of my mind, refusing to go away. "What about the sacred groves? Who do all those belong to?" I pointed to five or six hilltop clumps within a five-mile radius.

He didn't seem to know, or care much. "They must be ours," he said carelessly. "We've been here longest."

"And the mosques, the Muslim mausolea among them?"

"Well, this place is very important politically and militarily. If you're going to send Muslim soldiers here, you have to make places for them to worship."

This was superficial chit-chat, not hard information. I was surprised at the parochial view of this educated man, who had lived and worked in other societies besides his own.

Yet I had to admit that, had he quizzed me as closely on my own neighbours as I had him on his, I would probably have scored nothing at all.

*

I stocked up at a friendly greengrocer's before leaving Safita. A couple of kilos of carrots for Madfaa, bread and cheese and a melon for myself, and a can or two of Coke. The café next door spilled a few tables on to the street, and from the trays they bore I noticed with an internal groan that I was back in mâté territory. I would have to polish up a few excuses to have ready.

Beyond the town the countryside was one continuous olive grove, and it wasn't hard to find a spot for a very comfortable lunch. You haven't tasted melon until you've eaten one within half a mile of where it grew, ripened on the vine rather than in the plane or the supermarket shelf. The drawback - or the perfect excuse for gluttony - is that it's so juicy that once cut it must all be eaten immediately, or else left behind for fear of soggy saddlebags; and my mother taught me never to waste good food. Madfaa, knocking back half the carrots with a double handful of barley, approved of Safita's greengrocers as much as I did.

Both too full to move, we lingered until the late afternoon. Presently a group of gypsies found us, arriving from a camp across the road of several tents, Bedouin-style but made of rough sacking. A young mother engaged me in earnest conversation while the children gathered around my bags, looking just a bit too innocent for comfort. I packed up hastily, saddled Madfaa and left, surreptitiously counting my spoons.

I was making my way vaguely in the direction of Krak des Chevaliers; but without too much urgency, for it was a day or two's journey away. Quite prepared to be distracted, and meaning anyway to get off the main road for the night, I was willingly seduced by the distant glimpse of a fort which didn't appear on any of my maps. It was no more than a jumble of stones on the end of a low outcrop; wreathed in trees, topped with bushes and coloured sepia by the late sun, it looked like a nineteenth-century print.

Turning off the road without a second thought, I soon found myself among the first houses of a village. I couldn't see the castle any longer. But I knew that I hadn't imagined it, for large, well-cut blocks formed the lower walls of the houses, the now-familiar sign of recycled masonry.

I asked about lodging, and a handful of swaggering young men gathered around Madfaa as I led him up the road. Although I was a yard or two ahead of him, I suddenly felt a jolt run through him, and he stopped dead. One of the young toughs had taken a run and literally leapt into the saddle, banging his considerable weight down with a hefty thump.

Madfaa had gone a long way that day, and was weary. He was carrying the rest of the carrots and a huge bag of tibn as well as my own baggage. It was common enough among the young men I'd met on the way to see him as a sort of executive toy, and try to treat him accordingly; but this was way out of order. The little horse stood quivering, thoroughly upset but too well-mannered to react violently. I wasn't so tolerant. Through a sort of red haze, I grabbed the man's leg and tipped him backwards out of the saddle.

The others began to remonstrate. I swore at them, pointing at the heavy bags and pulling Madfaa behind me in a gesture that was purely symbolic. It was a good thing Nadia arrived when she did, or there might have been an Anglo-Syrian Diplomatic Incident.

*

You didn't argue with Nadia. Nobody argued with Nadia. Not that she was bad-tempered, or nagged, or nurtured any potential harpy characteristics; far from it, she was cheerful, good natured and end-lessly kind. She achieved her end through sheer energy, utter determination and the overwhelming force of her personality. One glance at her jawline, and the most intransigent male chauvinist pig would have put on a pinny and cleaned the loo.

Nadia was as attractive as she was charismatic. I tried to picture her in the setting of my own world, and cast her as a politician, perhaps; or a sporting star. Come to think of it, she was a dead ringer for the tennis champion Aranxa Sanchez Vicario. I could just see her putting the winning shot away with a merciless smash; or summarily demolishing hecklers on the back benches with the same blend of ease and ruthlessness which now had the young men slinking away.

As she bore Madfaa and me back to her house, the crowd that gathered was a protective escort, mostly women and children. They followed us to her gate, where the younger ones hovered. Mistaking the cause of my clenched teeth - for I was still gibbering faintly from the Incident - she apologised and tried to shoo them away; but I begged her not to, for they were a benevolent swarm. Once I'd divested Madfaa of his baggage I took him back outside for them to pat and stroke.

Meanwhile Nadia prepared a big bowl of alaf for him, with a bundle of maize stalks for afters. Her garden was large and secure, and she stared at me with disbelief when I tentatively broached the subject of sleeping outside with him. Clearly unnerved by such caprice, she decided that I was a guest who needed protecting from myself. Grabbing my arm, she frog-marched me into the guestroom and plonked me down on the sofa for tea and introductions. I'd been wearing the same clothes for days and was only fit for the cowshed; but had to obey, sitting gingerly on the edge of the seat and hoping I wouldn't leave an indelible stain.

At last Nadia took me in a friendly half-Nelson and led me to the bathroom, where I scrubbed the grime out of every pore. As I powdered myself liberally with the talc I'd bought in Lattakia I wrinkled my nose as usual, for it stank of disinfectant like a Victorian lavatory. I'd ignorantly supposed that the ladies of the Mediterranean coast needed something with a bit more wellie than lavender to soak up the effects of the climate, and therefore I probably needed it too. It was weeks before I idly took out my dictionary to read the small print on the bottle, and found that I'd been dusting my intimate regions with a fungicidal powder for treating athlete's foot. Such a muscular approach to hygiene, I imagine, would have entirely pleased Nadia.

I was repeating the soap and water treatment on my clothes when her daughters, set to guard the door in case I escaped to join Madfaa, took over. They had the same physical approach to domesticity as their mother. I tried to insist that I should do my own dirty work, but was hauled off forcibly, and led away to a very welcome supper.

Afterwards a stream of visitors came round. "Five lira a head!" laughed one of the girls. Two of them spoke English: a charming young man from next door and the local doctor. Between them they answered many of my remaining questions about the Alawis, and sorted out the confusion over the Nizaris (Isma'ilis), Nusayris (Alawis) and Nasara (Christians), which had been tying my brain in knots ever since Qadmus.

I didn't dare to argue with Nadia when she put me to bed indoors. But she gave me a room opening directly on to the veranda, so that I could check up on Madfaa whenever I wanted to. She remained anxious about my waywardness, however, for whenever I put my head out of the window, hers popped up the other side; and when I went out at two in the morning to look at his tether, she materialised instantly, like a djinn, escorting me every step of the way down the garden and seeing me safely back into bed.

*

"It's very, very old," said Fardit, Nadia's young neighbour. "There was a Jewish stronghold here first. That's how the village grew up."

He led me along a well-trodden path through an olive grove, among farmhouses in which the density of black and white stones was steadily increasing. "There is our own sacred grove." The trees looked haphazard and quite ordinary, only the scattering of tombstones denoting their status. The sacred places, I was finally beginning to understand, didn't have to be exclusively on hilltops. Clumps of trees seemed to possess a spiritual presence wherever they stood, and thus to be naturally associated with burial places.

Presently we reached what was left of the castle of Umm Khosh. Only the keep still stood, and little remained of three of its walls. The fourth rose to about forty feet, and bore traces of machicolation. I walked round to the far side, and found the signature which told me who had occupied and fortified, possibly even built, this castle: the splay-edged cross of the Knights Hospitaller, the emblem which acquired the name of the Maltese Cross from their later history. Almost as fresh and clear as the day it was first carved into the black basalt, it had defied the aspirations of stone-hungry builders for hundreds of years.

You could still see the arch of storerooms below, and one corner of the once-elegant vaulting which had supported the Great Hall. From the original stables and granaries surrounding the keep, animal pens and shelters had been built and rebuilt in continuous occupation and re-occupation. Fardit took me to the nearby farm, where utility had saved the biggest group of subsidiary buildings from the depredation which had reduced the keep. Here the stone vaulting of the storerooms was intact, and housed - as in the time of the Knights - a large flock of sheep and a dozen Friesian cows.

We crossed the farmyard on our way home to Nadia's house, and exchanged greetings with a group of men sitting in the shade of a tree and drinking mâté. The tea packet was lying open on the table. Something attracted my attention, and I picked it up for a closer look.

This particular brand came not from the Argentine but from Malta. It bore a Maltese Cross. What a strange journey that symbol had made, following the fortunes of the Knights from Umm Khosh to Cyprus, Rhodes and Malta; before making its way back, seven centuries later and via South America, to just a hundred yards from its prototype... on a packet of tea.

*

From an early hour faces popped up at the window, whispering sounded from the veranda, young heads peered hopefully round the door then, disappointed, retreated not-quite-soundlessly. I feigned sleep for as long as I decently could, but the moment my foot touched the floor the bedroom was full of people. The *levée* chez Nadia was a social ritual.

But it was a friendly and unpressurised ritual. By now I was getting rather more used to living my life in the public spotlight, to stripping, washing and dressing among hordes of people. And it no longer distracted me from my packing, or saddling up, or whatever it was I was trying to do. When I was finally ready to say my goodbyes, some twenty or thirty of Nadia's friends and neighbours gathered to see Madfaa and me on our way.

The country lanes around Umm Khosh felt comfortably familiar, the nearest thing to English countryside that I'd seen so far. I followed a cart track like a Yorkshire pack-horse trail, except for the dark volcanic rock from which it was cut; though the limestone was still here, too, and even the rough-built stone walls were patterned in black and white. I could put my map away and navigate by sight, for I could see my next destination. There it was on a distant hilltop: the fortress of Krak des Chevaliers staring back at me, watching every movement, as it had once kept its unsleeping eye on all nearby movements, friendly or hostile.

I turned Madfaa off the road on to a watermeadow where we might spend the afternoon. He took a couple of steps and baulked. Rather irritably I dragged my attention away from the view to take notice of what was going on around me. I was just in time to see a wicked-looking black snake, some four feet long, writhing across the track from literally under Madfaa's feet and into the nearby bushes.

We forded a stream and arrived at a patch of good grazing. Before I settled to rest myself I made a minute inspection of Madfaa's feet, looking for puncture marks. But, streetwise little horse that he was, he had frozen quickly enough to avoid frightening the snake into striking. The incident was a salutary reminder of the potential dangers here. "Watch the rocks for scorpions," I now remembered someone saying a few days ago; but I'd forgotten the warning until now. I was getting very careless. It was time to take myself in hand.

No sooner had I settled down to rest than a couple of bulldozers materialised from nowhere and started to excavate the ford we had just crossed. I stayed poised for flight, for any minute they would surely come over on to our side; but they vanished as suddenly as they had come, and peace descended once more. Now an elderly man appeared, sat down beside me and engaged me in conversation. I was desperate, for I was exhausted and badly wanted to rest, rather than struggling to make polite small-talk in a language I couldn't properly manage. In fact it was my incomprehension that was the problem; for it took me some time to understand that he was there not for chit-chat but as a courtesy. He was afraid that children might thieve from my baggage, and was there to keep watch while I slept. It was my second lesson in the space of one hour. How easy it was for westerners to misunderstand the degree of hospitality in this country, the sense of responsibility for any guest, especially a foreign guest; and how near I had come to being ungrateful to this kindly old man.

In the cool of late afternoon we resumed our slow progress towards Krak, and almost immediately stumbled over yet another castle. This, the road sign told me, was *Burj Arabi*, simply the Arab Tower. It was only half a mile off the road, so I turned off for a closer look.

The village - these castles never existed in isolation, unless like Marqab they were grand enough to contain their own village inside the outer walls - was built around a rough oval track. Did this plan, I wondered, mark out the original circuit of the walls? Once again, the houses were built with large, well-cut stone rather than concrete block, and you didn't have to look far to see why. The square tower I'd seen from the road was all that was left of the original fort.

That much, at least, was complete. The lowest of its three stories was used as a cowshed, but the other two were occupied. The owner beckoned me up, and I climbed a staircase of alternating steps - two basalt, one limestone - to the middle level. Astonishing to think that, in such a plain, utilitarian building, there was time to think about decoration, even of what lay under your feet.

These were the family quarters. An internal staircase led to what had been the Great Hall, and another to the roof, which was uneven and grassed over. The view was, of course, tremendous; but although Safita and Umm Khosh were clearly visible, for the first time that day I couldn't see Krak. Fardit had told me how all these castles could communicate by chains of bonfires within literally minutes of an emergency arising. But if, as its name suggested, Burj Arabi belonged to the Opposition, perhaps communication with Krak wasn't a high priority.

It reappeared as we rejoined the main lane. For the next four miles frenetic activity surrounded the building of a new road, until I thought we would have an easy time of the last bit of the journey. Not so. The velvet strip of new tarmac led us into a quarry and deposited us there with nowhere to go. Bulldozers roared and shovelled all around us.

"Krak?" I hopefully asked one of the drivers.

"Straight on!" He motioned to a bank of rubble. I climbed it obediently. On the other side the road had vanished. In its place a goat track rambled away up the hill among olive groves.

I looked back with disbelief. He waved me on irritably, his words drowned in the colossal voice of the machine. I took a deep breath and set Madfaa at the hillside.

It was a very pleasant ascent; except, I grumbled to myself, I wouldn't much like to do it all in reverse if it led nowhere. Krak, visible from so far away, had perversely disappeared. At least we were heading east, and up, both of which were right.

The path now disappeared completely, and I led Madfaa rather fearfully across terraces treacherous with sharp rock. I was about to give up hope when I spotted a good track winding away up the opposite side of the hill, with the obvious intent of getting to the top.

It got stronger as it went, acquiring first a good, solid footing and then a pair of stone walls. Before the olives closed in again I took a look back, to where the Lebanese mountains were just beginning to step out into the clearing light of evening. Suddenly the loneliness of the mountainside ceased to be hostile, and began to be beautiful, and rather romantic. Elation gripped me; we were winning. And I had come by a route that no other tourist had seen - unless Lawrence had come this way whilst footslogging through the mountains from one castle to the next.

Now a few people began to appear on stage; mostly small boys riding donkeys. We passed a little village and set off up the shoulder of the mountain on the last haul to the top, skirting the head of the valley. Looking back, I could see the quarry marked by puffs of dust and smoke; work was continuing late into the evening. Beyond, a dull meandering stripe marked the road from Umm Khosh. On an eggshell-blue skyline stood the cube of Safita Tower. I even convinced myself I could see the distant sea. Ahead, where a road hugged the top of the ridge, a plain white building topped by a cross beckoned us on.

At last, exhausted and winded, we struggled up the last few yards of the track and gained the road. Women came out from a little knot of houses and gave us a drink. Madfaa gratefully emptied a bucket, and I almost matched him, swallow for swallow.

"Come and stay with us!" they urged.

"Thank you, no, I want to get to Krak tonight."

Perhaps I shouldn't have turned down hospitality this late in the evening, I thought; but I couldn't bear to stop now, with only a couple of miles to go. The castle had reappeared, looking tantalisingly close; and the road to it was one of the most dramatic I'd seen yet.

It stepped airily along the highest part of the ridge, a moorland of dry grass stretching down either side of the granite walls that bordered it. Trees grew along its length, stunted and bent double by the force of the wind, like a row of old men. At a bend, the land dropped sheer away to the south to give a view across an eerily flat basin, before rising again higher - far higher - to the snow-capped reaches of Mount Lebanon.

So that was the Homs Gap. It was this corridor, this extraordinarily easy passage in such contrast with the tortuous mountains that surrounded it, that was Krak's *raison d'être*. An army intending to threaten the interior of Syria must pass the coastal mountains far to the north, or else come through this funnel. Whoever held the Gap held the balance of power hereabouts. And it was Krak, sitting on the high point at the southernmost tip of the Alawi Mountain, that was the secret to holding the Gap.

From here the ridge fell away gently to the north. The rocky outcrop at its end merged into the granite stones of the great castle. By the time Madfaa and I were crawling, like ants, under its outer walls the setting sun had coloured them gold.

A half-circle of the fortress brought us abruptly into shadow. At the junction we passed the road to the castle entrance, instead turning sharply downhill on slippery tarmac towards the town which sprawled on the gentler slopes below. Exhausted and still dehydrated, I was almost incoherent as I asked about stabling for Madfaa. Someone emerged from the crowd and took charge of us, and I have a dim recollection of stumbling after him down a maze of darkening streets which seemed to swallow us up, like tunnels leading deep into the earth.

*

"No, they're not here," said Raghdaa, leafing through the post. "Maybe they'll come tomorrow." She was anxiously awaiting the results of her Baccalaureate, to see whether she could go ahead and take up her offer of a place at Aleppo University.

Raghdaa, quiet and studious, was the academic member of her generation. Her elder sister Amira was the family housekeeper. It was their brother, Mustafa, who had rescued me from the streets of Krak town the night before.

The father, Murshid Ahmad, a gentle, rather highly-strung man dressed in a white dishdasha and lace skullcap, hardly looked strong enough to be the father of ten children. The retired schoolmaster of Burj Arabi, he vibrated with nervous enthusiasm, and a quick humour that reminded me of my own father.

The Ahmads lived in a big house in the Sarayah Quarter of the town. There were three floors: a central storey level with the main entrance, a rooftop one with a back door opening higher up the steeply-sloping hill, and a basement reached from outside by a zig-zagging rocky passage on the open mountain, down which Madfaa had climbed nervously in the dark the previous evening. This lowest room was where the family spent their leisure in summertime; for it was cool and pleasant, with a vine shading a quiet courtyard planted with a profusion of flowers.

There was a sudden commotion as the four Music Bears tumbled into the courtyard.

"How's Andros?"

They were the children of another brother, and I'd named them for the cartoon figures on the pyjamas they wore. Perhaps I was sub-consciously taking revenge, for they had from the first given Madfaa a new name, after a horse in a cartoon on Syrian television.

"Andros is very comfortable, thank you." Madfaa was just outside the back gate, in a stable built so deep into the hillside as to be almost a cave. He had displaced the donkey, last seen disappearing up the hill into yesterday evening's gloom led by the hospitable Mustafa. I had bought a big stock of tibn and barley that morning, and my tired companion was now resting well and happily tackling a pile of feed. Satisfied that he was well provided for, I could take a look at the town and renew acquaintance with its fortress, which I'd visited twice on previous travels in Syria.

Somehow I found my way back through the narrow lanes I'd traversed, blinking and comatose, the night before. Two crosses com-manded the foreground of the view up the main street to the castle, representing the Christian half of Krak's inhabitants. A number of old arches and several vaulted storerooms, effortlessly absorbed into the current century, anticipated the architecture to come.

Krak of the Knights was constructed in three main stages. Nobody can remember who originally occupied this natural fortress, but the eleventh century Emir of Homs entered the history books by building the first known castle, garrisoning it with Kurds and giving rise to its early name *Qala'at al-Akraad*, the Castle of the Kurds. Taken by the Crusaders in about 1110, Krak was one of a number of castles gifted to the upwardly-mobile Order of the Hospital in 1142-4 by Count Raymond II of Tripoli, who intended to create a defensive ring about his fief. The Hospitallers rebuilt on a grand scale, obliterating the Emir's and the earlier Crusaders' efforts under a fortress so massive that it would never be taken by assault. Saladin, who laid siege to Krak in 1188, failed to conquer it; two decades later his brother al-Malik al-Adil also admitted defeat. Even the formidable Mameluke Sultan Baybars, who penetrated its outer defences, had to resort to trickery to finish his work. A note purportedly from the Hospitaller Grand Commander at Tripoli induced the Knights to surrender after a five-week siege. Marching out under safe conduct to Tartous, they realised too late that they had been duped: the letter was a fake.

Age has not withered Krak's massive walls; even the earthquake that reduced Sheizar to rubble barely shook it. "The best preserved and most wholly admirable castle in the world" was Lawrence's verdict. Robin Fedden is more poetic: "The fortress buffets the wind and rides above the extended landscape with the confidence and mastery of a ship." A contemporary Arab chronicler tersely described it as "a bone stuck in the very throat of the Muslims".

More than eight centuries after the Hospitallers performed their mighty work, visitors come from six continents to marvel at Krak. Even at noon on this hot July day, huge buses crammed the tiny parking area before the gates. Armies of tourists spilled from their doors, each cohort following its own German or Japanese or even English-speaking commander, each pausing obediently in a well-drilled squad before the door while he delivered the first of his many lectures. "Here is the entrance gate, rebuilt by Baybars after his conquest. Please note the Arabic inscription above: 'In the name of Allah, our Sultan Baybars the Wise, the Righteous, the Brave, the Tenacious, protected by Allah, Pillar of the World and of the Faith, ordered the restoration of this blessed citadel...'" Behind the ranks of sunglasses, eyes were already starting to glaze.

Squeezing past, I paid my entry fee and began to climb the entrance tunnel. I tried to imagine myself a mediaeval knight returning from campaign, hot and sweaty under my armour, my tired horse slipping on the polished cobbles and breaking stride every few yards to mount a succession of low steps. After a few dozen yards a shaft of brilliant sunlight fell on an elbow bend. Here I would dismount and hand my horse to a groom, who would lead him away through the gateway to the stables beneath the outer walls; here an assailant, blinded already by the sudden glare, would be bombarded by stones, arrows or Greek fire from above.

A few more dark steps, and I emerged into the light once more with a ninety-degree turn into the cramped space of the courtyard. How could this castle possibly have housed up to four thousand men? Yet the lower yard was home to an entire village until 1935, when the government moved the people into the newly built houses of today's town, leaving the fort to the tourists. Twenty-six years earlier, Lawrence had stayed here with the governor, "...a most civilised French-speaking-Free-Masonic-Mahommedan-Young Turk: very comfortable." (Not entirely comfortable, though, for he commented more than once on the fleas.)

A flight of stairs took me to the upper level. Now I could walk on the roofs of the kitchens, storerooms and little chapel which so hemmed in the lower yard. Here was a much greater sense of light and air. The castle lay spread out before me as if on a map, heavy and powerful as a wrestler, crafted and graceful as an athlete.

Onwards, and upwards. Opposite the weakest point - the spur joining the fortress to the hillside - was the keep. From its top, the view rivalled those of Marqab and Safita, no mean feat among these enclosing mountains. The sea lay hidden under the mist of distance and heat; to the south the Lebanon ranges poked their heads above the shimmering layers of air, accentuating the eery flatness of the Homs Gap. Away to the right I could see the monastery which had watched over my ascent up the hillside of olive orchards.

I leaned over the coping stones of the highest tower, and peered giddily down the sloping, moss-covered wall to where frogs plopped and croaked in the slimy green waters of the moat in the outer ward.

The besieging Arabs, having mined one of the outer towers, actually penetrated this far. They must have thought they had broken Krak at last; but, staring gloomily up the great inner *talus* which they christened the Mountain, they realised that they had merely scratched its flanks.

A little further round, and I looked down on the town, tracing my path through its streets until I found the Ahmads' house. I could see just the two churches, both in the Street of the Citadel. The flat roofs of the houses all around were covered with wheat spread out to air, and shallow pans of tomato pulp drying and thickening in the sun.

From this vantage point I could plan my route to the south. The time had come to leave the Alawi Mountain and drop down to the Gap. The roads from here all ran in the wrong direction, seeking the easiest path through the hills. But I could just make out a promising-looking track running southwards down a precipitous cleft in the mountainside. A short-cut through, I thought eagerly; then banished the thought, crossing my fingers against the evil eye. No expectations. I'd find out the next morning if it was viable.

*

Cautiously, Madfaa made his way down a path so steep that it made our approach to Krak feel like a flat stroll by comparison. It wound dramatically back on itself to pass almost under the castle, towering above us on its crag like a malevolent dragon sitting on its pile of gold.

The family had gathered to see us off. At the last moment, as I prepared to mount, Amira pressed a small box into my hand. Opening it, I found earrings of amber set in gold. A few embraces, the odd snatch of last-minute advice, and we were off, clattering down the main street as so many riders had done so many centuries ago.

My non-expectations were rewarded. Considering the rapid height loss the track was very passable, snaking back and forth across the hillside among eucalyptus trees, joined by olives as we dropped lower. Was this the original approach from the Homs Gap? It must be, for I'd seen no other such direct route between the two yesterday. If so, pity the poor horses that had to labour up this road to the fortress under the weight of a knight's armour and weaponry.

Halfway down, a spring bubbled out from under a pile of bushes. The small trickle was joined by another from nearby rocks to make a tiny stream, which we followed to the foot of the valley. Krak glowered over us every step of the way, its heavy masonry receding to just a grim and forbidding outline writhing in the heat-haze.

*

The pink tail waving above the top of the drain pipe was getting longer, and longer. First just the tip, then a couple of inches, then a lot more. Somebody was doing a nifty bit of vertical reversing, preceded by what had to be the crowning glory of a rodent. A mouse, or a rat? At that length, it had to be a rat, surely? I hoped very much it was a rat. Preferably a big one. He might be an ally. He might be hungry.

He might eat cockroaches.

The rustling among the maize stalks had begun soon after I had laid out my bag and prepared to sleep. Don't fuss, I told myself. If you must sleep in the barn with a horse, be grateful there's a pile of maize stalks to lie on, instead of the bare concrete that's all Madfaa has. Who ever made a fuss about the odd beetle? Shut up and go to sleep.

The rustle got closer and louder. I ripped off my sleeping bag, struggled to my feet and hit the light switch. Half a dozen cockroaches froze in the act of closing in on me.

I'm not a great fan of cockroaches. I could thumb my nose at the *dad* and shake a stick at the *barda*, but cockroaches were different. They were real.

I took my sleeping bag into the middle of the concrete floor and laid it on the alternative bedding thoughtfully provided by generations of cows. Emptying my tiny bottle of bug powder, I made a protective ring around my bed like a necromancer warding off evil spirits. Then I forced myself to switch off the light and lie down again.

Don't think about them. Cockroaches know about self-preservation. Anything so revolting has to work that bit harder to stay alive. They'll know organo-phosphates well enough to stay outside spitting distance. If not, by the time they cross that barrier they'll be dead. Won't they?

I lasted about four minutes before going for the light again. And nearly retched.

The floor was dark with cockroaches. Big, black cockroaches two inches long, with quivering antennae, uniform as the toys out of a cornflake packet but minus the aesthetic appeal. There must have been about a hundred, motionless, paralysed by the sudden light. And although I'm sure they had all actually been heading in random directions, from where I stood they were all pointing towards my bed. That was when I'd seen the tail, spiralling out of a bit of piping that leaned against the doorpost.

A mouse, or a rat? It was a cliffhanger that went on for several moments. Climbing backwards out of a vertical pipe can't be easy. And when the potholer emerged, I cheered. Quietly, so I didn't frighten him off. For he was the largest, plumpest, most cheerful-looking rat you could imagine; straight from the pages of Beatrix Potter.

A pity I never found out if he was a cockroach-eating rat. He smoothed his whiskers, sat back and took a look around him, saw me and dived under a pile of sacking. Which left just me, and the cock-roaches. That was when I lost it for a few minutes, laying about me like a whirlwind with one boot, scattering corpses like Attila the Hun.

I couldn't kill them all. There was an inexhaustible supply. But something was happening. The numbers were dropping much faster than I was killing them. Then I realised. They couldn't bear the light.

The solution was easy. I simply kept the light on all night, and never saw another cockroach. Madfaa sighed and lay down to sleep, bare concrete, light and all, and I dozed a bit. But it was a long night.

*

I didn't see my host the next morning. When I'd turned down his hospitality to sleep in the stable with Madfaa, he had lost interest. Instead, I shared my breakfast with a neighbour, a girl who had come by last night to see what I was doing. She wore an eclectic mix of the dress codes so far: jeans, hijab and a baseball cap. I didn't remember to ask the prevailing religion in this village of Azan; but we passed both a church and a mosque.

As I walked Madfaa down the main road south out of Azan, only half my mind was on the desultory conversation with the girl. The Homs Gap presented me with a navigational problem, which I couldn't resolve properly until I reached it: the Lebanese border.

When I'd first visited Krak twenty years before, chugging out from the city of Homs in an elderly Volkswagen driven by a friend of Nabil's, the route had involved an obligatory detour through the

Lebanon. Actually, not a detour at all, for the road was straight; only the border, drawn arbitrarily on the map, made a loop slicing through the main road west from Homs, the only road through the Gap, at Tell Kalakh. The practical difficulties imposed by the border were solved in a typically Arab fashion: pretend it didn't exist. A couple of army checkpoints paid lip service to officialdom, but didn't go to the extreme of stopping the traffic. According to the rules, you just drove into Lebanese territory and straight out the other side, staying in your car so as not to set foot on foreign soil. In practice this code was ignored, and Nabil and his friend had strolled freely among the traders' stalls that lined the road, openly selling electrical goods, liquor and perfumes. It was a great duty-free shopping trip, and many a theoretical journey to Tartous and the coast never in fact went further than Tell Kalakh.

Now, though, a new motorway skirted the kink in the border, taking all the traffic westwards to Tartous and on up to Lattakia. That was no use to me, and my map showed no alternative. Would the old road still be open, I wondered, as I rode into the outskirts of Tell Kalakh? If so, would they let me through on a horse? I could always, I reckoned, promise not to dismount.

At the end of the road was a T-junction. Right, and west, for the coast. Left for the Lebanon, and Homs. The checkpoint was a few yards from the junction. The moment of truth had come.

The soldiers were friendly enough. I was optimistic, for I've always got on well with Syrian soldiers. Perhaps I could bluff my way through. But it was nothing doing. Had it been up to them, the guards would have turned a blind eye. But the army handbook didn't cover horses, and soldiers have to do things by the rules. I could always, they called after me helpfully as I turned disconsolately back, use the *autostrade*. Yes, of course I could take a horse on the autostrade.

From its distant hilltop, Krak watched us malevolently as we backtracked up the road. I could almost hear a low rumble of laughter.

After a mile, I found a track leading due east. Would it take us anywhere, or peter out and dump us in the middle of nowhere? I asked a few people, but they just stared at me as if I was simple and pointed up the road to the motorway. There wasn't an alternative, so I hoped for the best and started along the track.

Half an hour or so later it turned into a construction access track for an aqueduct coming towards me; access, that is, from the other end. Surely, then, it must get better as we went further. *In sha'llah.*

Almost at once it disappeared completely. I never did work out how the site labourers got to work. I was too busy extricating us both from a nightmare familiar from my days of travelling in Turkmenistan. It had all the same ingredients: low, flat land with heavy irrigation; drainage ditches and aqueducts blocking the way; and a steady convergence of autostrade and railway squeezing us between them. Eventually a river across our path brought us to a standstill. I scanned the horizon in vain for any sign of a bridge or even a ford for the construction traffic, for the Syrian equivalent of "heavy plant crossing"; but there was nothing even a small weed could have crawled over. Only the railway and the autostrade bridged the river.

Desperate times; desperate remedies. I turned on to the railway bridge. Looking across to the demonic traffic not far away, I congratulated myself on having chosen the safer option. Until I saw a train coming.

We were a hundred yards from either end. Urgently I kicked Madfaa forward into a canter. He responded instantly, his small, hard feet scrunching over the chippings beside the track. The distance was deceptive in that landscape; but so was speed. Although we made it to the other side quite comfortably, the train when it passed us a few minutes later was travelling at a rate which gave me nightmares for a long time.

In the end, there was no choice. "You'll be fine on the autostrade!" cried my latest informant. "There's a track beside it you can use." So there was; for about a quarter mile. After that, it was the hard shoulder or nothing. Madfaa was magnificent, hardly flicking an eyelid when the hugest of lorries thundered past with tarpaulin ripping in the wind. Just as well, for I was a gibbering wreck within five minutes.

Eventually - *al-hamdu li'llah* - we escaped on to the old road to Tell Kalakh, at the point where it disappeared across the border. Damn all politics, I thought as I passed within sight of the checkpoint. What an easy couple of miles that might have been.

Krak, whose all-seeing gaze had been following my crazy ramblings all morning, now had the decency to fade into the haze. The mountains of Lebanon, although closer than ever, had completely disappeared. Down here in the valley, the heat was oppressive.

I holed up for the afternoon in the shell of an Ottoman khan. Discreetly; for, as with so many old buildings in Syria, a house grew from one of its corners. The remainder was ruinous, with friendly brambles tumbling over the fallen black basalt stones. But the immense double span of its arches gave comfortable shade for Madfaa and me to lie up out of the sun.

When the heat faded a little, we crawled out of hiding and made our way ever eastwards, threading in and out of low hills. Behind these the presence of Krak, alternately appearing and disappearing with the rise and fall of the landscape, loosened its grip on us at last. With the tail end of the day we crossed back over the railway and followed the cows home into Hansa.

*

The bus station in Homs was frantic and shambolic; just as I had always known it. No, more so. The crowd was denser than ever, its pressure more intense. A greater multitude of traders made a more colossal noise, so that the private drivers shouting their destinations had to shout louder than ever to make themselves heard. At least there was plenty of choice when I looked for presents to replace my rapidly diminishing stock of gifts for future hosts.

I'd come into Homs in urgent need of cash. I was down to my last few lira, and Hansa was the nearest I would come to a town where I could change travellers' cheques. Madfaa remained in Hansa, comfortably stabled in a part-finished building next to the house of Ahmed Mohammed Khalil.

It had felt strangely exhilarating, after weeks of slow movement on horseback, to mount a *serviis* bus and whizz down the motorway I had tried so hard to avoid the day before. So much so, that I'd thought myself disloyal to Madfaa, and tried to stop enjoying the speed. After a long time in wild and largely empty countryside, Homs seemed a sparkling metropolis, instead of the miserable, rather grotty place of my memories. Only the bus station, with its hum and bustle, its chaotic unfocussed sense of purpose and, above all, its throbbing demand for departure to new and exciting horizons, had ever raised my pulse rate before. Here I'd sat eating falafel to the deafening roar of Vangelis bashing out the signature tune to Syrian radio; had perched, for lack of a remaining seat, on the engine cover of a rickety old charabanc itching for its departure to the Palmyrene desert. And here I'd been rescued by Ayman.

That was the year that proper snow fell on the Homs plateau, six inches of serious white stuff that paralysed the roads and trains, bringing all public and most private transport to a stop. On my way back from Palmyra to Damascus I'd made it thus far, only to find that it looked as if I'd be spending the night on the floor of the station while everybody waited for a thaw. That was when I fell in with Ayman and his chums. A bunch of army lads travelling south from their Aleppo barracks, they had just four days' leave to spend with their families in Damascus, and had no intention of wasting a minute of it.

Covering my shivering shoulders with a thick army jacket, they towed me with them round the town, visiting acquaintances and calling in favours until they persuaded someone to drive them south. There followed one of the hairiest journeys I have ever known. Given good conditions and a modern car, Syrians are not generically safe drivers. This guy, in an old banger with bald tyres - nobody with a posh car was prepared even to think about the journey - dealt with the snow by pretending it wasn't there. Over the next four hours I learned a whole new dimension to the idea of correcting a skid. The episode left me with my first grey hairs, and a permanent soft spot for Syrian soldiers.

I saluted Homs bus station with a banana milk shake, and started to look for a bank. Only it was Friday.

I'd lost the rhythm of weekdays while I was in the Mountain. Or perhaps, in reconnecting with modernity in the form of towns, buses and motorways, I'd subconsciously slipped back into a western cycle. Syria is secular, but the commercial week follows the Muslim pattern, with Friday as the Holy- or holiday. All the banks were closed. I had to find my way to a smart hotel on the outskirts to change money. Homs had indeed changed; when I was last here smart hotels were rarer than snow.

Before returning to the bus station I paid a brief visit to the old citadel. There's not much to see; but, having never spent time looking round Homs before, I felt obliged to take the trouble. Stone walls at the bottom of the old city mound must have dated back thousands of years, for you had to climb to the top to reach traces of the Romans. They left little: just the walls of a few outlying towers. But Roman Emesa was never a great player in world politics; just a middle-ranking *entrepôt* on the caravan routes, whose sole, dubious claim to fame was as birthplace of the mad transvestite Emperor, Elagabalus.

On the way back to Hansa I glimpsed Lake Qattinah, where a dam collects the waters of the Orontes to supply Homs. I looked for landmarks about it, but there were few points of reference in this flat country. And I needed some, for as far as my maps were concerned, the next stage was unmarked territory. I hoped to squeeze between *Buhayrat* Qattinah and the Lebanese border and reach the ancient city of Kadesh on the Orontes, and I wasn't sure if there was even a road.

My serviis whisked me back down the motorway as rapidly as a flying carpet. I had a moment's panic when I couldn't remember the name of Hansa, nor recognise the approach - all places look the same from a motorway, especially at whisking speed - and the driver fidgeted impatiently while I dithered in the doorway, deciding whether to jump before I was pushed. But the old benevolent spirit of Homs bus station had blessed my journey, for I got it right.

*

The railway, the motorway and the old road to Tell Kalakh converged at Hansa. It might thus have been buried by iron, concrete and the internal combustion engine. In reality it had managed to remain blessedly and determinedly rural. With its low, rough stone walls, its narrow streets scarcely wide enough for the passage of a small car, the village reminded me strongly of the Scilly Isles. All it needed was a few daffodils instead of sunflowers and olives in the tiny, stone-walled fields, perhaps a scattering of fuchsia and a few spikes of orange montbretia soaking up the sunlight, and the illusion would have been complete.

There were other parallels. The parochial nature of the society, for instance, with close relationships between not only neighbours but dwellers in opposite ends of the settlement. And the wind; a constant buffeting, tearing gale that whistled through the Homs Gap and ripped across the flat landscape. The main street ran north-south, and thus at an exact right-angle to the funnel of the Gap. It was a wonder, I thought as I struggled up it leaning into the blast, that everybody here didn't develop a permanent list to one side; though I suppose that walking home straightened them out again.

From the roof of their house, Ahmed's daughter Abiir pointed out a couple of old city mounds. They were bigger and more clearly defined than those I'd seen before. The whole valley of the Orontes - which I was now approaching once again - must have been closely settled in antiquity. Perhaps here, in the upper reaches of the river with its harsher landscape, old cities had a better chance of surviving than in the fertile alluvial plain of the Ghaab, where every inch of soil was fiercely coveted by succeeding generations.

Down in Abiir's living room, the news was on television. For some reason it was subtitled in French, so that for the first time I could follow what was going on around me on the higher stage in Syria. At a major conference, Hafez al-Assad had openly announced his intention that his son Bashar, the younger brother of the "martyr" Basel, should succeed him to the Presidency. The Republic of Syria, like that of Ancient Rome, seemed to be transforming itself into a monarchy.

"Will it really happen?" I asked Abiir.

She shrugged. "Why not?" She wasn't really interested. Her family were Alawi. They had no cause to fear the perpetuation of the ruling family.[6]

Not that you felt much sense of political alignment - which usually overlaps, in Syria, with religious alignment - in Hansa. Its mix of cultures - Sunni, Shi'ite, Alawi and Orthodox Christian - was a seamless blend of good neighbourliness.

"We're all the same," said Abiir. "We all love each other." A pity there aren't more places like Hansa in the world.

The wind, though, was more hostile than ever the next morning, and the landscape became bleaker with every step onwards away from Hansa. It became increasingly difficult to tell human intervention from the hand of nature in the outcrops of rock among the walls, and apart from a few half-hearted attempts to grow maize, there was little effort to coerce profit from the grudging soil. My impression of the Scillies gave way to visions of the Outer Hebrides. When I passed a wide,

---

[6] Not long after, Hafez-al-Assad died, and Bashar duly became President.

shallow lake with reeds at its edge and a knot of pines on the central island, I felt myself a thousand miles from Syria.

How on earth could wide, shallow lakes survive in a hot climate? Though in truth it was almost cold today. Even after the immense variation in the types of country I'd travelled in recent weeks, I felt disorientated by these surroundings. It seemed that, in leaving my large-scale map and making this rather romantic dive into (for me) uncharted territory, I'd left behind everything familiar and stepped into a parallel universe.

Madfaa was eating fire. Well-rested, he was bursting with energy and ready to run. He had skittered down the main street this morning frightening everybody who came near him. I should make pretty good mileage today, I reckoned, if the leg held up to pressure. It should do; the tendon was now completely flat, with all sign of swelling gone.

The wind dropped and the sun came out, while the miles rolled past. Excellent progress. Away to my left I could see Buhayrat Qattinah. A signpost told me that it was only thirty kilometres from here to the Damascus road. This was reassuring, but rather dented my sense of remoteness and adventure. I restored it by noting down the villages I passed through, adding their names to my empty map: Qabtah, Jawbatiyyah, Al-Haw…

By the time I reached the village of Na'iim, I could see a mound in the distance which had to be Kadesh. "Tell Nebi Mend?" I asked the lady whose grass Madfaa was guzzling. Nobody around here, I guessed, had used the ancient name for a couple of thousand years.

She nodded encouragingly, and I asked some more questions. "What religion is this village? How do the local people live?" The latter question had pricked my curiosity more and more urgently, as I passed through this increasingly lunar landscape.

It was, I discovered, another place where people of all denominations co-existed happily. "Most people either work on the land, or have jobs in the Lebanon." She pointed out the road I must take, a left turn which I would otherwise have trotted carelessly past.

Beyond Na'iim, the fertile artery of the Orontes reached a few capillaries up into these low hills. The idea of "working on the land" began to seem less surprising, more feasible. Though whatever the people here did live on, it arrived in plastic bags. Plastic was strewn about the place more thickly than anywhere else in Syria. White plastic, black plastic - no other colours - covered every inch of open ground. Geology had taken millennia to colour this land black and white in basalt and limestone. Modern Syrians had taken perhaps a decade to achieve the same effect in plastic.

The old city mound rose from the horizon and swelled to fill my view. No need of a map, here. In a surreal moment we left the last tiny village of al-Haw and tripped over a great four-lane highway, which stopped dead at a T-junction with a minor road. It solved the problem of how we were to cross the river, a worry which had been nagging at me all morning.

Just as well, for, defying both the map and the history books, the Orontes flowed to the east of Kadesh and must be crossed before we could reach the old city mound. I suppose the main course of a river can change in three thousand years - there are enough subsidiary channels, as Pharaoh Ramses II found to his cost - but it was reasonable to hope that the American satellites which had inspired my newest map might have got it right. I took an unnecessary detour into a building site to avoid the highway, but was forced to backtrack and cross by the new bridge. A good job that the road went nowhere except to a remote area of the Lebanon, and was almost unused.

The Orontes here resembled the Cherwell, running sluggishly through low banks fringed with willow and edged by sandbanks. People idled beside it, and small boys jumped and dived like porpoises in the clear water, while sunbeams cut like diamond through the fountains they sent up. Seen through such a foreground the dry, crumbling mud of the ancient city, rising high above the houses on the riverbank, seemed more alive.

Madfaa and I crossed the last spur of water, fielded a few good-natured catcalls from the boys, and climbed the hill.

*

The *tell* at Kadesh was already high, heaped up by more than a thousand years of crumbled mud brick, everyday rubbish and general detritus of human occupation, when around 1280 BC Pharaoh Ramses II marched carelessly up its western side on his way to engage the Hittite army which he believed was waiting near Aleppo.

At least, the hill was high and wide enough to hide the two thousand five hundred Hittite war chariots crouching in ambush behind it.

Ramses had every reason to be confident as he marched on "the false city of Kadesh". Less than two centuries before, his predecessor Tuthmosis III had crushed the King of Kadesh at the Battle of Armageddon. Since then, however, the Hittites had extended their sphere of influence southward into Syria, threatening the security of the trade routes. Egypt needed to reassert her power over her former vassal, who had begun to look to the north for her friends. With false information placing the Hittites far away, Pharaoh's confidence was buoyant.

As Ramses, with the vanguard of his twenty thousand men, made his camp to the north-west of the city, the Hittites emerged from the south, forded the river and smashed into the second of the four Egyptian divisions. With their army spread out, split by tributaries of the Orontes and now broken in two, the Egyptians scattered. Ramses and his men should have been annihilated; but the triumphant Hittites stopped to plunder his camp, leaving him time to rally his personal escort and fight his way to safety.

"I was by myself, for my soldiers and my horsemen had forsaken me," boasted Ramses, celebrating the battle in hieroglyphics on temple walls from Luxor to Aswan. We will never know whether it was he personally, or some anonymous commander, who gathered the soldiers around the Pharaoh, cut through the Hittite ranks to rejoin the rest of the army, and withdrew the survivors to safety. Ramses would scarcely have hesitated to overrate his own contribution, when he was brash enough to proclaim as a great victory what was at best a drawn contest - and one in which he was lucky to escape with his life from culpable negligence. Ramses knew how to "spin" as well as any modern politician, and was at rather greater liberty to do so. Informed only by Royal proclamation, most of his subjects probably never even knew that the outcome of the long Hittite wars was no better than a mutual non-aggression pact.

How on earth, I wondered, could this mound have hidden the colossal Hittite army? Perhaps the cultivation was more extensive than today, with more than a just a few fruit trees and willows to give cover. But five thousand horses could scarcely have been kept silent and still. Had Ramses not even bothered to send any scouts out? Or were the twenty thousand men attributed to each side just one more exaggeration?

Kadesh today was virtually abandoned. These days people no longer retreat to the heights for safety, and the inhabitants of the town bearing the name of Tell Nebi Mend live on the plain at the foot of the earthen mound. The few mud-brick houses that remained on its top were crumbling and empty. There were no children playing in the streets. Deserted yards stood open to the wind, which was howling down as fierce as ever off the Lebanon ranges. I half expected to hear saloon doors crashing behind me in the gale, the ultimate cliché of the ghost town.

Heavy iron doors still guarded one or two of the yards, with a few goats and sheep huddling behind them. And as Madfaa and I made our way through the silent streets, heads popped out from a couple of houses to see who was passing. It wasn't completely dead after all; moribund, though, with no lingering memory of its former glory.

From its far side, I spotted the path of a dry stream running parallel to the Orontes on the west side. This must be what my American satellite map had shown, which I'd taken to be the main river. It explained another mystery of the battle: how had the Hittite chariots forded the river quickly enough to wreak such havoc on the marching Egyptians? If it had been only this minor channel that they crossed, the ambush seemed much more feasible. Doubtless it was modern irrigation, as well as the season, which had sucked it so dry.

Irrigation had long been practised here. From my vantage point I could see evidence to the east of older workings. A system of passages occupied differing levels, retaining water at a greater height than the slowly dropping river. It was beautiful, clear water, and wherever I looked I could see little boys swimming in it.

The western stream bed ran among well-watered fields with good grass, perfect for Madfaa. Descending the hill, I tethered him and walked on down the valley, still trying to reconstruct the battle. A few hundred yards to the south, the stream bed broadened into what had obviously been a ford. Astride the shallows - it would be fully in the water when the stream was running - stood an old building. Very old; Byzantine at the latest, judging by the marble columns and remains of a marble pediment built into the walls. It suggested that the spot had been a ford for two thousand years at the very least; and significant enough to merit a guard post. Could this be where the Hittites crossed? It fitted perfectly the geography of the battle; though the closeness to the city, and the consequent lack of room for large armies to manoeuvre, again seemed to downsize the scale of the encounter.

At some later date the little fort had been converted to a mill. Piers outside directed the water into rectangular channels passing directly underneath. The remains of a wall showed how the flow had been concentrated from a riverbed which, in these shallows, ran naturally very wide. The mill had been maintained until comparatively recently, for concrete shored up the piers, and a railway sleeper had replaced one of the rotten beams inside. Maybe it had outlived its usefulness when the Homs dam was built.

I sat eating my lunch under a bramble hedge beside a field of maize, while Madfaa grazed a ditch rampant with rye grass and clover. A man strolled over to us. I thought him a local, arriving for a pleasant chat. I was wrong.

"Passport!"

He wore ordinary clothing, but the terseness, the expectation of instant obedience, marked him out.

Syria is said to have many levels of secret police. They are universally loathed by the people for the control they exercise, and for the sanctions that can be applied by those at the top of their hierarchy. Amnesty International has a long file on Syria.

I'd met one or two of these characters on my way. An expensive Toyota would pass, turn round and pull over, and a man in plain jeans and shirt would alight and demand to check over my papers. I took good care to be courteous, but never showed my documents until I'd asked for identification. I wasn't going to pull my money belt out from under my shirt until I knew who I was dealing with, especially on a lonely road. More than once ordinary people had pretended to be secret policemen just to wind me up, or from curiosity to look at an English passport.

"OK. May I see your authorisation?"

Now the fun began. He was just being nosey, for he wasn't on duty. And he'd left his own papers at home. So I wasn't getting mine out. On principle, of course.

"You say you're a policeman. How do I know? You haven't any identification. Real policemen have identification."

He got more and more stroppy, while I remained politely obstructive. Limited by my Arabic, the argument wasn't an intelligent debate; rather, it went along the lines of, "Oh, yes, you must!" "Oh, no, I shan't!"

One or two passers-by stopped to watch the pantomime, and within minutes a crowd was gathering. With the protection of my foreign status, I could get away with baiting the poor man in a way the locals couldn't. They were heartily enjoying his discomfiture.

It might have gone on for hours, but his pal turned up. Number Two was a colleague.

"Passport!"

It might have been a repeat performance; except that Number Two had his identification papers with him.

Of course, Officer. Three bags full, Officer. I handed it over obligingly. He passed it at once to Number One, who checked it, gave it back to Number Two, and cleared off almost before I had it back in my belt. Number Two asked a few cursory questions until honour was satisfied all round, and then followed him. The fat lady had sung, and the crowd drifted away.

It made good sport. I felt no compunction. Whereas Syrians in uniform were invariably decent men doing their job, the secret police were a different breed. But it was sobering to reflect that only the privilege of my nationality allowed me to play the game at all.

*

We rejoined the Orontes one last time at the old Roman bridge of Antara, and came into the outskirts of Qusair at evening, having made excellent time on arrow-straight roads running in the right direction. By my reckoning we covered close on forty kilometres that day.

For the last hour I'd been looking unsuccessfully for accommodation. Now the town's suburbs rose beyond the orchards through which we were approaching. I was about to tie Madfaa under an orange tree and bivvy, when Abu Mohammed spied us and called us over.

He was sitting in his yard enjoying a last glass of tea before going home. A cacophony of moos, bleats and clucks came from the assortment of barns behind him. In no time he had made a space for Madfaa in the biggest barn, and installed me in the one-roomed building that served as night-watchman's hut. The night-watchman himself was Abu Mohammed's younger son Adham, who arrived five minutes after me, handed the car keys to his father and settled down to sleep.

I had plenty of food for Madfaa, but nothing for myself bar a bottle of Coke that I'd bought from the café at Antara. Abu Mohammed, though, had just finished the evening milking, and gave me a great beaker of milk. It filled the void nicely, and I had enough to share with the little marmalade-and-white cat which came scrounging as soon as I'd rolled myself in my sleeping-bag.

It was a wonderfully early night. There was no question of getting up to check on Madfaa, for all the barns were locked and a particularly ferocious dog stood guard. If I'd even tried to squint over the wall, it would have raised the neighbourhood. So I took a deep breath and went to sleep, sure that he would be fine.

He was as right as a trivet the next morning, though covered with dung from having again lain down on bare concrete to rest. Abu Mohammed arrived with a contingent of his family. Umm Mohammed immediately set to doing the milking, while her daughter Jude joined Adham and their father unloading tibn into the granary next to the hut. By the time they had finished, Umm Mohammed had returned with frothing pails of warm, fresh milk. The little marmalade-and-white cat had a bowl to itself; then hung around taking every opportunity to thieve someone else's.

Abu Mohammed owned a lot of land as well as the dairy. Gesturing in all directions, he listed the fruits he grew. The farm itself was an absolute menagerie. Studiously, I revised my Arabic vocabulary from the names painted on to the mud-brick walls: chickens here, ducks there, geese somewhere else. I was puzzled by the label which seemed to tell me that one hut was a bath-house. My dictionary showed me I'd fallen into an old linguistic elephant trap in Arabic. Instead of writing a doubled consonant twice, you write it once with a squiggle over the top. The squiggle, together with all the vowel signs - themselves not part of the word but mere commas or dashes above or below - is then routinely discarded. The written word thus consists entirely of consonants; filling in the missing bits is a breeze, a guessing game or a nightmare, depending on whether you are respectively an adult, a child, or a foreign halfwit. *Hammaam*, bath, said the dictionary. *Hamaam*, pigeon.

"*Warda.*" Jude continued the lesson, pressing a rosebud into my hand as I left. I put it into my lapel, and its scent tickled my nose as I rode into the first streets of Qusair through a morning like an English October, its dreamy sunshine wreathed in waves of mist spiralling down off the Lebanon mountains.

Little was stirring yet. Now and again open doors gave glimpses into courtyards, where elderly men in white keffiyahs lingered over their early morning glasses of tea. Further in, merchants blocked the roads while they unloaded the day's goods: boxes of cucumbers, crates of aubergines, a whole truckload of tomatoes the size of tennis balls. The wide ledge outside a mosque hade been made into an impromptu counter. The road sign in the main square brought home with a thump the closeness of Lebanon with, among the signs to Damascus and Homs, one quite casually pointing to Baalbek, site of the spectacular Roman ruins in the Beka'a Valley.

The delivery trucks were parked on the pavements. Over and over again Madfaa and I were forced into the road to pass. It meant playing chicken with the growing traffic, and I dismounted to walk between Madfaa and the cars. This worked quite well until an impatient bus driver, angry at having to share his road with a horse, came straight for us with deliberate intent.

He probably only meant to scare me, and chase us out of his way. But there was nowhere to jump. At the last moment before what looked like certain annihilation I spun the stallion round, spreading my arms across him in a completely futile gesture of desperation and screaming obscenities at the driver. The bus squealed to a stop almost touching my feet, and some passers-by, furious on my behalf, jumped into its open door to give the driver a dressing-down. It had to have been quite bad, I thought as I wrung the sweat from my shirt, to have registered on the local Traffic Incident scale.

This was my abiding memory of Qusair, for we left it almost at once behind us. Our road led straight up the Beka'a Valley parallel to the river. Alongside ran a disused railway, its tracks now covered with asphalt. An old station of the French Colonial period materialised splendidly among the concrete block and mud-brick architecture of rural Syria.

We turned left across the tracks and headed away from the river, directly towards the eastern of the two mountain ridges cradling the

Orontes valley. It was slightly daunting to be heading for more mountains. But this was a much shorter route than the dog-leg round the north end of the mountain spur, which would take us almost to Homs before we could branch south. Besides, after this morning's Incident, the last thing I wanted to see was a major road.

As the mountain ridge loomed ahead, it actually felt rather pleasant to be approaching a Geographical Feature again, after all that flat plain of the last few days. I began to experience a twinge of that gut-churning excitement which goes with fresh horizons. And now, to the eternal question "Where are you going?" I could answer "Damascus!"

Very soon the irrigation was drying up, the land becoming coarser. A number of broad *wadis* reached up from the valley floor to end abruptly in nothing. It was as if the Orontes, having spilled down out of those dramatic mountains to hit the plain, had let freedom go to its head and run riot in all directions, only to run out of steam against the rising ground. I passed an Artesian well, the first I'd seen. Normally water came from a deep spring via an electric pump. I'd arrive at a house and ask for water, and the owner would go inside and reach for a switch. Water would gush from a hose, often into a large concrete basin into which Madfaa would be invited to sink his nose. Abu Mohammed's basin, with all that stock to water, was about four times the size of everyone else's - and he kept fish in it. I'd been taken aback when I spotted them flapping eerily in its depths, as for once there was no label. I suppose to write "fish" on the water tank was a bit superfluous, even for his tidy mind.

Soon I would say goodbye for good to the Orontes Valley. Now the landscape was changing rapidly; no villages, just a few scattered homesteads. People stopped work and leaned on their hoes to watch us pass, or threw open windows and called out from inside the house.

"*Faddali!*" Come in!

"I can't. I've got a long journey."

"*Shwaiyya!*" Just a little.

"Sorry!"

"*Wayn bit'ruuhi?*" Where are you going?

"Damascus!"

"*Sham? Ba'iid jiddan!*" It's a very long way.

"I know!"

There was one last settlement before the mountains. It was an odd, frontier-town affair; perhaps a dozen houses in all, half old mud-brick, half new concrete block. Most were closed and empty, and several had begun to disintegrate. Below the village trailed the last of the irrigation attached to the Orontes valley; above, a few valiant fingers of green stretched a mile or so into brown, dry, crumbly mountain. Nothing except geology linked this elevated desert with the fertile, populous uplands of the Anti-Lebanon. Though, judging by the number of rock-littered wadis that scarred the hillside, the mountain wasn't always this dry. The road snaked away up towards the pass, making a light brown stain in a darker background.

"You won't like it," they'd told me back in Qusair when I'd asked about this road. "It's very difficult. It's an unmade road, and it's hard."

By hard, I had understood them to mean steep. But it couldn't be that much worse than all the upping and downing we'd had to do in the Jebel al-Alawiyiin. Besides, anything discouraging to traffic had to be good news.

In fact, although it was rough enough underfoot to be bad going for a car, Madfaa was more than equal to it. And the gradient was gentle. While my map told me that the mountains reach three-and-a-half thousand feet hereabouts - and five thousand just over the Lebanese border - the road I could see passing over the saddle ahead of me was very little higher than the village.

Agriculture was creeping up the hill beside it. Up here the fruit trees were tiny, in their first few years of growth, and the pumps that fed them shiny and new. I passed a party of engineers, the men charged with making this desert bloom. It looked an unrewarding task, for it was hard to imagine anything growing in a topsoil that was no more than crumbled rock fallen off the mountaintop. But the results spoke for themselves, and even if the melons were a tad smaller than those in Qusair's market, the tomatoes made up for them.

I begged a last bucket of water from the engineers for Madfaa. A few yards further on, I picked up a couple of watermelons that had fallen literally off the back of a lorry. I still had some tibn in my saddlebags. At least we were both well provided for as we resumed the steady uphill plod. Just as well, for the last of the irrigation dribbled to a few drops, and now the desert began for real.

V

THE DESERT

The pass was easy. The road, by now running over great slabs of rock, changed so little in gradient that it was barely perceptible. There was little sense of a summit, no view down the far side.

High up to my right, clouds belched skywards. Something was burning, or steaming, violently. I watched it with some anxiety as we approached. For all I could see from here, it might as well be a crashed aircraft.

A series of booms rattled my ears and made Madfaa jump. Another cloud mushroomed skywards. Quarry dust. We were coming into the edge of the mining belt. There's not much you can do with these hills, I suppose, except dig things out of them.

Halfway down from the pass the Damascus Highway came into sight, unwrapping itself from a succession of low hills which tried to mask the view. From this distance it was uncharacteristically silent. For once I wasn't dismayed by the sight of the traffic. The autostrade might guide us, but would not, this time, suck us in. Where there is neither habitation nor cultivation, nor are there any fences. From now on Madfaa and I might go where we liked.

An ugly but perfectly adequate concrete hut gave us some shade and the excuse for a food stop. I sank a whole melon in one go, with no shame; all I'd had to eat that day was a few biscuits in Qusair. Madfaa, meanwhile, lunched off alaf and tibn, followed by melon and tibn, and stood contentedly slobbering over the pool of melon juice left in the bottom of the bucket. With perfect timing, a jeep rolled down the dusty track and disgorged two army lads, who completed Madfaa's refuelling with a generous bucket of water.

In mid-afternoon we came down out of the Anti-Lebanon towards the Damascus Highway, through a land too dry and bare to support so much as a single goat. Even the crickets had abandoned it, and the only sound was that of the wind sifting through a handful of tinder-dry stalks. We turned south, and came almost at once to the village of Hassyah.

It gave us a very warm welcome. Madfaa quickly gathered a crowd at the little shop, where I bought biscuits, cheese and canned tuna. It didn't sell bread, but the shopkeeper kindly fetched me a round from his own kitchen, refusing payment. Someone brought Madfaa a bucket of water while I sank a couple of cans of Coke and answered the usual questions: where are you from, where are you going, how old are you, have you any children... As we left, a little boy came running after us and thrust a couple of tomatoes into my hand.

I stopped in the shade of a water tower to eat a second lunch; then sat for a bit, feeling thoroughly sated, while Madfaa browsed thriftily on the dried stalks of what had been grass a couple of months earlier. Should we stop here, or move on? It had been a hard day already; but, for all the welcome, there had been no spontaneous invitations to stay, and I baulked at asking. Surely, from now on there would be a con-tinuous stream of villages along the autostrade. OK, there was a big gap on the map; but that had meant nothing on its last empty section between Hansa and Kadesh.

From here low mountains ran south, parallel to the road. Tracks ran across the mile or two of desert in between. They were tempting, but unpopulated; there would be time enough to go exploring in the days to come. For now I stayed near the road, to make sure I wouldn't miss the next settlement.

But there was nothing, nothing and more nothing. At least I'd found the perfect compromise between ease of travelling, and safety. The old road, pre-autostrade, the one I'd travelled in past decades, marched through the quarter-mile gap between the two carriageways of the motorway. From time to time buildings appeared on the horizon, creeping closer with painful slowness while I scanned them anxiously, only to find here an army camp, there a refinery. By now the sun was sitting on top of the mountain ridge and my shadow was reaching to the northbound carriageway of the autostrade, fifty yards away.

Passing over a small hill, I came upon a truck driver who had pulled off on to the old road and stopped for a cigarette.

"How far's the next village?"

He ground his heel on the cigarette butt, pausing for a minute while he thought.

"Thirteen kilometres."

My heart hit my boots with a clunk. I opened my mouth to swear, but the words died on my lips as I came over the top of the rise at that very moment to see a cluster of houses some four or five kilometres away. We weren't, after all, going to be spending the night camped out on the motorway.

On the outskirts of the village was a service station. I found a bucket of water for Madfaa and saw off two more cans of Coke. But there was no hanging about, for Madfaa, who had long had enough of the road and was now also freaked out by the new experience of car headlights, threw a tantrum and nearly squashed the children who were beginning to press about him. Wearily I led him back to the tarmac and entered the little town. Welcome to al-Brayj, said the sign.

The shell of a former police post, abandoned when the old road fell out of use, was the first building we came to. That would do us very nicely, I thought. I could tether Madfaa in the outer part and sleep in one of the inner rooms. It was a pity about the goat droppings, but they were dry and would brush cleanly off the floor. I had a full stomach and some food left, and some spare water from the service station. All I needed was some tibn.

I went to the nearest house and knocked on the door. It was thrown open with breathtaking speed. As I held out my tibn bag like a suppliant, stammering something unintelligible in my frightful Arabic, I was dimly aware through the haze of exhaustion that there were an awful lot of people, and that they were exceptionally well dressed. I felt that I had opened a door and walked into a world which wasn't in the script.

Within moments Madfaa was stabled and eating heartily, and I was going to a party.

*

My host reminded me of Sean Connery. Not only did he look astonishingly similar, and was of comparable age; he had the same range of amused facial twitches, the fierce and eloquent eyebrows; the same brisk, competent control of all situations, without once losing his good humour. I half expected to hear him introduce himself with, "The name's Salim. Hassan Ahmad Salim."

His elder daughter-in-law continued the theatrical theme, her features, her air of enthusiastic enquiry and a mouth that readily turned up at the corners making her a dead ringer for Jemma Redgrave. Like her sisters-in-law, she wore a white headscarf, with a rather nunnish big safety-pin at the throat. I was back in no-knickers-on-the-line territory.

But there was absolutely nothing subservient about these girls. On the contrary; irrepressibly extrovert, they exchanged banter with their husbands, thumped them heartily from time to time and were quite clearly equal partners in all things. Apart from the wimples, they were dressed in peacock colours for the party, a glamorous change from the rather drab village costume I'd been getting used to, and their wrists sparkled with gold.

I was rapidly dispatched to the bath-house to make myself presentable. By the time I emerged, still embarrassingly shabby in my clean change of clothes, another knock had rattled the door - the one they'd been expecting, this time - and the real guests had arrived. Friends and family blew into the house like a gale, and in a remarkably short time introductions were completed and the party had separated into male and female rooms. We were seated around a banquet, a mez-zeh of assorted vegetables, fruits, humous, laban and mixed salads, and the company became as noisy and jolly as a party of students - without needing a drop of alcohol to fuel their mirth. The conversation ran fast, furious and completely incomprehensible as far as I was concerned. It gave me an excuse to sit quietly and reply with just a smile now and then. I was in no state that night to be a lively guest.

Nor to hit the road the following morning. Hassan willingly said I might stay another day, and I idled around the house catching up on some sleep.

Madfaa, too, needed to rest. At around forty-three kilometres, the previous day had been a marathon. He was comfortably eating tibn and barley in a stable more elegant than many houses in the herring-bone pattern of its mud-brick. A black and white sheep shared his manger, and cattle browsed on maize stalks in the yard outside. With a security born of many companions, he had scarcely bothered last night with his now-customary evening habit of licking my arm and holding it for a moment.

Hassan ran the village dairy, as well as a poultry farm. A man of many parts, he also worked as a builder and long-distance lorry driver, a calling shared by his sons. Their work had taken them all over the Arab world and beyond. They were one of the wealthier families in the village. It was evident, from the respect with which their neighbours treated them, that they were held in high esteem. I wondered if Hassan were the equivalent of a local councillor. It would have sat well with his air of relaxed yet brisk authority, with my feeling that this was the man people would turn to in a crisis. From the speed with which he had gathered me and Madfaa into his family to the efficient, good-humoured ordering of his household, I never saw him either hesitate or hurry.

His oldest grandson was also called Hassan Ahmad Salim.

"It's a family tradition," said Hassan senior, "to name the grandson after the grandfather."

"How long for?" I asked. "I mean, how many times?"

"Oh, at least ten times."

Twenty generations. Perhaps four or five centuries. Right back to the early days of the Ottoman Empire.

The family had a strong tradition of transmitting their history, the *hadith* that is usual among the Bedouin but which I hadn't been aware of in my encounters so far with villagers. They had originally come, said Hassan, from a village near Deir ez-Zor on the Euphrates, and had crossed the Badiat ash-Sham to settle here about two hundred and fifty years ago. Al-Brayj was called Burj 'Atash then. It was a strange name: the "Tower of Thirst".

In the afternoon I joined the girls on the water run. With a couple of wheelbarrows they carried half a dozen containers to the tap near the mosque. It might have been a drudgery, but custom had transformed it into a social outing. Here the women met to gossip and exchange news, to comment on each others' clothes, to play with the children and exclaim at their growth. What a pain, I'd thought at my first visit to a village well, to have to fetch all your water from down the road. By now I'd realised that a private water supply probably did as much to stifle community interaction as the invention of television.

Back at the house they brewed *za'atar babunish*, a local green tea with mint in it. "Soothing to the body," explained Hassan, whereas the black tea, it seemed, was bracing. The heat by now had climbed to an intensity that was new to me, and I was glad I wasn't plodding through the desert. The girls slaked their thirst greedily, not bothering with a cup but raising the heavy water drum to pour a jet of water into their mouths from six inches away. I tried to copy them. It wasn't as easy as it looked. After I'd wasted half a pint down my shirt front and then choked on the rest, I gave it up and fetched a glass.

When the sun slipped low and the heat dropped to a tolerable level, I went on to the roof and gazed out in each direction in turn. Across the street an old army barrack stood empty, the solid iron gates closed on the parade ground. A repeating motif of crossed swords was roughly drawn in the red ochre of its walls. Beyond the crumbling, ill-defined roofs of the village houses rose the continuation of the mountain ridge we'd crossed yesterday, darkened in the sunset to the same colour as the walls below me.

As I turned to face in the opposite direction and look eastward out to the desert, the Imam began the call to evening prayer. For the first time in weeks, I felt myself fully in Syria. Why should this arid, barren landscape make my soul expand in such a way? Was it because this was the face of Syria that I saw first, the face that I had known longest and was most familiar with? Or was something stirring of the old romantic longing of someone from a green well-watered country, perversely yearning for endless bare horizons? Whatever subconscious thoughts were moving and slotting into place inside me, I felt suddenly than the journey was beginning to mesh with my fantasies.

Beyond Hassan's yard, there was pretty well nothing between me and the Euphrates. I sat until it grew dark, looking at the low hills that formed the horizon. A number of tracks turned their backs on the village and the nearby motorway to lead off into the void. For two pins, I'd have saddled Madfaa and ridden out on one of them.

Of course, I knew damn well that if I had, within an hour or so I'd have been fed up beyond endurance with the heat, the hard going, the emptiness, the unchanging scenery and the lack of water. But it was a beguiling thought to go to bed on; perhaps all the sweeter for knowing that for now, at least, it would remain just a pipedream.

"Are you happy that you stayed here?" asked Hassan's daughter Halima, sitting up suddenly in bed as if the thought had just arisen and urgently needed an answer.

"Yes," I replied. "Very happy. Very, very happy."

*

In the morning, the family gathered to wish us on our way.

"*Fii amaani'llah*," said Hassan formally. Go in the safekeeping of God.

"*Allah yesallimak*," I replied. May God give you peace. A last wave, and we were clattering down the village street, past the mosque with its tap, and out on to the empty road.

At the first opportunity I turned off the road on to a track leading diagonally westwards towards the mountain ridge. This was the nearest I'd get to realising my desert fantasies. It would do very nicely, I thought practically, as the roar of the motorway faded and al-Brayj dwindled to a low outline of roofs. From now on a rambling network of tracks took us roughly south. I could choose my way by inclination and instinct, for the mountain ridge would keep me company all the way from now to Damascus, and was all the guide necessary.

In the village of Qara we spoilt the day of the watermelon man, who did a double-take when he saw Madfaa walking up the main street. His head screwed over his shoulder while his hands continued mechanically undoing the tailgate of his truck, with the result that his cargo rolled into the street and half his melons split.

From the top of the village I could see a large solitary building about a mile away near the foot of the mountains. Its crisp white outline was the only clear landmark in a world which was sinking without resistance into the haze of another very hot day. Somebody told me it was a monastery. I went to see for myself; then seduced by its neatly-kept gardens and the sound of running water, decided to take a closer look on the pretext of a drink for Madfaa.

Heaps of building material and a couple of trucks blocked the approach. Major renovation was in progress. I tethered Madfaa under a fig tree while I went to ask a workman for water. He passed me up the line of command and in no time I found myself talking to Aziz Farah, the *mudir* - foreman - who gave me the guided tour. He very quickly corrected my first misapprehension.

"No, it's not a monastery, it's a convent." The fifty nuns, though, were living in the village while the workmen were in situ. Aziz took me into the church.

"It belongs to St. Yacoub. It was first built in 550 AD. After the Christians, it became a temple of the *Arami*." It took a moment for the word to click. Arami - the Aramaeans. Not far south of here, I knew, were villages where Aramaic is still spoken today.

Around 1500, the Christians - now Franciscan Catholics - had returned and repossessed their former church. It was an unpretentious edifice: small, not more than twenty yards in length, and simple; three circular pairs of arches led to an apse at the far end. The walls were smooth and unadorned. In one corner was a small, vaulted chamber which was, at more than a thousand years old, the oldest part of the convent. Some of the plaster had fallen or been stripped off the wall, showing traces underneath of a faded fresco. Building materials filled the nave, and the only life was a family of cats. One of these, a kitten that looked too small to do anything more than suckle, was hungrily devouring a sparrow.

Outside was a typically Middle Eastern courtyard surrounding a marble fountain. Pillared arches supported two storeys of covered walkways around the perimeter. Was this Middle Eastern pattern, I wondered suddenly, a blueprint for the mediaeval cloister? Wooden beams of round, unworked poplar made the roof, and a series of eight-point stars decorated the walls.

Tibn blew about the yard from the pile in the corner. No bricks without straw; and mud-brick was an essential part of the restoration being lovingly carried out. The mud-brick, as an original material, was as important as the new slabs of fine marble waiting to be cut. Much of the brickwork followed the herring-bone layering that I'd seen all the way from the Jebel al-Alawiyiin to Hassan's yard.

I still hadn't filled my bucket for Madfaa. Aziz took me to where a small stone channel carried crystal clear water to the gardens.

"The Romans built this. The water comes off the mountains." He gestured behind him to the ridge, now levitating in the fog of the intense heat. It was hard to believe that anything wet could come from there. Or, indeed, remain wet on the journey here. Aziz quickly solved the second riddle.

"The main channel is fifteen feet down."

Now I understood. It was a *qanat*, a man-made underground stream. I'd spent many fruitless hours searching for them in Central Asia, where they had all long ago fallen in.

A real-life qanat, and still working! I was well pleased with my excursion to St. Yacoub's convent.

*

From below, the huddle of buildings on the hilltop looked more like a Moroccan *kasbah* than a Syrian village. No sign of life moved in or around it. Was it inhabited, or empty? If it was inhabited, I thought, I'd ask for a bucket of water, and half a bucket of tea. If it was empty, I'd take it over for the afternoon.

It was empty. And it was almost a kasbah. The greater part was a single complex of houses, stables and yards, presenting a blank face to the outside, and intruders. Nevertheless we intruded easily, for the gate swung readily on its hinges and most of the houses lacked doors. A large corral filled much of the interior, beside a smaller yard on to which fronted houses and barns alike, semi-derelict. Mud-brick formed the walls, their plaster fallen off here and there to show the familiar herring-bone style. The roofs were of brushwood supported by ancient beams, some fifteen inches thick and bleached as white as the surrounding desert. The accumulation of centuries of animal-dung caked the barn floors.

A smaller but similar complex was separated from the main one by the nearest thing to a street that the little settlement possessed. I offsaddled Madfaa and left him with a feed, then went on a tour of discovery. The smaller yard was in better repair than the first, its roofs and ceiling completely intact, thorn brush still embedded in the mud plaster. One completely separate block turned out to be a bakehouse, with a clay oven, and walls and ceiling all blackened with soot. In a barn I found treasure - a huge pile of tibn - and scrumped a bucketful for Madfaa.

A rough wooden ladder against the wall took me to the roof, where a single second-storey room stood out like an observation post. I looked across to where Madfaa was mooching in the first yard, tweaking the odd dried stalk, his barley finished; then on and up to the mountains, a line of pale brown mounds with which this deserted homestead was completely in harmony.

If it really was deserted; the tibn suggested otherwise. Although past ghosts whispered in the corners, the present was here too, somewhere. The owners might have shut the far gate behind them at exactly the moment I'd walked in the near one, the echo of their footsteps still hovering among the rustle of the leaves in the roofing twigs.

While I was away, Madfaa had done some exploring of his own. He had already searched the corral for anything edible, and been dis- appointed. I came back to find him emerging from one of the stables, having long since learned to associate "inside" with food. So I left him inside a barn where he could eat his stolen tibn as privily as possible.

A good thing too, for later that day a lad appeared from nowhere; one of the owners, come to check me out. The settlement was called Khayza, he told me. Its inhabitants had all moved away to the town. He pointed into the distance, in the direction of Qara.

It was probably only ever occupied for part of the year, for it was pretty exposed up on this ridge. Fried now, in late July, it must have been bleak in January. Nowadays, irrigation stitched a green thread of orange and fig trees across the valley below, and a couple of miles away beyond the line of electricity pylons tiny matchbox cars ran soundlessly along the road. But a hundred years ago there would have been nothing to see but the mountains and the desert, except perhaps for a brief splash of green in the wadi at a kindly time of year.

Way beyond the road, a flickering outline began to detach itself from the haze as the day wore on. The Jebel ash-Sharqiyya an-Nabk, the eastern mountain ridge that would squeeze my route between itself and the Anti-Lebanon, sucking me into the funnel that led down to Damascus.

*

"Let me answer your question like this," replied Hussein Nayf Bakr. "If you had two brothers, and one of them beat the other, what would you think of him?" Automatically he picked up the pot and made another circuit, filling each glass with black tea, syrupy with sugar.

All roads, in conversations about Arab politics, led to one of two ends: Palestine or Saddam Hussein. Or rather, one end with two faces. In hurling rhetoric and the odd scud missile towards Israel while funding Palestinian terrorist groups, the Iraqi megalomaniac had cleverly and effectively driven a wedge through the middle of the global Arab nation. In the one corner, those who deplored the destitution visited on his people by his home and foreign policies, and the brutal hand that maintained them; in the other, those who saw him thumb his nose at western imperialism and champion (even while admitting to themselves that it was largely with hot air, and so ill-directed as to scorch rather than warm) the Palestinian cause.

According to BBC World Service reports that I'd heard in the last few days, the current rapprochement between Israel and Turkey was causing some realignment within the Arab world. In particular, Damascus was moving cautiously in the direction of Baghdad. Recently the two governments, long-term bitter rivals under their parallel Ba'athist regimes, had been talking to each other again. Hussein Bakr was the man on the Jarajir omnibus. What, I asked, did he think of his namesake?

"The Syrian people love the Iraqi people. We are brothers," he went on. "But Saddam Hussein is a lunatic."

It was a relief to hear it. A few days ago I'd met an enthusiastic supporter of Saddam. Here, in Hussein's house in Jarajir, there was a bit of English spoken to add to my Arabic. It was a chance to canvas local opinion more thoroughly than usual. His guests warmed to the theme - is there an Arab in any country across the world who doesn't eagerly discuss politics, especially with a foreigner - and reminded me that Syria had sent a force to join the Allies in the Gulf in 1991.

"Were you afraid then that, if he went on to invade Saudi Arabia after Kuwait, sooner or later he would attack Syria also?"

"Well, think of Hitler," was the answer. "Saddam Hussein is like Hitler. Once you start gobbling up other countries, it can get to be a habit." I seemed to have heard this line once or twice before; we might have been in Westminster. Who had taken their cue from whom, I wondered? Was Downing Street plumbed in to al-Jazira, or did Hussein pick up CNN on his satellite dish? I shrugged and gave up. Perhaps they'd all gone to bed with a volume of Nostradamus.[7]

Now it was my turn to be grilled. "What do the English think about the Arabs? Do they believe that we're just a people who do nothing but make war?"

"Thirty years ago," I replied, "that might have been the attitude. Now, though, we have very good news reporting. People are much better informed. For example, we know exactly what's happening in the West Bank and Gaza. Western people, on the whole, have very great sympathy for the Palestinians, and deplore the way they are treated by the Israeli government."

The company, in its turn, relaxed. Perhaps we were all relieved to learn that, whatever the position of our respective governments, we, the ordinary people, could agree without too much difficulty. There was an easing of tension I hadn't realised was there, and conversation passed to lighter subjects.

"So you're going to Yabrud and Ma'alloula? The *Jebel ad-Din*?"

The Mountain of Faith. I'd known that the mountains south of here were strongly Christian; St Yacoub's Convent had been just an outrider.

"Did you know that we have a Christian holy man here? That the Lebanese revere a saint they call the Patriarch of Jarajir?"

"Did you know," somebody added, "that they still speak Assyrian in the Jebel ad-Din?"

*

A neighbour of Hussein's, a man riding a three-wheeled scooter, showed me the road to Yabrud. I was grateful, for Jarajir sat in a

---

[7] Michel de Nostradame, a sixteenth century mystic who predicted the rise of Hitler ("Hister") and Napoleon ("Napoleron") and foretold the coming of a third great Antichrist in Asia around the end of the twentieth century.

hollow that swallowed up all sense of direction, and its streets were a labyrinth.

I waved goodbye from the top of the hill, then drew rein and sat a little, transfixed by the mountains to the east. How was it, I wondered, that something so barren could be so beautiful? Shape, I decided; their beauty was a function of their graceful curves, their folds and cusps, picked out by the early morning sun as cosmetics highlight the contours of a beautiful face.

It was a good track, picking the easiest path through gently rolling hills. Even from the higher points I could never be sure what lay more than a quarter-mile ahead; when I came to a fork, the mountains and the sun guided my choice. Frequent watercourses scored the land. There were no bridges; the track would drop into them and wind up the other side. No doubt road maintenance was a regular task every spring.

We came over a saddle to the head of a wide valley. The road fell quite sharply into it, then led away into the distance in a gentle, inviting arc, a white streak across a brown landscape flecked with the grey-green of sage brush. To the right, a ridge swept down from the Anti-Lebanon, barring progress to all but goats. To the left an arête, curving parallel to the road beneath, rose to a conical summit. Distantly framed in the V between the two huddled the dark, angular outlines of a conurbation. Yabrud.

From now on we would be among the foothills of the mountains. New country; though not so new. The rocky outcrops that now bubbled up from the high ground were familiar. They heralded the start of country I had long wished to set my foot upon.

For twenty years, travelling between Damascus and the north, I had been fascinated by the ridge running alongside the road for fifteen miles or more. Above a smooth slope of scree ran an unbroken line of sheer sandstone, like foam topping a breaking wave. One day, I'd promised myself, I would go behind the ridge, climb it maybe, taste and feel the mountains, perhaps walk along the crest of that frozen wave. Until now there had always been another agenda, another destination, a plane to catch, no time. Now there was time.

As yet, the rock at the crest of each hill appeared as a tor, an isolated geological afterthought. Further south, the hills became more con-tinuous, the outcrops began to coalesce. By the time we neared Yabrud, I could see how the rock strata leaned gently from east to west, then broke off abruptly. To my left, long sandy slopes led up the offshore edge of the wave to a relatively dull horizon. To my right, the scarp rose sharply to the foot of yet another magnificent sandstone ridge.

A few straggling vines marked the approach to Yabrud's outlying villages. Underneath the luminous green dome of a mosque, a parked tractor reminded me that we were re-entering the modern world. Now we picked up an asphalt road again; but there was a smooth earthen track to the side of it, and only another mile or so into Yabrud.

One hundred thousand years of human settlement, they say of Yabrud. Looking at the cliffs above the town, I could see why - and where. The rockface was densely pitted with holes burrowed into the soft sandstone. Huge boulders balanced precariously on the scree slopes, many of them hanging above areas of dense housing. Whether they would stay put for the next hundred minutes, or the next hundred years, or the next hundred centuries, was anybody's guess.

Massive stones might have been the theme of Yabrud. The cathedral sat on them - cubes, this time, hewn by Roman masons who built a temple to Jupiter. The first Christian Emperor, Constantine, took their work over for Christianity, and to this day it remains the preserve of Greek Catholics.

They have filled it with icons, illuminated by the glass chandeliers which seem to light all Asiatic churches. A row of paintings marched across the top of the iconostasis, and a procession of saints clustered about the pulpit to lend gravity to the preacher.

I reclaimed Madfaa from the attention of a kindly shopkeeper, and went to forage for our lunch. At a shop selling watermelons as big as footballs and tomatoes as big as watermelons, I bought an enormous cabbage for Madfaa and bananas, a melon and some Coke for myself. It was just past mid-day and the heat was blistering. It was forty in Damascus, said the greengrocer as he put a bucket of water under Madfaa's nose. And forty-six in Palmyra, he added as an afterthought.

Outside on the street, people sat out the heat of the day under awnings, drinking mâté. Here, it was to be expected. The majority of the considerable Syrian diaspora in South America hailed from Yabrud and its surroundings. The town had even provided an Argentinian President, for the family of Carlos Menem emigrated from here.

Just outside the town I found the tombs of the Romans who had worshipped Jupiter in his temple at Yabrud before Constantine had so

radically moved the ecclesiastical goalposts. They were not very special; unpretentious caverns with two or three chambers to a tomb, long
emptied by animal or archaeological scavengers. The privilege of burial
here lay in the surroundings: those spectacular cliffs, their creamy
orange sandstone fretted by millennia of weather and freckled with tens
of thousands of years of human history.

They narrowed to a gorge, then briefly spread out enough to allow
cultivation. Even here there was tibn; I begged a bagful for Madfaa,
then tied up under a stand of pine trees to sit out the worst of the heat.

As we made our way slowly southward in the cool of the evening, I
accomplished what I had desired for so many years: the exploration of
the other side of that tremendous crested ridge that follows the main
road all the way down to Damascus. With the same eastward list in the
strata as before Yabrud, the layer of sandstone sloped gently towards
the top. Bleak rock, the bare bones of the earth, dusted here and there
with sand and seamed with wadis, it ran up to a peak which, far from
the flat table I had long visualised, was discontinuous, cracked and
broken by erosion and the constant fidget of the earth's mantle below it.
So much for my aspirations to walk along it. You'd need wings; or to
be a very good longjumper.

To the right, meanwhile, were the mountains of the Anti-Lebanon,
those mountains which I had grown to love so much while they had
been keeping me company and guiding my steps over the last week.
They were drawing away, now; across about five miles of open desert
rose first the foothills, then the main ridge itself. Lest the colour of the
landscape become too uniform, dark green blobs of orange orchard
broke the pattern, under a china-blue sky dotted with brilliant white
splashes of cloud. No wonder that so many religious foundations chose
to settle themselves here. There could be few better places to
contemplate the glory of Creation.

I passed an army barracks, where bored young soldiers whiled away
their off-duty hours in a swimming pool hard by the road. "Come and
join us!" they called. Hot and sticky, I was sorely tempted; but it could
have been a bit complicated, and discretion got the better part of valour.
Besides, time was getting on, and I was starting to wonder if we'd
make it to Ma'aloula before dark.

It was a stroke of pure luck that nightfall caught up with us on the road. Otherwise I might have bypassed Sarha with never a guess at the secret it bore.

As it was, I stopped in the village and, using a tactic that had proved useful before, asked at the village shop about somewhere to stay. Heads were scratched, then shaken; a crowd gathered, and Madfaa began to feel harassed. I was about to remount and move on, when Wahidi arrived to claim us.

*

I should, strictly speaking, write "Wahida", as that was how her name was spelt. But Syrian dialect gives an upward inflexion to the feminine ending, and it was as Wahidi that I knew her.

There was something of Anne Boleyn about Wahidi. Perhaps the black coif (worn in respect for a recently deceased brother-in-law), with its edging of gold beads, put me in mind of the jewelled head-dress of the famous painting. Or perhaps it was something in her eyes, a worldly-wise and faintly cynical expression; although there was nothing there of sexual awareness. She was about thirty, older than your average unmarried daughter. Looking at her lithe, slender figure and intelligent features, I was surprised that no-one had claimed her thus far.

To my discomfort, she read my thought.

"Syrian men don't like skinny women."

She regarded me with a quizzical detachment, her thin, mobile face twitching with amusement, the corners of her mouth curving upwards with quirky irony. She had good reason to be amused at my antics.

By now trembling with exhaustion, I was quite inarticulate. As I bumbled my way through introductions and explanations, I must have seemed like a babbling idiot. And I couldn't even feed myself properly.

After all my practice with the flat Arab loaves, used at table as a scoop, a spoon, a mop and whatever else you need to minimise the cutlery, I was usually fairly dexterous in my eating habits. Tonight, every attempt at eating ended in slop on the communal tray, or slop down my own clothing. After watching me for some minutes in silent embarrassment, someone quietly and tactfully handed me a spoon, as though I were an infant. No wonder that subsequently, when I rose to go to the privy, members of the family courteously escorted me, waited for me and led me back to the house, as though I were not safe to cross the yard without getting lost. It must have been a source of great bewilderment to all that I had somehow found my way all round Syria, without taking a wrong turn and ending up in Baghdad.

I also failed to close the padlock correctly on Madfaa's door, an omission which was disapprovingly corrected by Umm Khalid, Wahidi's mother. Again, I wasn't allowed near the stable without an escort. This was a bit awkward.

The basement of a neighbour's house, it was the biggest and most pleasant stable Madfaa had yet occupied. There was no window, and the only light came from the open door. But it was roomy, and a thick litter covered the floor. Outside, it was almost dark. Madfaa would be comfortable here for the night, as long as I got him out of here quickly in the morning when daylight made him aware of his own darkness within.

But, as I led him in, Umm Khalid gestured to the ring in the manger. Even where there was no possibility of escape, no competition with other animals, it was, it seemed, *de rigueur* that an animal should be tethered. After my experiences with the harpy, I knew that to leave him loose would cause surprise, consternation even, complicated by my inability to explain properly in Arabic. And here, I seemed to be having more difficulty than usual in understanding anybody. So I obediently knotted the lead rope - for now.

Later, returning on the excuse of giving Madfaa an extra feed, I groped my way across the stable in complete darkness with my bucket of tibn while the old lady stood at the door. Furtively slipping the headcollar off, I got out again just in time to stall Wahidi, who had considerately fetched a cigarette lighter to help me see, from coming inside and finding me out. Better to keep the situation under wraps. That way, everyone was happy; most importantly, Madfaa.

Over supper, my communication difficulties continued. I could follow Wahidi a little - as much as I could anyone - when she spoke to me directly, but I couldn't pick up a word of family conversation. Suddenly, I realised why.

Ma'alloula is famous as the place where Aramaic, the ancient lan-guage of the Middle East which is the parent of both Arabic and

Hebrew, is still spoken. And Ma'alloula was only a few miles up the road. Excitedly, I turned to Wahidi.

"Do your family speak Aramaic?"

"No," she answered. "We speak Assyrian. We *are* Assyrian."

*

Had I been travelling these parts a little under three thousand years ago, I should not have willingly gone home with an Assyrian. The very word was synonymous with violence and destruction.

It was in 745 BC, after half a millennium of false starts, that the men of Assur erupted from their city on the upper Tigris to overrun Mesopotamia and the Levant, devouring in the process the mighty Babylon, the seaboard city-states of the Phoenicians, the kingdom of their inland cousins the Aramaeans and the small, fragile kingdom of Israel, and compelling even the Egyptian Pharaoh to pay tribute. Around 700 BC they moved their capital to Nineveh, which became the symbol of arrogance and oppression to her subject nations.

"The well-favoured harlot, the mistress of witchcrafts, that selleth nations through her whoredoms, and families through her witchcraft..." thus fulminated the prophet Nahum against Nineveh, while Sennacherib rampaged throughout the Levant. But the city was to predominate for less than a century before Medes and Scythians joined a Chaldean-led insurgency from Babylon, and reduced Nineveh to ashes. An exiled government ruled a rump state from Harran in southern Turkey for three more years before being finally overrun. Their end was just as Nahum had foretold: "Thy people is scattered upon the mountains, and no man gathereth them."

But he did not have the last word. Safe in their mountain retreats from Mesopotamia's latest superpower, a new-born Babylon, the Assyrians maintained their identity with the extraordinary tenacity that characterises so many Asiatic clans. They spread through the mountains from northern Mesopotamia into Syria, embracing Christianity somewhere along the way. Periodically repressed both on their own account and by geographical or religious association with persecuted groups, they lost an estimated 90,000 in the Turkish massacres of Armenian Christians less than a century ago. Today only a small handful of scattered communities survive, mostly in the north of Syria and Iraq. I hadn't expected to meet them here; but, given the cultural and ethnic diversity of the Levant's coastal mountains, I should have been ready for any surprise.

*

That night, there was a wedding in Sarha. It was celebrated with very loud music, which seemed to consist of one phrase played over and over again. This was joined at intervals by rifle shots and bursts of automatic fire, which made it sound as if a coup were in progress; as if Sennacherib was reborn and had come to claim his empire. In the morning the only sound was that of a single flute, piping a wistful melody that made the hillside echo to Arcadian rhythms.

I rescued Madfaa from his dungeon and tethered him in the garden. When he was settled, Wahidi and her brothers Fatoum, Ahmed and Mohammed took me to visit Sarha's Church of St. Andrew.

From outside, it looked like a plain village house, with not so much as a cross to identify it. "There are no Christians in Sarha," explained Wahidi. "People come from Ma'alloula every so often to hold services."

Inside, a few rather gaudy icons cheered up what was essentially a very simple building. The altar, in a separate room at the back which you approached through an archway, was a flat slab of limestone rest-ing on four concrete pillars. The ceiling was plain wood laid across naked beams, from which dangled a single glass chandelier.

On the way back I noticed the mosque, which I'd failed to spot on the way up the hill.

"How long has this village been Muslim?" I had thought that all Assyrians were Christian.

"About six or seven hundred years."

That meant, from just about the time that Arabic had become fully established as the dominant language, almost totally eliminating Ara-maic from Syria. It suggested an answer to another question that I lacked the vocabulary to ask. Why had Wahidi stressed that her language was Assyrian? Hadn't her ancestors, adopting the *lingua franca* of their conquered territories to replace their own Akkadian-related speech, themselves used Aramaic and spread it throughout their dominions, contributing to its preservation for nearly three millennia?

Were not, therefore, the Assyrian language of Sarha and the Aramaic of nearby Ma'alloula one and the same?

Perhaps they had been − seven centuries ago. Maybe the Aramaic of Sarha, of the few Muslim Assyrians, had evolved and changed a little, while that of the Christians, enshrined in liturgy and scholarship, had remained static. I suppose a language may be allowed to generate a slight variety in dialects over three thousand years, or even seven hundred.

You could see how easily it could have happened that way. At home, I began to realise, the family slipped bilingually between Arabic and Assyrian; although, strain as I might, I couldn't always tell which they were currently using. To be fair, it wasn't just my limitations. Aramaic or Assyrian, their language was very close to modern Arabic.

I asked Wahidi's father, Abu Khalid, to allow me to record him on my dictaphone. He agreed with enjoyment, making a speech in a wonderfully clear and sonorous voice, and saying how pleased he was that, in making my journey round Syria, I had come to stay with him.

*

If I'd known how close I was to Ma'alloula, I might never have discovered Sarha's hidden treasure. We had covered barely a couple of miles when the road took us to the summit of the ridge, then pitched us down a fissure which opened in the mountain to swallow us.

It was suddenly very dark, and deliciously cool. It was also very slippery. Madfaa's shoes were becoming very worn; the "chairs" had long since worn away. The descent was hairy, and I dismounted to coax him one careful step at a time down between two long pillars of pink sandstone. It was a relief when the crack widened out again, the gradient eased, and Ma'alloula spread itself before us.

The village dangled precariously from the rockface. Houses climbed up the mountain at a crazy angle, one man's basement resting on his neighbour's roof, right up to the foot of a vertical cliff. Further down the valley where the cliff ended abruptly, great rocks were lodged high above the town on patches of scree, as at Yabrud; any one of them could wipe out a dozen houses, were it to break loose and tumble down the hillside. You had to admire the faith of the people of Ma'alloula, who could build their houses under such a threat.

"They've been there for a thousand years," said Umm Sabir. "They'll last a bit longer."

I certainly hoped so; for her house, where I pitched camp, was right underneath them.

*

We stayed in her orchard, with Madfaa attached to an orange tree while I bivvied alongside. Here for once there was proper grass for him to pick at, instead of the dried stalks which were all that he normally found along the way. But it wasn't the most restful place for him. Several horses were kept nearby but not close enough for company, which accentuated his loneliness. And he had time and energy to think about them, for he was fit and corned up, but we had done only short stages in the last few days.

He burned off quite a bit of that energy in the night, walking round and round on his tether and flattening the irrigation channels that watered his part of the orchard.

"I'm sorry," I said in the morning to Umm Sabir.

"Don't worry," she said airily. "They're not mine. The orchard belongs to my neighbour." She had billeted us there without asking him, she added, for he was away in Damascus. I hoped he wasn't due back just yet.

Ten or twelve churches served Ma'alloula, she told me; rather fewer than the forty-odd that are sometimes claimed. I set out to visit the highest one, which gave me an excuse to plunge into the deep thicket of houses clinging to the hillside.

I'd wondered how on earth you went among houses woven into each other so tightly that you could see no passage between them. Very often the answer was, you didn't; you went under them instead. Up and up; through a tunnel, up a stairway, through another tunnel. I stooped under beams grey with age to emerge suddenly into blinding light; passed doorways framed with marble which was surely recycled from earlier building; peered down miniature alleys at front doors leading to what could barely be more than hobbit-holes. Twisting and turning, I would have lost all sense of direction, but for the insistent, magnetic pull of "upwards". When I finally arrived at the end of the road, it wasn't somebody's back garden, but a hundred feet of sheer rockface.

The church I was seeking had entirely disappeared, and I gave up trying.

The chapel of St. Thekla, Ma'alloula's patron saint, was easier to reach, lying at the foot of a gorge musical with the sound of running water. Water defined Ma'alloula. Water had chiselled out the dramatic gorge which, in turn, imparted to the settlement below a mystique, a sense of awe that had stepped easily over the narrow dividing line into sanctity. Now that water was diverted from far up the hillside into a number of streams. Wherever you looked, little channels barely a foot wide ran with water so crystal clear that you were tempted to drink it; until you remembered the piles of rubbish you'd seen lying beside it elsewhere.

The gorge itself was a smaller edition of Petra's famous *siq*. Writhing back and forth through echoing sandstone cliffs, it was honeycombed with caves and tombs cut high into the rock, some bearing the remains of stairways. As I climbed slowly on bare rock - there was little here to resemble a path - I passed sweeping, undercut caverns hewn by centuries of floodwater. High on the cliff were the remains of the aqueduct which had once lifted the stream from its bed. Now the water ran unconstrained through its original path, here neither concreted nor piped - nor filled with rubbish.

At the top I came back into daylight via an archway leading to a grove of willows and poplars. Away to my left I could see the monastery of Mar Sarkis; but not very clearly, for there was an impediment to the view.

For fourteen centuries Mar Sarkis has perched in splendid isolation on its crag above the village, allowing solitude and silence to focus the monks' devotion and reflecting the elevated nature of their calling. No longer so.

A garish new hotel towers over the self-effacing, plain cube of the monastery. How arrogant is man, to think that by depositing an intrusive building hard by the object of his interest he can not only facilitate his own enjoyment of it, but somehow enhance it by his own proximity. What a limitless capacity we have to destroy beauty. And how privileged I was, in that I had come here many years ago and seen the monastery before it was spoiled.

Not that the hoteliers were the first to take up residence outside the monastery. The hillside all about was scarred with caves: Roman tombs, anchorites' dwellings … present-day incumbents. For people still lived in these caves. Some were barred with heavy iron doors; one, high up the cliff-face, was reached by a twenty-foot ladder. Another was a stable, where a tiny donkey stood on a thick litter made from decades of droppings mixed with tibn. Against this continuation of unimaginably ancient occupation Mar Sarkis itself, you had to admit, was a modern intrusion.

*

The heavy old door was of wood, with brass hinges. It couldn't have been more than five feet high, and I had to stoop low to step inside. At once I was fielded by Father Michael, who greets all visitors to the monastery – "two hundred thousand of them every year," he said, "and that's not counting the local people."

He handed me sweet, local wine in a small metal cup like a tiny chalice. Thus the monks of the Basilian Salvatorian Order of Greek Catholics welcome all visitors to their monastery of Mar Sarkis. The ritual welcome performed, I was able to wander freely about the church.

It is one of the oldest in the Middle East, dating from the time of Constantine and built on a foundation of heavy Roman blocks. Two further features mark it as exceptional.

The first is the form of its altars. Behind a gorgeously decorated iconostasis, the main altar was semi-circular and hollow, with a lip around the edge: the form of a pagan altar shaped to collect the blood of the sacrificial victim. The style, with its echoes of an older faith, is unique to Mar Sarkis. It was repeated in the altar of the side chapel dedicated to the Virgin Mary. Square, this time, and resting on a curious plinth of tapering cylinders, its indented surface looked even older and more worn than the first. It bore a cross of wood inlaid with pearl, the hallmark of Damascus work. A dome-shaped canopy hovered above, painted deep blue with golden stars and resting on pink marble columns; heaven and earth represented in miniature for human comprehension.

The second glory of Mar Sarkis lies in its icons. Faded icons from the thirteenth century, icons of the sixteen-hundreds donated from Poland, icons whose still-brilliant colours were painted as recently as

1813... One paid its compliments to the monastery's other distinction: the Last Supper, whose feast is laid on a semi-circular table following the pattern of the main altar. And here was the Icon of the Passion, painted around 1300 AD, just as the last of the Crusaders were being violently ejected from Syrian territory not so many miles from here.

Before I left I bought a cassette tape ("We have it in twenty languages, including Finnish, Armenian and Czech," said Father Michael with justifiable pride). It told the story of Ma'alloula and its saints, and bore the Lord's Prayer in Aramaic... the language in which Christ first delivered it.

*

The contemporary icons in Ma'alloula's central café showed a prudent Respect of Persons. President Assad occupied the central position of honour, while Christ and the Virgin Mary hovered deferentially to either side, and lower down.

I bought a huge bottle of Coke and carried it back triumphantly to Madfaa in his shady garden. Irrigating myself inside and out, I went back again and again between long, cool swigs from my bottle to the channels of water which splashed through the orchard. I washed my clothes, and then myself, and then some more clothes, and then my hair. I couldn't keep away from the enticing, cool water; when I ran out of excuses I went and sat with my feet in it for about twenty minutes until they ached with the cold.

At a height of five thousand feet, Ma'alloula is famous for its cool, clear air. Today's air was neither; the temperature was around forty, and a pall of haze hung over the town. It wasn't conducive to going anywhere in a hurry.

I wasn't going anywhere in a hurry. There remained only one item on my itinerary.

*

At Ma'alloula I'd crossed the main escarpment, and was now riding south directly underneath the sandstone ridge. From here, it was more striking than ever: a series of flattish tops, scarred by small gullies and split by deeper ones, growing out of the smooth yellow scree slope like an endless jawbone bearing well-worn, heavily discoloured teeth in a long-buried skull.

Madfaa and I covered eighteen kilometres that day, heading towards Sednaya. There followed a horrible night. I bought tibn and barley in a village, but couldn't find anywhere to stay. Too exhausted to go further, I took refuge on a deserted building site – plenty of these in the mountains, so close now to Damascus – hiding Madfaa and myself in the back yard.

Too late, I realised that we were just across the road from a chicken processing plant. The stench of rotting carcasses swirled about us all night long like a malevolent fog. I slept with an open deodorant bottle under my nose, vainly trying to blot out the smell. Madfaa didn't even have that degree of relief, and was miserable. I'd thought I had plenty of food for him; but he ate up very early, then crunched around on the building rubble all night. Although I'd very carefully cleared all the loose stone from his patch so that he could lie down, he didn't rest at all.

In the morning his tether rope was barely intact, frayed by constant chafing against the square concrete pillar to which he was tied. I knotted the weak patch and made a mental note to avoid that happening again; though I had no intention of spending another such night. The rising sun lifted the smell of dead chicken to a new intensity, and a million flies vied for my breakfast. I had to wave every piece of food like a manic conductor hurling his baton about, to get it into my mouth without adding to the ration.

From here on, the road was more heavily built up. As each new settlement appeared I berated myself. Could that place ahead be somewhere comfortable where we might have slept the past night if I'd only plodded on a bit further? The answer was always, no. This one was another chicken factory, that one a huge army camp, the other a chicken factory again. You could always tell the chicken factories well in advance by the stench. This area seemed to be Syria's centre for packing chickens. I might have thought of it as Sun Valley, if I hadn't been halfway up a mountain.

It was another eleven kilometres to Sednaya, and not one of them offered a better alternative to my building site. I had forgiven myself by the time the town rose on its hill, and the convent came into sight.

It is one of the two retreats for which Sednaya is famous. The other houses zealots of a different type of faith, held forcibly behind closed doors to reflect on their heresies, unwilling postulants to a secular cloth; for Sednaya Prison is the ultimate sink into which dissidents of all colours disappear. But then, life isn't all that comfortable at the convent itself.

For centuries it has been disputed, its possession tossed back and forth between Greek Orthodox monks and Greek Catholic nuns. These Christians do not love one another. Fighting with words, they exchange insult and propaganda. Presumably it has been so ever since the Catholics evicted the Orthodox in the mid-eighteenth century. Certainly the war was in full swing fifty years ago when Fedden observed it, mentioning in passing that the male protagonist in the convent was "an unsavoury character who goes by the title - a little startling for one who moves among female votaries - of *le procureur*."

From the bottom of the hill, nothing much in Sednaya was appealing. With masses of new apartment blocks under construction, it looked like one large building site. Brown grass covered the few bits of land that weren't under concrete; desiccated stalks that might have spent centuries withering to less substance than dandelion seeds. Those empty shells of houses might have been falling down, rather than going up; in the throes of death rather than the pangs of birth. It looked, to my jaded eye, as if the mountainside had been used as a nuclear test site.

The most depressing thing, though, was the hill itself.

Mentally and physically, I'd just about shot my bolt by the time we reached its foot. It was lucky that Madfaa had strength enough for both of us. I took it very slowly, stopping frequently so that he could rest, appeasing his hunger on those unappetising wisps of blasted vegetation. As the convent took shape above us, it seemed to grow higher and higher. I could hardly think how I was going to climb its final crag on my own.

At the top of the hill we entered the real Sednaya, the old village at the heart of the mushrooming new town. It was as attractive, and as busy, as the outskirts had been ugly and inanimate. The enormous number of churches was out of all proportion to its size. Big, opulent churches crowned with splendid, three-dimensional crosses, little caves in the rock identifiable only by a symbol painted on the wall, and all sorts and conditions in between.

"Nearly everyone here is Christian. It's only ten per cent Muslim," said the friendly shopkeeper who refreshed Madfaa with two buckets of water, and me with a couple of glasses of ice-cold water from his fridge. It went down a treat with both of us, and nerved me for the final assault on the convent itself.

Just as well, for the prospect was daunting. The first of four storeys grew out of a forty-foot crag over the front entrance. A set of very worn stone steps climbing the crag were reserved for the faithful, while new paved ones had been built for the tourists who come here by the coach-load. I tied Madfaa to the rails at the bottom and climbed slowly, stopping at the corner of each zig-zag to gather my breath, using the pause to watch the little stallion for a few minutes and check that he was standing quietly.

Once inside the main doorway I found a maze of passages and steps, with a succession of little courtyards on different levels; like an Escher drawing, or a tiny Ma'alloula in marble and limestone. Self-effacing nuns flitted about the corridors, going about their daily tasks, bearing trays of coffee or piles of laundry. The interior of the church was more gorgeous than the most ornate Roman Catholic cathedral.

In common with eastern fashion it was domed, not arched, the central dome painted sky blue and covered with stars. The intricately carved wooden panels beneath were almost completely covered by icons: icons more magnificent than any I had yet seen, their brilliantly fresh colours framed by panels of gold. Golden belts encircled the angels' robes, golden bracelets hung from the Virgin's wrists, every saint bore a halo of finely-beaten gold plate. But in this house also were many mansions, and among the celestial beings there was room for the earthly faithful. In the four corners of the church pious men sat at their desks, a benevolent angel or a tempting demon hovering at their shoulders.

Devout ladies moved along the iconostasis, touching each painting in turn and then crossing themselves. A curtain shut off the altar, overlooked by the Last Supper. Near it was the Holy of Holies: the shrine of the Virgin Mary, patroness of the convent, worker of miracles. The mundane was represented by a washbasin and tap in one dark corner, and a big, heavy fuse box in another.

I climbed another flight of stairs to the highest point of the convent, just below the belltower. Peering over the roof I could see Madfaa, some eighty feet below, and reassure myself that he was OK. As I began to descend, the clock struck the hour with an unexpectedly feeble, tinny sound. Eleven strokes. The eleventh hour of our journey.

Now, nothing remained but to get ourselves back to Damascus.

*

There were no more chicken farms on the Damascus road. Instead, a dreary succession of restaurants lined the highway, a monoculture relieved only once by a rather garish new monastery. At least I now knew who was eating all those chickens.

I bought a big watermelon to share with Madfaa for one last lunch on the road. Nowhere, though, could I find anywhere to lie up out of the sun. The temperature seemed to climb with every mile, and the dryness of the atmosphere was unlike anything I'd known before, even in Central Asia. Though it was, I reminded myself, the end of July. A bloody silly time of year to be doing something like this, I swore savagely into my dictaphone.

After several miles I found a fig tree, hard by the entrance to an army barrack. I'd hoped to hide under it unnoticed, for by now I was beyond any attempt at socialising in any language, and just wanted to spend a few hours comatose. But Madfaa needed water, so I summoned my reserves to chat up the soldiers at the gate and beg a bucketful.

It was a mistake. A couple of minutes later a kindly young officer emerged, bearing tea, conversation and a very reasonable curiosity as to who I was and what I was doing. But, exhausted and desperate for solitude, I couldn't face company; while my scrambled brain could hardly at that moment have delivered a few coherent words of English, let alone Arabic. With unforgiveable - and, no doubt, to him, inexplicable - discourtesy, I gathered up my half-eaten watermelon, flung the saddlebags over Madfaa's back, and fled.

Half a mile down the road I found a small olive tree and tied up under its sparse shade. A large slice of melon and a litre and a half of Coke went some way to stiffen my sinews and patch a few holes in my resolve. But after weeks of travelling I was mentally, physically and emotionally threadbare.

I watched Madfaa slurping happily in an inch of watermelon juice as he chased the last few seeds around the bottom of the bucket. A good thing he had enough grit to see us both through the last couple of days.

*

For the second and last time we passed through the sandstone ridge. It had been creeping up unnoticed from the east; now a great cleft opened up, as a gap in the teeth and a crack in the jawbone itself. The road poured itself over and down like a waterfall. Littered like boulders stemming the flow were the first houses of Mnine; caves pockmarked the cliffs above. Had the village grown up in this rather cramped, uncomfortable spot out of a need for someone to guard the pass?

Madfaa's shoes were now worn as flat as skis. I dismounted to make it easier for him as he slipped and slithered. Across the road at the bottom was the only thing I ever saw to slow a Syrian driver down: a speed ramp. It was a strange thing to see in a main road; but needful, for now the road plunged through another gap in a second, lower ridge which had been hiding beneath the first, and at this second step of the staircase the gradient was even steeper.

As we emerged from the gorge I craned for a sight of Damascus. But rolling hills obscured the road, which continued to descend gently. For the third time in eight kilometres or so, a sign placed Damascus at a steady twenty kilometres ahead. Was it running away from me as fast as I approached?

Mnine ran seamlessly into the town of at-Tall. As the houses climbed to several storeys and shops enveloped the street, I felt myself already in a suburb of the capital. A stream had joined the road in its course down the valley; from time to time I glimpsed it across an open space, a thread of coolness and moisture from the mountains that was yet strong enough to nurse gardens and orchards along its banks.

Just beyond at-Tall was a village sitting high on the hillside. It was now getting towards sunset; here was my last chance to find somewhere Madfaa and I could spend the night. A store selling vege-tables looked a likely place to enquire, and I began by asking where I might buy bran, barley and tibn before putting the burning question. As I'd hoped, the shopkeeper knew somewhere for us to stay.

He was just shutting up shop, and when he'd finished he led us in his truck by a long, rambling road up the hill. At the very top lived Abid.

The shopkeeper had chosen well. Abid kept a horse to work his farm, and a row of stabling ran along the bottom storey of his big house. He was unfazed to have a dirty, exhausted pair of guests unexpectedly thrust upon him, and welcomed us with wide open arms. Better still, Abid's horse was a mare, so that for the first time in weeks Madfaa had congenial company. He expressed his delight noisily; but his furious stamping and trumpeting ended abruptly when Abid placed a great pile of tibn and barley under his nose.

I asked to sleep alongside him in the stableyard. Fayiz' yard was on the opposite side of Damascus from here, and for safety's sake I wanted to be through the city centre before the traffic built up. I intended to be up at an ungodly hour the next morning, and didn't want to wake the house.

But Abid wouldn't hear of it. With hearty goodwill he carried me inside, wisely sent me to the bathroom and then introduced me to the family.

Abid's father was known as Hajji, which meant that he had made the pilgrimage to Mecca. His mother was a lady of large proportions and an uncompromising countenance. She received me warmly, sitting in state on a step in the courtyard with her feet apart, her hands firmly on her knees and her shoulders aggressively squared, like an earth goddess or a tribal chieftain sitting in judgement. A lovely old grandmother was as sweet and delicate as the mother was formidable. She questioned me intently about my travels, with a deep courtesy tempering her gentle amusement at my stumbling Arabic and my story of whimsical ramblings round Syria.

Abid's family had a telephone, a luxury uncommon among the people with whom I'd been staying. At last I had a chance to phone Basil, and let him know of the continuing safety and imminent return of his horse. It was a brief conversation, for people were arriving. Once again, I had unintentionally gatecrashed a party.

What luck, to join a celebration here at the end of my journey. But I fear I was a dull guest, for exhaustion numbed my brain and turned my legs to jelly. I excused myself early and went to bed, making the family promise that they would not get up at my horribly early departure.

It was a hard thing to ask of Syrian hospitality. But I managed to convey how embarrassed I would be to cause such disruption; and was grateful that they allowed me to have my way.

*

I left at five in the morning, slipping out without waking anybody and parting a reluctant Madfaa from his lady friend.

"Don't worry," I said as I put his saddle on for the last time. "In a few hours you'll be back with all your old mates."

We minced carefully down the steep and slippery hill, and joined the terrifying Damascus Highway. It wasn't light yet, and the headlights that Madfaa so hated were still raking the darkness. Plenty of them; if I'd thought to have the roads to myself at this hour, I was cruelly disappointed. Cars roared down at breakneck speed, their drivers all racing to get into work and finish their day early, before the heat built up to unsustainable levels.

I'd chosen my stopping place well, for it was in fact the very last one possible. Immediately the road entered a gorge dropping over the northern shoulder of Mount Kassioun, the crumbling sandy ridge that forms Damascus' north-west boundary. As the gorge widened out it began to accommodate the first houses of the Salhiyeh suburb that climbs up the mountain. With rapidly increasing density, they swallowed the road and blocked out sight of all but the couple of hundred yards of road straight ahead. Unlike the Prophet Mohammed, who stood here long ago dazzled by the vision of an earthly Paradise, I was to have no sudden, breathtaking view of the city I had striven for so long to reach. I felt cheated, robbed of a small moment of triumph.

Nor was there any chance to take my bearings and look for a quiet route through. So we came into the city with the commuters; taking the high road, following the road signals, waiting at traffic lights and dodging the cars. It was desperately slow progress. For there was no longer any hard shoulder for Madfaa, and he had to brave the tarmac on shoes which were dangerously smooth.

At first I used the pavements. They were very high off the road, with a twelve-inch step down the kerb which Madfaa baulked at, stepping down gingerly whenever we had to cross the road. At one of these hazards he almost fell, banging his hind foot and limping for a moment or two. After this I decided that the traffic was the lesser of two evils, and stuck to the tarmac.

We followed the main road all the way past the great sports stadium and nearly to the centre. By now, although it was barely six, it might have been mid-day for the volume of traffic. It lent weight to the resolve that had been growing in me since this morning: that I would go straight through the middle of the Old Quarter. That would be much easier than trying to navigate around it, for it was the part of Damascus that I knew best. More, it would give us both some respite from the traffic.

I followed my instincts and turned down a side street. It led me straight past the end of the Saddlers' Souk to the Bab al-Faraj. The Gate of Deliverance; aptly named, I thought with relief, as I led Madfaa away from the hooting, roaring cars.

President Assad smiled down on us from strips of bunting as we passed under the old gateway with its massive bronze doors, through the short, dark tunnel and into the blissful silence of Old Damascus. Here, at least, my judgement was good, for most of the shops still had their shutters down and few people stirred. We frightened one or two well-wrapped ladies, their headscarves blotting out the sound of approaching hoofsteps. But by and large the streets were quiet and the going easy.

Left, then right, left, then right, taking a diagonal path through the grid... Retracing some of the steps of my earlier route, we passed close to Saladin's tomb and reached the Great Mosque at the corner of its main entrance, by the Roman columns. Here we picked up the end of the Souk Hamidiyeh; left, right and left again, ducking under the canopies of vines that drape the road past the long side of the Mosque.

Now I made a bad choice, turning right again up a hill. The road here was like glass. Poor Madfaa slipped and fell to his knees. He scrambled to his feet shaken, though unhurt. But it was the last straw.

Something had to be done about his mobility. I tied up and rummaged in my Useful Bag for anything that might help.

The first thing I found was baling twine. I tried tying it round his shoes, wedging it under the loosened heels, to give him some grip. Then I saw a piece of sacking lying in the gutter, and had a better idea. I was trying to put it into practice when a friendly shopkeeper threw up his shutters, prepared to open his haberdashery store, and saw me struggling.

Wonderful man; he came to the rescue with two large pieces of strong canvas. Together we made pads for Madfaa's hind feet. Wrapped like poultice boots and tied around the pasterns with baling twine, they gave enough friction for the little horse to continue safely.

Now the going got easier. Left again, for the last time. A Roman arch at the junction told me that we had reached the main street of the old Roman layout, the *via recta*: the Biblical "Street called Straight", where the blind St. Paul lodged in the house of Ananias. From here down to Bab Sharqi, the East Gate, is the Christian Quarter. The Greek Orthodox Church of the Virgin Mary was the first of several churches, among them chapels to Ananias and to St. Paul; the latter commemorates the spot where the Apostle was lowered from the walls in a basket to escape his pursuers.

In this quiet corner are some fine old Damascus houses. Most of those I passed were still closed up at this hour, turning blind walls to the road and hiding behind solid iron doors furnished only with a brass hand-and-ball door-knocker and a heavy padlock. But I had wasted more time than I realised over Madfaa's boots, and people were beginning to come and go. Wherever I chanced to see through an open door, it was to look on an essentially uniform pattern. A quadrangle of housing, surrounding a courtyard shaded with vines and planted with flowers; and always in the centre a fountain, celebrating the water that is more than just the theme of Damascus: it is the life-blood of the vast oasis, the city's *raison d'être*.

After less than half a mile we arrived at Bab Sharqi, the biggest of the city gates. The roar of traffic warned me that we had to leave the safety of the Old Quarter and launch ourselves on to the busiest street yet. And it was late, far too late; already nine o'clock, with the rush hour at its height.

The other side of Damascus: the home straight.

*

Along the city walls, hugging the pavement, under the square tower of St. Paul's Chapel, to the terrifying roundabout where the airport road branches south along a six-lane highway. Our road.

I can't remember how we made it across the roundabout; only that somehow we reached the other side unscathed. But Madfaa was slipping again. The boots had worn right through.

Again I searched my baggage for inspiration. All my kit, at this stage, was expendable. Perhaps I could cut up a shirt to make another pair. I looked in my washing bag, and found something better.

I wouldn't need those socks again. Anyway, the thought of washing them revolted me; they'd been worn far too long already. Madfaa had more need of them than I had. Secured with red sticky tape over his hind feet, they made him look really rather dashing. A pity it was an odd pair; but you can't win 'em all.

It wasn't the last problem, for I was stopped by police just short of the Babileh turning. The road was blocked off with cones, and cars were turning round to go back and find another way.

I didn't know another way. I pleaded with the policeman to let me pass; surely a horse could go where a car could not. I couldn't understand his reply, but he was adamant. In despair I turned about; so close, only to face another delay. And I simply had to get off this road. In another hour the traffic would be even heavier, even more dangerous. I cursed the traffic, the building heat, most of all I cursed myself. I shouldn't have a horse out on this road at all. I should have started by night, and been through the city by dawn.

Seeing my desperation, the policeman called me back, motioning me to wait. I sat beside Madfaa in the road for ten minutes, wondering what would happen next. Suddenly all was clear. A ministerial motorcade swept past on its way to the airport; half a dozen sleek black cars, one bearing flags on each wing. Within seconds the cones had vanished, and the traffic flowed as if it had never been absent. The smiling policeman waved us on our way.

Now all impediments disappeared, and the last miles rolled away. With relief I turned Madfaa on to the road for Babileh. Trees shaded our path as we approached the quiet suburb. No matter that the socks had worn through, for now dried mud edged the road and for the most part I could avoid the tarmac.

It was mid-day when we entered Fayiz' yard, and an ecstatic Madfaa had been announcing our return for the last quarter-mile.

*

Fayiz brought him an enormous pile of fresh lucerne, a luxury he hadn't tasted since Lattakia.

For the last time I washed him off, and rubbed him down. I stood a little scratching his back, saying my goodbyes. I offered him my hand to lick, in the usual ritual; but it was a security blanket he no longer needed.

Instead he called to the horse in the next stable, reassuring himself that his old friends were near. Then he buried his nose in the lucerne, and got to work.

BIBLIOGRAPHY

Bartlett, W.B., *The Assassins: The Story of Medieval Islam's Secret Sect,* Sutton Publishing Ltd., 2001

Breasted, James Henry, *Ancient Times: A History of the Early World,* Ginn and Company, 1935

Castle, Wilfrid T.F., *Syrian Pageant,* Hutchinson & Co. Ltd., 1947

Ceram, C.W., *Gods, Graves & Scholars: The Story of Archaeology,* translated by E.B. Garside and Sophie Wilkins, Book Club Associates, 1971

Cottrell, Leonard, *The Warrior Pharaohs,* Evans Brothers Ltd, 1968

Fedden, Robin, *Syria: An Historical Appreciation,* Robert Hale Ltd., 1955

Homer, *The Iliad,* translated by E.V. Rieu, Penguin Classics, 1950

Hourani, Albert, *A History of the Arab Peoples,* Faber and Faber Ltd. 1991

Hyland, Ann, *The Endurance Horse,* J.A. Allen & Co. Ltd., 1988

ibn-Munqidh, Usamah, *Memoirs of an Arab-Syrian Gentleman Warrior,* trans. by Philip K. Hitti, Columbia University Press, 2000

Lawrence, T.E., *Crusader Castles,* Immel Publishing Ltd. 1992

Nicholson, Helen, *The Knights Hospitaller,* The Boydell Press, 2001

Read, Piers Paul, *The Templars,* Weidenfeld & Nicolson, 1999

Rihaoui, Abdulkader, *Die Burg Crac des Chevaliers,* Veroeff Entlichungen der Generalverwaltung der Antiken und Museen, 1982

Rosebault, C.J., *Saladin, Prince of Chivalry,* Cassell and Company, Ltd., 1930

Runciman, Stephen, *A History of the Crusades,* Cambridge University Press, 1951

Arabic Glossary

Aba'a long cloak
Alaf heavily milled grain
Alawis a minority sect living mostly in the Alawi Mountain
Al-hamdu li'llah praise be to God
Buhayra lake
Burj tower
Dishdasha man's long gown
Durra, dhurra milled grain
Fasaha classical Arabic
Ghizz traditional Arwad fishing-boat
Ghouta the Damascus oasis
Hadith oral tradition
Hammaam bath-house
Hijab Scarf covering hair and neck
Imam In general, a prayer-leader; also applied historically to each of
the twelve successors of Mohammed as divinely inspired leader of all
Muslims
In sha'llah if God wills
Isma'ilis a schismatic Shi'ite sect
Jebel al-Alawiyiin Mountain of the Alawis
Keffiyah headcloth
Kelaam 'adi colloquial Arabic
Khan caravanserai, caravan merchants' inn
Laban yogurt
Mezzeh assorted plates of food
Nahr al-'Asi River Orontes
Nasrani Christian
Nizaris the Syrian branch of the Isma'ilis
Noria Roman water-wheel of the Orontes Valley
Nusayris another name for the Alawis
Qala'a castle
Serviis shared taxi or bus
Shabb, pl. *shebaab* boys, gang
Sheikh old man, elder
Shi'ite member of the *Shii'at Ali,* Party of Ali
Sunni follower of the *Sunna,* the consensual interpretation of Islam
Souk market
Tell hill, ancient city-mound
Tibn straw chaff

Qirsh one-hundredth part of a Syrian pound
Wahash wild animals
Wa-wa ants

OUR CURRENT LIST OF TITLES

Abdullah, Morag Mary, *My Khyber Marriage* - Morag Murray departed on a lifetime of adventure when she met and fell in love with Sirdar Ikbal Ali Shah, the son of an Afghan warlord. Leaving the comforts of her middle-class home in Scotland, Morag followed her husband into a Central Asia still largely unchanged since the 19th century.

Abernathy, Miles, *Ride the Wind* – the amazing true story of the little Abernathy Boys, who made a series of astonishing journeys in the United States, starting in 1909 when they were aged five and nine!

Beard, John, *Saddles East* – John Beard determined as a child that he wanted to see the Wild West from the back of a horse after a visit to Cody's legendary Wild West show. Yet it was only in 1948 – more than sixty years after seeing the flamboyant American showman – that Beard and his wife Lulu finally set off to follow their dreams.

Beker, Ana, *The Courage to Ride* – Determined to out-do Tschiffely, Beker made a 17,000 mile mounted odyssey across the Americas in the late 1940s that would fix her place in the annals of equestrian travel history.

Bey, A. M. Hassanein, *The Lost Oases* - At the dawning of the 20th century the vast desert of Libya remained one of last unexplored places on Earth. Sir Hassanein Bey, the dashing Egyptian diplomat turned explorer, befriended the Muslim leaders of the elusive Senussi Brotherhood who controlled the deserts further on, and became aware of rumours of a "lost oasis" which lay even deeper in the desert. In 1923 the explorer led a small caravan on a remarkable seven month journey across the centre of Libya.

Bird, Isabella, *Among the Tibetans* – A rousing 1889 adventure, an enchanting travelogue, a forgotten peek at a mountain kingdom swept away by the waves of time.

Bird, Isabella, *On Horseback* in *Hawaii* – The Victorian explorer's first horseback journey, in which she learns to ride astride, in early 1873.

Bird, Isabella, *Journeys in Persia and Kurdistan, Volumes 1 and 2* – The intrepid Englishwoman undertakes another gruelling journey in 1890.

Bird, Isabella, *A Lady's Life in the Rocky Mountains* – The story of Isabella Bird's adventures during the winter of 1873 when she explored the magnificent unspoiled wilderness of Colorado. Truly a classic.

Bird, Isabella, *Unbeaten Tracks in Japan, Volumes One and Two* – A 600-mile solo ride through Japan undertaken by the intrepid British traveller in 1878.

Blackmore, Charles, *In the Footsteps of Lawrence of Arabia* - In February 1985, fifty years after T. E. Lawrence was killed in a motor bicycle accident in Dorset, Captain Charles Blackmore and three others of the Royal Green Jackets Regiment set out to retrace Lawrence's exploits in the Arab Revolt during the First World War. They spent twenty-nine days with meagre supplies and under extreme conditions, riding and walking to the source of the Lawrence legend.

Boniface, Lieutenant Jonathan, *The Cavalry Horse and his Pack* – Quite simply the most important book ever written in the English language by a military man on the subject of equestrian travel.

Bosanquet, Mary, *Saddlebags for Suitcases* – In 1939 Bosanquet set out to ride from Vancouver, Canada, to New York. Along the way she was wooed by love-struck cowboys, chased by a grizzly bear and even suspected of being a Nazi spy, scouting out Canada in preparation for a German invasion. A truly delightful book.

de Bourboulon, Catherine, *Shanghai à Moscou (French)* – the story of how a young Scottish woman and her aristocratic French husband travelled overland from Shanghai to Moscow in the late 19th Century.

Brown, Donald; *Journey from the Arctic* – A truly remarkable account of how Brown, his Danish companion and their two trusty horses attempt the impossible, to cross the silent Arctic plateaus, thread their way through the giant Swedish forests, and finally discover a passage around the treacherous Norwegian marshes.

Bruce, Clarence Dalrymple, *In the Hoofprints of Marco Polo* – The author made a dangerous journey from Srinagar to Peking in 1905, mounted on a trusty 13-hand Kashmiri pony, then wrote this wonderful book.

Burnaby, Frederick; *A Ride to Khiva* – Burnaby fills every page with a memorable cast of characters, including hard-riding Cossacks, nomadic Tartars, vodka-guzzling sleigh-drivers and a legion of peasant ruffians.

Burnaby, Frederick, *On Horseback through Asia Minor* – Armed with a rifle, a small stock of medicines, and a single faithful servant, the equestrian traveler rode through a hotbed of intrigue and high adventure in wild inhospitable country, encountering Kurds, Circassians, Armenians, and Persian pashas.

Carter, General William, *Horses, Saddles and Bridles* – This book covers a wide range of topics including basic training of the horse and care of its equipment. It also provides a fascinating look back into equestrian travel history.

Cayley, George, *Bridle Roads of Spain* – Truly one of the greatest equestrian travel accounts of the 19th Century.

Chase, J. Smeaton, *California Coast Trails* – This classic book describes the author's journey from Mexico to Oregon along the coast of California in the 1890s.

Chase, J. Smeaton, *California Desert Trails* – Famous British naturalist J. Smeaton Chase mounted up and rode into the Mojave Desert to undertake the longest equestrian study of its kind in modern history.

Chitty, Susan, and Hinde, Thomas, *The Great Donkey Walk* - When biographer Susan Chitty and her novelist husband, Thomas Hinde, decided it was time to embark on a family adventure, they did it in style. In Santiago they bought two donkeys whom they named Hannibal and Hamilcar. Their two small daughters, Miranda (7) and Jessica (3) were to ride Hamilcar. Hannibal, meanwhile, carried the baggage. The walk they planned to undertake was nothing short of the breadth of southern Europe.

Christian, Glynn, *Fragile Paradise: The discovery of Fletcher Christian, "Bounty" Mutineer* - the great-great-great-great-grandson of the *Bounty* mutineer brings to life a fascinating and complex character history has portrayed as both hero and villain, and the real story behind a mutiny that continues to divide opinion more than 200 years later. The result is a brilliant and compelling historical detective story, full of intrigue, jealousy, revenge and adventure on the high seas.

Clark, Leonard, *Marching Wind, The* - The panoramic story of a mounted exploration in the remote and savage heart of Asia, a place where adventure, danger, and intrigue were the daily backdrop to wild tribesman and equestrian exploits.

Clark, Leonard, *A Wanderer Till I Die* - In a world with lax passport control, no airlines, and few rules, the young man from San Francisco floats effortlessly from one adventure to the next. When he's not drinking whiskey at the Raffles Hotel or listening to the "St. Louis Blues" on the phonograph in the jungle, he's searching for Malaysian treasure, being captured by Toradja headhunters, interrogated by Japanese intelligence officers and lured into shady deals by European gun-runners.

Cobbett, William, *Rural Rides, Volumes 1 and 2* – In the early 1820s Cobbett set out on horseback to make a series of personal tours through the English countryside. These books contain what many believe to be the best accounts of rural England ever written, and remain enduring classics.

Codman, John, *Winter Sketches from the Saddle* – This classic book was first published in 1888. It recommends riding for your health and describes the septuagenarian author's many equestrian journeys through New England during the winter of 1887 on his faithful mare, Fanny.

Cunninghame Graham, Jean, *Gaucho Laird* – A superbly readable biography of the author's famous great-uncle, Robert "Don Roberto" Cunninghame Graham.

Cunninghame Graham, Robert, *Horses of the Conquest* –The author uncovered manuscripts which had lain forgotten for centuries, and wrote this book, as he said, out of gratitude to the horses of Columbus and the Conquistadors who shaped history.

Cunninghame Graham, Robert, *Magreb-el-Acksa* – The thrilling tale of how "Don Roberto" was kidnapped in Morocco!

Cunninghame Graham, Robert, *Rodeo* – An omnibus of the finest work of the man they called "the uncrowned King of Scotland," edited by his friend Aimé Tschiffely.

Cunninghame Graham, Robert, *Tales of Horsemen* – Ten of the most beautifully-written equestrian stories ever set to paper.

Cunninghame Graham, Robert, *Vanished Arcadia* – This haunting story about the Jesuit missions in South America from 1550 to 1767 was the inspiration behind the best-selling film *The Mission.*

Daly, H.W., *Manual of Pack Transportation* – This book is the author's masterpiece. It contains a wealth of information on various pack saddles, ropes and equipment, how to secure every type of load imaginable and instructions on how to organize a pack train.

Dixie, Lady Florence, *Riding Across Patagonia* – When asked in 1879 why she wanted to travel to such an outlandish place as Patagonia, the author replied without hesitation that she was taking to the saddle in order to flee from the strict confines of polite Victorian society. This is the story of how the aristocrat successfully traded the perils of a London parlor for the wind-borne freedom of a wild Patagonian bronco.

Dodwell, Christina, *Beyond Siberia* – The intrepid author goes to Russia's Far East to join the reindeer-herding people in winter.

Dodwell, Christina, *An Explorer's Handbook* – The author tells you everything you want to know about travelling: how to find suitable pack animals, how to feed and shelter yourself. She also has sensible and entertaining advice about dealing with unwanted visitors and the inevitable bureaucrats.

Dodwell, Christina, *Madagascar Travels* – Christina explores the hidden corners of this amazing island and, as usual, makes friends with its people.

Dodwell, Christina, *A Traveller in China* – The author sets off alone across China, starting with a horse and then transferring to an inflatable canoe.

Dodwell, Christina, *A Traveller on Horseback* – Christina Dodwell rides through Eastern Turkey and Iran in the late 1980s. The Sunday Telegraph wrote of the author's "courage and insatiable wanderlust," and in this book she demonstrates her gift for communicating her zest for adventure.

Dodwell, Christina, *Travels in Papua New Guinea* – Christina Dodwell spends two years exploring an island little known to the outside world. She travelled by foot, horse and dugout canoe among the Stone-Age tribes.

Dodwell, Christina, *Travels with Fortune* – the truly amazing account of the courageous author's first journey – a three-year odyssey around Africa by Landrover, bus, lorry, horse, camel, and dugout canoe!

Dodwell, Christina, *Travels with Pegasus* – This time Christina takes to the air! This is the story of her unconventional journey across North Africa in a micro-light!

Duncan, John, *Travels in Western Africa in 1845 and 1846* - The author, a Lifeguardsman from Scotland, tells the hair-raising tale of his two journeys to what is now Benin. Sadly, Duncan has been forgotten until today, and we are proud to get this book back into print.

Ehlers, Otto, *Im Sattel durch die Fürstenhöfe Indiens* – In June 1890 the young German adventurer, Ehlers, lay very ill. His doctor gave him a choice: either go home to Germany or travel to Kashmir. So of course the Long Rider chose the latter. This is a thrilling yet humorous book about the author's adventures.

Farson, Negley, *Caucasian Journey* – A thrilling account of a dangerous equestrian journey made in 1929, this is an amply illustrated adventure classic.

Fox, Ernest, *Travels in Afghanistan* – The thrilling tale of a 1937 journey through the mountains, valleys, and deserts of this forbidden realm, including visits to such fabled places as the medieval city of Heart, the towering Hindu Kush mountains, and the legendary Khyber Pass.

Gall, Sandy, *Afghanistan – Agony of a Nation* - Sandy Gall has made three trips to Afghanistan to report the war there: in 1982, 1984 and again in 1986. This book is an account of his last journey and what he found. He chose to revisit the man he believes is the outstanding commander in Afghanistan: Ahmed Shah Masud, a dashing Tajik who is trying to organise resistance to the Russians on a regional, and eventually national scale.

Gall, Sandy, *Behind Russian Lines* - In the summer of 1982, Sandy Gall set off for Afghanistan on what turned out to be the hardest assignment of his life. During his career as a reporter he had covered plenty of wars and revolutions before, but this was the first time he had been required to walk all the way to an assignment and all the way back again, dodging Russian bombs *en route*.

Galton, Francis, *The Art of Travel* – Originally published in 1855, this book became an instant classic and was used by a host of now-famous explorers, including Sir Richard Francis Burton of Mecca fame. Readers can learn how to ride horses, handle elephants, avoid cobras, pull teeth, find water in a desert, and construct a sleeping bag out of fur.

Glazier, Willard, *Ocean to Ocean on Horseback* – This book about the author's journey from New York to the Pacific in 1875 contains every kind of mounted adventure imaginable. Amply illustrated with pen and ink drawings of the time, the book remains a timeless equestrian adventure classic.

Goodwin, Joseph, *Through Mexico on Horseback* – The author and his companion, Robert Horiguichi, the sophisticated, multi-lingual son of an imperial Japanese diplomat, set out in 1931 to cross Mexico. They were totally unprepared for the deserts, quicksand and brigands they were to encounter during their adventure.

Hanbury-Tenison, Marika, *For Better, For Worse* – The author, an excellent story-teller, writes about her adventures visiting and living among the Indians of Central Brazil.

Hanbury-Tenison, Marika, *A Slice of Spice* – The fresh and vivid account of the author's hazardous journey to the Indonesian Islands with her husband, Robin.

Hanbury-Tenison, Robin, *Chinese Adventure* – The story of a unique journey in which the explorer Robin Hanbury-Tenison and his wife Louella rode on horseback alongside the Great Wall of China in 1986.

Hanbury-Tenison, Robin, *Fragile Eden* – The wonderful story of Robin and Louella Hanbury-Tenison's exploration of New Zealand on horseback in 1988. They rode alone together through what they describe as 'some of the most dramatic and exciting country we have ever seen.'

Hanbury-Tenison, Robin, *Mulu: The Rainforest* – This was the first popular book to bring to the world's attention the significance of the rain forests to our fragile ecosystem. It is a timely reminder of our need to preserve them for the future.

Hanbury-Tenison, Robin, *A Pattern of Peoples* – The author and his wife, Marika, spent three months travelling through Indonesia's outer islands and writes with his usual flair and sensitivity about the tribes he found there.

Hanbury-Tenison, Robin, *A Question of Survival* – This superb book played a hugely significant role in bringing the plight of Brazil's Indians to the world's attention.

Hanbury-Tenison, Robin, *The Rough and the Smooth* – The incredible story of two journeys in South America. Neither had been attempted before, and both were considered impossible!

Hanbury-Tenison, Robin, *Spanish Pilgrimage* – Robin and Louella Hanbury-Tenison went to Santiago de Compostela in a traditional way – riding on white horses over long-forgotten tracks. In the process they discovered more about the people and the country than any conventional traveller would learn. Their adventures are vividly and entertainingly recounted in this delightful and highly readable book.

Hanbury-Tenison, Robin, *White Horses over France* – This enchanting book tells the story of a magical journey and how, in fulfilment of a personal dream, the first Camargue horses set foot on British soil in the late summer of 1984.

Hanbury-Tenison, Robin, *Worlds Apart – an Explorer's Life* – The author's battle to preserve the quality of life under threat from developers and machines infuses this autobiography with a passion and conviction which makes it impossible to put down.

Hanbury-Tenison, Robin, *Worlds Within – Reflections in the Sand* – This book is full of the adventure you would expect from a man of action like Robin Hanbury-Tenison. However, it is also filled with the type of rare knowledge that was revealed to other desert travellers like Lawrence, Doughty and Thesiger.

Haslund, Henning, *Mongolian Adventure* – An epic tale inhabited by a cast of characters no longer present in this lackluster world, shamans who set themselves on fire, rebel leaders who sacked towns, and wild horsemen whose ancestors conquered the world.

Heath, Frank, *Forty Million Hoofbeats* – Heath set out in 1925 to follow his dream of riding to all 48 of the Continental United States. The journey lasted more than two years, during which time Heath and his mare, Gypsy Queen, became inseparable companions.

Hinde, Thomas, *The Great Donkey Walk* -

Holt, William, *Ride a White Horse* – After rescuing a cart horse, Trigger, from slaughter and nursing him back to health, the 67-year-old Holt and his horse set out in 1964 on an incredible 9,000 mile, non-stop journey through western Europe.

Hopkins, Frank T., *Hidalgo and Other Stories* – For the first time in history, here are the collected writings of Frank T. Hopkins, the counterfeit cowboy whose endurance racing claims and Old West fantasies have polarized the equestrian world.

James, Jeremy, *Saddletramp* – The classic story of Jeremy James' journey from Turkey to Wales, on an unplanned route with an inaccurate compass, unreadable map and the unfailing aid of villagers who seemed to have as little sense of direction as he had.

James, Jeremy, *Vagabond* – The wonderful tale of the author's journey from Bulgaria to Berlin offers a refreshing, witty and often surprising view of Eastern Europe and the collapse of communism.

Jebb, Louisa, *By Desert Ways to Baghdad and Damascus* – From the pen of a gifted writer and intrepid traveller, this is one of the greatest equestrian travel books of all time.

Kluckhohn, Clyde, *To the Foot of the Rainbow* – This is not just a exciting true tale of equestrian adventure. It is a moving account of a young man's search for physical perfection in a desert world still untouched by the recently-born twentieth century.

Lambie, Thomas, *Boots and Saddles in Africa* – Lambie's story of his equestrian journeys is told with the grit and realism that marks a true classic.

Landor, Henry Savage, *In the Forbidden Land* – Illustrated with hundreds of photographs and drawings, this blood-chilling account of equestrian adventure makes for page-turning excitement.

Langlet, Valdemar, *Till Häst Genom Ryssland (Swedish)* – Denna reseskildring rymmer många ögonblicksbilder av möten med människor, från morgonbad med Lev Tolstoi till samtal med Tartarer och fotografering av fagra skördeflickor. Rikt illustrerad med foto och teckningar.

Leigh, Margaret, *My Kingdom for a Horse* – In the autumn of 1939 the author rode from Cornwall to Scotland, resulting in one of the most delightful equestrian journeys of the early twentieth century. This book is full of keen observations of a rural England that no longer exists.

Lester, Mary, *A Lady's Ride across Spanish Honduras in 1881* – This is a gem of a book, with a very entertaining account of Mary's vivid, day-to-day life in the saddle.

MacDermot, Brian, *Cult of the Sacred Spear* - here is that rarest of travel books, an exploration not only of a distant land but of a man's own heart. A confederation of pastoral people located in Southern Sudan and western Ethiopia, the Nuer warriors were famous for staging cattle raids against larger tribes and successfully resisted European colonization. Brian MacDermot, London stockbroker, entered into Nuer society as a stranger and emerged as Rial Nyang, an adopted member of the tribe. This book recounts this extraordinary emotional journey, regaling the reader with tales of pagan gods, warriors on mysterious missions, and finally the approach of warfare that continues to swirl across this part of Africa today.

Maillart, Ella, *Turkestan Solo* – A vivid account of a 1930s journey through this wonderful, mysterious and dangerous portion of the world, complete with its Kirghiz eagle hunters, lurking Soviet secret police, and the timeless nomads that still inhabited the desolate steppes of Central Asia.

Marcy, Randolph, *The Prairie Traveler* – There were a lot of things you packed into your saddlebags or the wagon before setting off to cross the North American wilderness in the 1850s. A gun and an axe were obvious necessities.

Yet many pioneers were just as adamant about placing a copy of Captain Randolph Marcy's classic book close at hand.

Marsden, Kate, *Riding through Siberia: A Mounted Medical Mission in 1891* - This immensely readable book is a mixture of adventure, extreme hardship and compassion as the author travels the Great Siberian Post Road.

Marsh, Hippisley Cunliffe, *A Ride Through Islam* – A British officer rides through Persia and Afghanistan to India in 1873. Full of adventures, and with observant remarks on the local Turkoman equestrian traditions.

MacCann, William, *Viaje a Caballo* – Spanish-language edition of the British author's equestrian journey around Argentina in 1848.

Meline, James, *Two Thousand Miles on Horseback: Kansas to Santa Fé in 1866* – A beautifully written, eye witness account of a United States that is no more.

Muir Watson, Sharon, *The Colour of Courage* – The remarkable true story of the epic horse trip made by the first people to travel Australia's then-unmarked Bicentennial National Trail. There are enough adventures here to satisfy even the most jaded reader.

Naysmith, Gordon, *The Will to Win* – This book recounts the only equestrian journey of its kind undertaken during the 20th century - a mounted trip stretching across 16 countries. Gordon Naysmith, a Scottish pentathlete and former military man, set out in 1970 to ride from the tip of the African continent to the 1972 Olympic Games in distant Germany.

O'Connor, Derek, *The King's Stranger* – a superb biography of the forgotten Scottish explorer, John Duncan.

Ondaatje, Christopher, *Leopard in the Afternoon* - The captivating story of a journey through some of Africa's most spectacular haunts. It is also touched with poignancy and regret for a vanishing wilderness – a world threatened with extinction.

Ondaatje, Christopher, *The Man-Eater of Pununai* – a fascinating story of a past rediscovered through a remarkable journey to one of the most exotic countries in the world — Sri Lanka. Full of drama and history, it not only relives the incredible story of a man-eating leopard that terrorized the tiny village of Punanai in the early part of the century, but also allows the author to come to terms with the ghost of his charismatic but tyrannical father.

Ondaatje, Christopher, *Sindh Revisited* – This is the extraordinarily sensitive account of the author's quest to uncover the secrets of the seven years Richard Burton spent in India in the army of the East India Company from 1842 to 1849. "If I wanted to fill the gap in my understanding of Richard Burton, I would have to do something that had never been done before: follow in his footsteps in India..." The journey covered thousands of miles—trekking across deserts where ancient tribes meet modern civilization in the valley of the mighty Indus River.

O'Reilly, Basha, *Count Pompeii – Stallion of the Steppes* – the story of Basha's journey from Russia with her stallion, Count Pompeii, told for children. This is the first book in the *Little Long Rider* series.

O'Reilly, CuChullaine, (Editor) *The Horse Travel Handbook* – this accumulated knowledge of a million miles in the saddle tells you everything you need to know about travelling with your horse!

O'Reilly, CuChullaine, (Editor) *The Horse Travel Journal* – a unique book to take on your ride and record your experiences. Includes the world's first equestrian travel "pictionary" to help you in foreign countries.

O'Reilly, CuChullaine, *Khyber Knights* – Told with grit and realism by one of the world's foremost equestrian explorers, "Khyber Knights" has been penned the way lives are lived, not how books are written.

O'Reilly, CuChullaine, (Editor) *The Long Riders, Volume One* – The first of five unforgettable volumes of exhilarating travel tales.

Östrup, J, *(Swedish), Växlande Horisont* - The thrilling account of the author's journey to Central Asia from 1891 to 1893.

Patterson, George, *Gods and Guerrillas* – The true and gripping story of how the author went secretly into Tibet to film the Chinese invaders of his adopted country. Will make your heart pound with excitement!

Patterson, George, *Journey with Loshay: A Tibetan Odyssey* – This is an amazing book written by a truly remarkable man! Relying both on his companionship with God and on his own strength, he undertook a life few can have known, and a journey of emergency across the wildest parts of Tibet.

Patterson, George, *Patterson of Tibet* - Patterson was a Scottish medical missionary who went to Tibet shortly after the second World War. There he became Tibetan in all but name, adapting to the culture and learning the language fluently. This intense autobiography reveals how Patterson crossed swords with India's Prime Minister Nehru, helped with the rescue of the Dalai Lama and befriended a host of unique world figures ranging from Yehudi Menhuin to Eric Clapton. This is a vividly-written account of a life of high adventure and spiritual odyssey.

Pocock, Roger, *Following the Frontier* – Pocock was one of the nineteenth century's most influential equestrian travelers. Within the covers of this book is the detailed account of Pocock's horse ride along the infamous Outlaw Trail, a 3,000 mile solo journey that took the adventurer from Canada to Mexico City.

Pocock, Roger, *Horses* – Pocock set out to document the wisdom of the late 19th and early 20th Centuries into a book unique for its time. His concerns for attempting to preserve equestrian knowledge were based on cruel reality. More than 300,000 horses had been destroyed during the recent Boer War. Though Pocock enjoyed a reputation for dangerous living, his observations on horses were praised by the leading thinkers of his day.

Post, Charles Johnson, *Horse Packing* – Originally published in 1914, this book was an instant success, incorporating as it did the very essence of the science of packing horses and mules. It makes fascinating reading for students of the horse or history.

Ray, G. W., *Through Five Republics on Horseback* – In 1889 a British explorer - part-time missionary and full-time adventure junky – set out to find a lost tribe of sun-worshipping natives in the unexplored forests of Paraguay. The journey was so brutal that it defies belief.

Rink, Bjarke, *The Centaur Legacy* - This immensely entertaining and historically important book provides the first ever in-depth study into how man's partnership with his equine companion changed the course of history and accelerated human development.

Ross, Julian, *Travels in an Unknown Country* – A delightful book about modern horseback travel in an enchanting country, which once marked the eastern borders of the Roman Empire – Romania.

Ross, Martin and Somerville, E, *Beggars on Horseback* – The hilarious adventures of two aristocratic Irish cousins on an 1894 riding tour of Wales.

Ruxton, George, *Adventures in Mexico* – The story of a young British army officer who rode from Vera Cruz to Santa Fe, Mexico in 1847. At times the author exhibits a fearlessness which borders on insanity. He ignores dire warnings, rides through deadly deserts, and dares murderers to attack him. It is a delightful and invigorating tale of a time and place now long gone.

von Salzman, Erich, *Im Sattel durch Zentralasien* – The astonishing tale of the author's journey through China, Turkistan and back to his home in Germany – 6000 kilometres in 176 days!

Schwarz, Hans *(German)*, *Vier Pferde, Ein Hund und Drei Soldaten* – In the early 1930s the author and his two companions rode through Liechtenstein, Austria, Romania, Albania, Yugoslavia, to Turkey, then rode back again!

Schwarz, Otto *(German), Reisen mit dem Pferd* – the Swiss Long Rider with more miles in the saddle than anyone else tells his wonderful story, and a long appendix tells the reader how to follow in his footsteps.

Scott, Robert, *Scott's Last Expedition* – Many people are unaware that Scott recruited Yakut ponies from Siberia for his doomed expedition to the South Pole in 1909. Here is the remarkable story of men and horses who all paid the ultimate sacrifice.

Shackleton, Ernest, *Aurora Australis* - The members of the British Antarctic Expedition of 1907-1908 wrote this delightful and surprisingly funny book. It was printed on the spot "at the sign of the Penguin"!

Skrede, Wilfred, *Across the Roof of the World* – This epic equestrian travel tale of a wartime journey across Russia, China, Turkestan and India is laced with unforgettable excitement.

Stevens, Thomas, *Through Russia on a Mustang* – Mounted on his faithful horse, Texas, Stevens crossed the Steppes in search of adventure. Cantering across the pages of this classic tale is a cast of nineteenth century Russian misfits, peasants, aristocrats—and even famed Cossack Long Rider Dmitri Peshkov.

Stevenson, Robert L., *Travels with a Donkey* – In 1878, the author set out to explore the remote Cevennes mountains of France. He travelled alone, unless you count his stubborn and manipulative pack-donkey, Modestine. This book is a true classic.

Strong, Anna Louise, *Road to the Grey Pamir* – With Stalin's encouragement, Strong rode into the seldom-seen Pamir mountains of faraway

Tadjikistan. The political renegade turned equestrian explorer soon discovered more adventure than she had anticipated.

Sykes, Ella, *Through Persia on a Sidesaddle* – Ella Sykes rode side-saddle 2,000 miles across Persia, a country few European woman had ever visited. Mind you, she traveled in style, accompanied by her Swiss maid and 50 camels loaded with china, crystal, linens and fine wine.

Trinkler, Emile, *Through the Heart of Afghanistan* – In the early 1920s the author made a legendary trip across a country now recalled only in legends.

Tschiffely, Aimé, *Bohemia Junction* – "Forty years of adventurous living condensed into one book."

Tschiffely, Aimé, *Bridle Paths* – a final poetic look at a now-vanished Britain.

Tschiffely, Aimé, *Mancha y Gato Cuentan sus Aventuras* – The Spanish-language version of *The Tale of Two Horses* – the story of the author's famous journey as told by the horses.

Tschiffely, Aimé, *The Tale of Two Horses* – The story of Tschiffely's famous journey from Buenos Aires to Washington, DC, narrated by his two equine heroes, Mancha and Gato. Their unique point of view is guaranteed to delight children and adults alike.

Tschiffely, Aimé, *This Way Southward* – the most famous equestrian explorer of the twentieth century decides to make a perilous journey across the U-boat infested Atlantic.

Tschiffely, Aimé, *Tschiffely's Ride* – The true story of the most famous equestrian journey of the twentieth century – 10,000 miles with two Criollo geldings from Argentina to Washington, DC. A new edition is coming soon with a Foreword by his literary heir!

Tschiffely, Aimé, *Tschiffely's Ritt* – The German-language translation of *Tschiffely's Ride* – the most famous equestrian journey of its day.

Ure, John, *Cucumber Sandwiches in the Andes* – No-one who wasn't mad as a hatter would try to take a horse across the Andes by one of the highest passes between Chile and the Argentine. That was what John Ure was told on his way to the British Embassy in Santiago-so he set out to find a few certifiable kindred spirits. Fans of equestrian travel and of Latin America will be enchanted by this delightful book.

Warner, Charles Dudley, *On Horseback in Virginia* – A prolific author, and a great friend of Mark Twain, Warner made witty and perceptive contributions to the world of nineteenth century American literature. This book about the author's equestrian adventures is full of fascinating descriptions of nineteenth century America.

Weale, Magdalene, *Through the Highlands of Shropshire* – It was 1933 and Magdalene Weale was faced with a dilemma: how to best explore her beloved English countryside? By horse, of course! This enchanting book invokes a gentle, softer world inhabited by gracious country lairds, wise farmers, and jolly inn keepers.

Weeks, Edwin Lord, *Artist Explorer* – A young American artist and superb writer travels through Persia to India in 1892.

Wentworth Day, J., *Wartime Ride* – In 1939 the author decided the time was right for an extended horseback ride through England! While parts of his country were being ravaged by war, Wentworth Day discovered an inland oasis of mellow harvest fields, moated Tudor farmhouses, peaceful country halls, and fishing villages.

Von Westarp, Eberhard, *Unter Halbmond und Sonne* – (German) – Im Sattel durch die asiatische Türkei und Persien.

Wilkins, Messanie, *Last of the Saddle Tramps* – Told she had little time left to live, the author decided to ride from her native Maine to the Pacific. Accompanied by her faithful horse, Tarzan, Wilkins suffered through any number of obstacles, including blistering deserts and freezing snow storms – and defied the doctors by living for another 20 years!.

Wilson, Andrew, *The Abode of Snow* – One of the best accounts of overland equestrian travel ever written about the wild lands that lie between Tibet and Afghanistan.

de Windt, Harry, *A Ride to India* – Part science, all adventure, this book takes the reader for a thrilling canter across the Persian Empire of the 1890s.

Winthrop, Theodore, *Saddle and Canoe* – This book paints a vibrant picture of 1850s life in the Pacific Northwest and covers the author's travels along the Straits of Juan De Fuca, on Vancouver Island, across the Naches Pass, and on to The Dalles, in Oregon Territory. This is truly an historic travel account.

Younghusband, George, *Eighteen Hundred Miles on a Burmese Pony* – One of the funniest and most enchanting books about equestrian travel of the nineteenth century, featuring "Joe" the naughty Burmese pony!

We are constantly adding new titles to our collections, so please check our websites:

www.horsetravelbooks.com and **www.classictravelbooks.com**

Lightning Source UK Ltd.
Milton Keynes UK
UKOW042238231012

201056UK00003B/7/A